WHAT IS
TO BE DONE?

*Burning Questions
of Our Movement*

by V. I. LENIN

INTERNATIONAL PUBLISHERS
New York

11th Printing, 1992

This edition is based upon the text as it appeared in
V. I. Lenin, *Collected Works* (English edition), Vol. 5,
Progress Publishers, Moscow, 1961, translated by Joe
Fineberg and George Hanna, edited by Victor J. Jerome.
Corrections have been made in accordance with the fifth
Russian edition of the *Collected Works*. All references
to Lenin, *Collected Works* in the editor's footnotes are
to the English edition.

SBN 7178-0218-3

Library of Congress Catalog Card Number: 69–18884.

Printed in the United States of America

PUBLISHER'S NOTE

Among Lenin's most significant theoretical contributions, *What Is To Be Done?*[1] has long been a classic on the role of a revolutionary socialist party. Soon after his return from Siberian exile in 1900, he began to write on the "burning question" which confronted the Marxist movement in Russia and to seek the answers. At that time the revolutionary movement, growing rapidly and spontaneously, comprised conflicting trends and had not yet produced a party capable of playing a leading role. After some preliminary articles, Lenin wrote the present work in which he elaborated the theoretical premises upon which the Bolshevik, or Communist, Party was founded.

The book was published a year before the Second Congress of the Russian Social-Democratic Labor Party, which was held in London in July-August 1903. At this Congress, two trends emerged clearly: one represented by Lenin and his followers, which came to be known as Bolshevik (from the Russian word *bolshinstvo,* meaning majority) and an opportunist trend, a minority at the Congress, called Menshevik (from the Russian word *menshinstvo,* meaning minority). Lenin's book played a central role in winning the majority of the party to the revolutionary position. "As a trend of political thought and as a political party," Lenin was to write later, "Bolshevism has existed since 1903."

In Lenin's concept a leading, a vanguard party could be only a party of revolutionary Marxism and this required at the outset a clear definition and rejection of opportunism. In this book, therefore, Lenin concerned himself largely with what he considered the major problem—the distinction, in all major aspects, between a party of reform and a party of revolution. Thus, in the first years of the 20th century, Lenin took up the fight against the opportunist trend in Russia, which he saw as an aspect of opportunism in the world Marxist movement, represented by the Bernstein revisionists.

The Russian form of opportunism was Economism, the rough equivalent of which in the United States was known as "pure and simple trade unionism." The Economists maintained that the struggle of the workers for the improvement of their immediate conditions should be the chief preoccupation of the labor movement, while the political struggle against tsarism was to be left to the leadership of the liberal bourgeoisie. Lenin considered such views a complete break with the Marxist concept of the working class movement and its goal of attaining power. He opposed any effort to separate the political from the economic tasks and to subordinate the working class to liberal bourgeois leadership. In his view, the Russian proletariat confronted an "immediate task" of great revolutionary import: the overthrow of tsarist absolutism. "The fulfillment of this task, the destruction of the most powerful bulwark, not only of European, but (it may now be said) of Asiatic reaction," he wrote, "would make the Russian proletariat the vanguard of the international revolutionary proletariat."

Lenin's concept of a revolutionary Marxist party emerged from his dynamic theory of revolution, and the leading role of the working class in it. He saw the need for a vanguard party that, in the midst of the spontaneity of the mass movement, would impart socialist consciousness to the workers. Recognition of the socialist aims, he said, can come only from the "outside" —from the party—since it is not an automatic result of the class struggle. Such a role, he emphasized throughout, "can be fulfilled only by a party that is guided by the most advanced theory." Here is found his famous phrase: "Without revolutionary theory there can be no revolutionary movement." In the course of establishing these views, Lenin discussed problems which have remained paramount in world Marxism, such as party theory and education, the approach toward students and other nonproletarian forces, the role of terrorism, a revolutionary approach to reform, overcoming primitive and amateurish methods of work, the role of the press, and making use of experiences of other countries. With respect to the latter, he wrote, "What is required is the ability to treat these experiences critically and to test them independently." The kind of party he sought was "an organization of revolutionaries capable of guiding the *entire* proletarian struggle for emancipation."

To help place this work in perspective it will be helpful to recall that only three years after it was written the Bolsheviks were to play an important role in the Revolution of 1905 which Lenin later characterized as the dress rehearsal for the Socialist Revolution of 1917. The party principles Lenin developed early in the century were in accordance with his view that a revolutionary Marxist party must go beyond the recognition of the historical necessity of socialism to ask *what is to be done,* under the given circumstances, for its realization.

JAMES S. ALLEN

Contents

PREFACE   5

I. DOGMATISM AND "FREEDOM OF CRITICISM"   8

  A. What Does "Freedom of Criticism" Mean?   8
  B. The New Advocates of "Freedom of Criticism" 12
  C. Criticism in Russia 17
  D. Engels on the Importance of the Theoretical Struggle . . 24

II. THE SPONTANEITY OF THE MASSES AND THE CON-
SCIOUSNESS OF THE SOCIAL-DEMOCRATS 28

  A. The Beginning of the Spontaneous Upsurge 30
  B. Bowing to Spontaneity. *Rabochaya Mysl* 35
  C. The Self-Emancipation Group and *Rabocheye Dyelo* . . 44

III. TRADE-UNIONIST POLITICS AND SOCIAL-DEMOCRATIC
POLITICS 54

  A. Political Agitation and Its Restriction by the Economists . 54
  B. How Martynov Rendered Plekhanov More Profound . . 65
  C. Political Exposures and "Training in Revolutionary Activity" 68
  D. What Is There in Common Between Economism and
    Terrorism? 74
  E. The Working Class as Vanguard Fighter for Democracy 78
  F. Once More "Slanderers", Once More "Mystifiers" . . . 93

IV. THE PRIMITIVENESS OF THE ECONOMISTS AND THE
ORGANISATION OF THE REVOLUTIONARIES 97

  A. What Is Primitiveness? 98
  B. Primitiveness and Economism 101
  C. Organisation of Workers and Organisation of Revolution-
    aries 108
  D. The Scope of Organisational Work 124
  E. "Conspiratorial" Organisation and "Democratism" . . . 131
  F. Local and All-Russian Work 139

V. THE "PLAN" FOR AN ALL-RUSSIAN POLITICAL NEWS-
PAPER 149

    A. Who Was Offended by the Article "Where To Begin" . 150
    B. Can a Newspaper Be a Collective Organiser? 156
    C. What Type of Organisation Do We Require? 167

CONCLUSION 175

APPENDIX:

THE ATTEMPT TO UNITE *ISKRA* WITH *RABOCHEYE DYELO* 178

CORRECTION TO *WHAT IS TO BE DONE?* 186

NOTES 188

> "...Party struggles lend a party strength and vitality; the greatest proof of a party's weakness is its diffuseness and the blurring of clear demarcations; a party becomes stronger by purging itself...."
>
> (*From a letter by Lassalle to Marx, of June 24, 1852.*)

PREFACE

According to the author's original plan, the present pamphlet was to have been devoted to a detailed development of the ideas expressed in the article "Where To Begin" (*Iskra*,[2] No. 4, May 1901).* We must first apologise to the reader for the delay in fulfilling the promise made in that article (and repeated in response to many private inquiries and letters). One of the reasons for this delay was the attempt, undertaken in June of the past year (1901), to unite all the Social-Democratic organisations abroad. It was natural to wait for the results of this attempt, for, had the effort proved successful, it would perhaps have been necessary to expound *Iskra*'s conceptions of organisation from a somewhat different approach; in any case, such a success promised to put an end very quickly to the existence of the two trends in the Russian Social-Democratic movement. As the reader knows, the attempt failed, and, as we propose to show, was bound to fail after the new swing of *Rabocheye Dyelo*,[3] in its issue No. 10, towards Economism. It was found to be absolutely essential to begin a determined struggle against this trend, diffuse and ill-defined, but for that reason the more persistent, the more capable of reasserting itself in divers forms. Accordingly, the original plan of the pamphlet was altered and considerably enlarged.

Its main theme was to have been the three questions raised in the article "Where To Begin"—the character and main content of our political agitation; our organisational

---

* See *Collected Works*, Vol. 5, pp. 13-24.—*Ed.*

tasks; and the plan for building, simultaneously and from various sides, a militant, All-Russian organisation. These questions have long engaged the mind of the author, who tried to raise them in *Rabochaya Gazeta*[4] during one of the unsuccessful attempts to revive that paper (see Chapter V). But the original plan to confine the pamphlet to an analysis of only these three questions and to set forth our views as far as possible in a positive form, without, or almost without, entering into polemics, proved wholly impracticable, for two reasons. On the one hand, Economism proved to be much more tenacious than we had supposed [we employ the term Economism in the broad sense, as explained in *Iskra*, No. 12 (December 1901), in the article entitled "A Talk With Defenders of Economism", which was a synopsis, so to speak, of the present pamphlet*]. It became clear beyond doubt that the differences regarding the solution of the three questions mentioned were explainable to a far greater degree by the basic antithesis between the two trends in the Russian Social-Democratic movement than by differences over details. On the other hand, the perplexity of the Economists over the practical application of our views in *Iskra* clearly revealed that we often speak literally in different tongues and therefore *cannot* arrive at an understanding without beginning *ab ovo*, and that an attempt must be made, in the simplest possible style, illustrated by numerous and concrete examples, *systematically to "clarify"* *all* our basic points of difference with *all* the Economists. I resolved to make such an attempt at "clarification", fully realising that it would greatly increase the size of the pamphlet and delay its publication; I saw *no other way* of meeting my pledge I had made in the article "Where To Begin". Thus, to the apologies for the delay, I must add others for the serious literary shortcomings of the pamphlet. I had to work *in great haste*, with frequent interruptions by a variety of other tasks.

The examination of the above three questions still constitutes the main theme of this pamphlet, but I found it necessary to begin with two questions of a more general nature—why such an "innocent" and "natural" slogan as

---

* See *Collected Works,* Vol. 5, pp. 313-20.—*Ed.*

"freedom of criticism" should be for us a veritable war-cry, and why we cannot come to an understanding even on the fundamental question of the role of Social-Democrats in relation to the spontaneous mass movement. Further, the exposition of our views on the character and substance of political agitation developed into an explanation of the difference between trade-unionist politics and Social-Democratic politics, while the exposition of our views on organisational tasks developed into an explanation of the difference between the amateurish methods which satisfy the Economists, and the organisation of revolutionaries which we hold to be indispensable. Further, I advance the "plan" for an All-Russian political newspaper with all the more insistence because the objections raised against it are untenable, and because no real answer has been given to the question I raised in the article "Where To Begin" as to how we can set to work from all sides simultaneously to create the organisation we need. Finally, in the concluding part, I hope to show that we did all we could to prevent a decisive break with the Economists, a break which nevertheless proved inevitable; that *Rabocheye Dyelo* acquired a special significance, a "historical" significance, if you will, because it expressed fully and strikingly, not consistent Economism, but the confusion and vacillation which constitute the distinguishing feature of *an entire period* in the history of Russian Social-Democracy; and that therefore the polemic with *Rabocheye Dyelo*, which may upon first view seem excessively detailed, also acquires significance, for we can make no progress until we have completely put an end to this period.

N. Lenin

February 1902

I

Dogmatism and "Freedom of Criticism"

A. What Does "Freedom of Criticism" Mean!

"Freedom of criticism" is undoubtedly the most fashionable slogan at the present time, and the one most frequently employed in the controversies between social-ists and democrats in all countries. At first sight, nothing would appear to be more strange than the solemn appeals to freedom of criticism made by one of the parties to the dispute. Have voices been raised in the advanced parties against the constitutional law of the majority of European countries which guarantees freedom to science and scientific investigation? "Something must be wrong here," will be the comment of the onlooker who has heard this fashionable slogan repeated at every turn but has not yet penetrated the essence of the disagreement among the disputants; "evidently this slogan is one of the conventional phrases which, like nicknames, become legitimised by use, and become almost generic terms."

In fact, it is no secret for anyone that two trends have taken form in present-day international* Social-Democ-

---

* Incidentally, in the history of modern socialism this is a phenomenon, perhaps unique and in its way very consoling, namely, that the strife of the various trends within the socialist movement has from national become international. Formerly, the disputes between Lassalleans and Eisenachers,[5] between Guesdists and Possibilists,[6] between Fabians[7] and Social-Democrats, and between Narodnaya Volya[8] adherents and Social-Democrats, remained confined within purely national frameworks, reflecting purely national features, and proceeding, as it were, on different planes. At the present time (as is now evident), the English Fabians, the French Ministerialists, the German Bernsteinians, and the Russian Critics— all belong to the same family, all extol each other, learn from each other, and together take up arms against "dogmatic" Marxism. In

8

racy. The conflict between these trends now flares up in a bright flame and now dies down and smoulders under the ashes of imposing "truce resolutions". The essence of the "new" trend, which adopts a "critical" attitude towards "obsolete dogmatic" Marxism, has been clearly enough *presented* by Bernstein and *demonstrated* by ·Millerand.

Social-Democracy must change from a party of social revolution into a democratic party of social reforms. Bernstein has surrounded this political demand with a whole battery of well-attuned "new" arguments and reasonings. Denied was the possibility of putting socialism on a scientific basis and of demonstrating its necessity and inevitability from the point of view of the materialist conception of history. Denied was the fact of growing impoverishment, the process of proletarisation, and the intensification of capitalist contradictions; the very concept, *"ultimate aim"*, was declared to be unsound, and the idea of the dictatorship of the proletariat was completely rejected. Denied was the antithesis in principle between liberalism and socialism. Denied was *the theory of the class struggle*, on the alleged grounds that it could not be applied to a strictly democratic society governed according to the will of the majority, etc.

Thus, the demand for a decisive turn from revolutionary Social-Democracy to bourgeois social-reformism was accompanied by a no less decisive turn towards bourgeois criticism of all the fundamental ideas of Marxism. In view of the fact that this criticism of Marxism has long been directed from the political platform, from university chairs, in numerous pamphlets and in a series of learned treatises, in view of the fact that the entire younger generation of the educated classes has been systematically reared for decades on this criticism, it is not surprising that the "new critical" trend in Social-Democracy should spring up, all complete, like Minerva from the head of Jove. The content of this new trend did not have to grow

this first really international battle with socialist opportunism, international revolutionary Social-Democracy will perhaps become sufficiently strengthened to put an end to the political reaction that has long reigned in Europe?

and take shape, it was transferred bodily from bourgeois to socialist literature.

To proceed. If Bernstein's theoretical criticism and political yearnings were still unclear to anyone, the French took the trouble strikingly to demonstrate the "new method". In this instance, too, France has justified its old reputation of being "the land where, more than anywhere else, the historical class struggles were each time fought out to a decision..." (Engels, Introduction to Marx's *Der 18 Brumaire*).[9] The French socialists have begun, not to theorise, but to act. The democratically more highly developed political conditions in France have permitted them to put "Bernsteinism into practice" immediately, with all its consequences. Millerand has furnished an excellent example of practical Bernsteinism; not without reason did Bernstein and Vollmar rush so zealously to defend and laud him. Indeed, if Social-Democracy, in essence, is merely a party of reform and must be bold enough to admit this openly, then not only has a socialist the right to join a bourgeois cabinet. but he must always strive to do so. If democracy, in essence, means the abolition of class domination, then why should not a socialist minister charm the whole bourgeois world by orations on class collaboration? Why should he not remain in the cabinet even after the shooting-down of workers by gendarmes has exposed, for the hundredth and thousandth time, the real nature of the democratic collaboration of classes? Why should he not personally take part in greeting the tsar, for whom the French socialists now have no other name than hero of the gallows, knout, and exile *(knouteur, pendeur et déportateur)*? And the reward for this utter humiliation and self-degradation of socialism in the face of the whole world, for the corruption of the socialist consciousness of the working masses—the only basis that can guarantee our victory—the reward for this is pompous *projects* for miserable reforms, so miserable in fact that much more has been obtained from bourgeois governments!

He who does not deliberately close his eyes cannot fail to see that the new "critical" trend in socialism is nothing more nor less than a new variety of *opportunism*. And if we judge people, not by the glittering uniforms they don or by the high-sounding appellations they give themselves, but by their actions and by what they actually advocate, it will be clear that "freedom of criticism" means freedom for an opportunist trend in Social-Democracy, freedom to convert Social-Democracy into a democratic party of reform, freedom to introduce bourgeois ideas and bourgeois elements into socialism.

"Freedom" is a grand word, but under the banner of freedom for industry the most predatory wars were waged, under the banner of freedom of labour, the working people were robbed. The modern use of the term "freedom of criticism" contains the same inherent falsehood. Those who are really convinced that they have made progress in science would not demand freedom for the new views to continue side by side with the old, but the substitution of the new views for the old. The cry heard today, "Long live freedom of criticism", is too strongly reminiscent of the fable of the empty barrel.

We are marching in a compact group along a precipitous and difficult path, firmly holding each other by the hand. We are surrounded on all sides by enemies, and we have to advance almost constantly under their fire. We have combined, by a freely adopted decision, for the purpose of fighting the enemy, and not of retreating into the neighbouring marsh, the inhabitants of which, from the very outset, have reproached us with having separated ourselves into an exclusive group and with having chosen the path of struggle instead of the path of conciliation. And now some among us begin to cry out: Let us go into the marsh! And when we begin to shame them, they retort: What backward people you are! Are you not ashamed to deny us the liberty to invite you to take a better road! Oh, yes, gentlemen! You are free not only to invite us, but to go yourselves wherever you will, even into the marsh. In fact, we think that the marsh is your proper place, and we are prepared to render *you* every assistance to get there. Only let go of our hands, don't clutch at us and don't besmirch the grand word freedom, for we too are "free" to go where we please, free to fight not only against the marsh, but also against those who are turning towards the marsh!

B. The New Advocates of "Freedom of Criticism"

Now, this slogan ("freedom of criticism") has in recent times been solemnly advanced by *Rabocheye Dyelo* (No. 10), organ of the Union of Russian Social-Democrats Abroad,[10] not as a theoretical postulate, but as a political demand, as a reply to the question, "Is it possible to unite the Social-Democratic organisations operating abroad?": "For a durable unity, there must be freedom of criticism" (p. 36).

From this statement two definite conclusions follow: (1) that *Rabocheye Dyelo* has taken under its wing the opportunist trend in international Social-Democracy in general, and (2) that *Rabocheye Dyelo* demands freedom for opportunism in Russian Social-Democracy. Let us examine these conclusions.

Rabocheye Dyelo is "particularly" displeased with the "inclination of *Iskra* and *Zarya*[11] to predict a rupture between the *Mountain* and the *Gironde* in international Social-Democracy".*

"Generally speaking," writes B. Krichevsky, editor of *Rabocheye Dyelo*, "this talk of the *Mountain* and the *Gironde* heard in the ranks of Social-Democracy represents a shallow historical analogy, a strange thing to come from the pen of a Marxist. The *Mountain* and the *Gironde* did not represent different temperaments, or intellectual trends, as the historians of social thought may think, but different classes or strata—the middle bourgeoisie, on the one hand, and the petty bourgeoisie and the proletariat, on the other. In the modern socialist movement, however, there is no conflict of class interests; the socialist movement in its entirety, in *all* of its divers forms [Krichevsky's italics], including the most pronounced Bernsteinians, stands on the basis of the class interests of the proletariat and its class struggle for political and economic emancipation" (pp. 32-33).

---

* A comparison of the two trends within the revolutionary proletariat (the revolutionary and the opportunist), and the two trends within the revolutionary bourgeoisie in the eighteenth century (the Jacobin, known as the Mountain, and the Girondist) was made in the leading article in No. 2 of *Iskra* (February 1901). The article was written by Plekhanov. The Cadets,[12] the Bezzaglavtsi,[13] and the Mensheviks to this day love to refer to Jacobinism in Russian Social-Democracy. But how Plekhanov came to apply this concept for the first time against the Right wing of Social-Democracy—about this they prefer to keep silent or to forget. (Author's note to the 1907 edition.—*Ed.*)

A bold assertion! Has not Krichevsky heard of the fact, long ago noted, that it is precisely the extensive participation of an "academic" *stratum* in the socialist movement in recent years that has promoted such a rapid spread of Bernsteinism? And what is most important—on what does our author found his opinion that even "the most pronounced Bernsteinians" stand on the basis of the class struggle for the political and economic emancipation of the proletariat? No one knows. This determined defence of the most pronounced Bernsteinians is not supported by any argument or reasoning whatever. Apparently, the author believes that if he repeats what the most pronounced Bernsteinians say about themselves his assertion requires no proof. But can anything more "shallow" be imagined than this judgement of an entire trend based on nothing more than what the representatives of that trend say about themselves? Can anything more shallow be imagined than the subsequent "homily" on the two different and even diametrically opposite types, or paths, of party development? (*Rabocheye Dyelo*, pp. 34-35). The German Social-Democrats, in other words, recognise complete freedom of criticism, but the French do not, and it is precisely their example that demonstrates the "bane of intolerance".

To this we can only say that the very example B. Krichevsky affords us attests to the fact that the name Marxists is at times assumed by people who conceive history literally in the "Ilovaisky[14] manner". To explain the unity of the German Socialist Party and the disunity of the French Socialist Party, there is no need whatever to go into the special features in the history of these countries, to contrast the conditions of military semi-absolutism in the one with republican parliamentarism in the other, to analyse the effects of the Paris Commune and the effects of the Exceptional Law Against the Socialists,[15] to compare the economic life and economic development of the two countries, or to recall that "the unexampled growth of German Social-Democracy" was accompanied by a strenuous struggle, unique in the history of socialism, not only against erroneous theories (Mühlberger, Dühring,*

---

* At the time Engels dealt his blows at Dühring, many representatives of German Social-Democracy inclined towards the latter's

the *Katheder*-Socialists[17]), but also against erroneous tactics (Lassalle), etc., etc. All that is superfluous! The French quarrel among themselves because they are intolerant; the Germans are united because they are good boys.

And observe, this piece of matchless profundity is designed to "refute" the fact that puts to rout the defence of the Bernsteinians. The question whether or not the Bernsteinians *stand* on the basis of the class struggle of the proletariat is one that can be completely and irrevocably answered only by historical experience. Consequently, the example of France holds greatest significance in this respect, because France is the only country in which the Bernsteinians attempted *to stand* independently, on their own feet, with the warm approval of their German colleagues (and partly also of the Russian opportunists; cf. *Rabocheye Dyelo*, No. 2-3, pp. 83-84). The reference to the "intolerance" of the French, apart from its "historical" significance (in the Nozdryov[18] sense), turns out to be merely an attempt to hush up very unpleasant facts with angry invectives.

Nor are we inclined to make a present of the Germans to Krichevsky and the numerous other champions of "freedom of criticism". If the "most pronounced Bernsteinians" are still tolerated in the ranks of the German party, it is only to the extent that they *submit* to the Hanover resolution,[19] which emphatically rejected Bernstein's "amendments", and to the Lübeck resolution,[20] which (notwithstanding the diplomatic terms in which it is couched) contains a direct warning to Bernstein. It is debatable, from the standpoint of the interests of the

views, and accusations of acerbity, intolerance, uncomradely polemics, etc., were hurled at Engels even publicly at a Party Congress. At the Congress of 1877, Most, and his supporters, introduced a resolution to prohibit the publication of Engels's articles in *Vorwärts*[16] because "they do not interest the overwhelming majority of the readers", and Vahlteich declared that their publication had caused great damage to the Party, that Dühring too had rendered services to Social-Democracy: "We must utilise everyone in the interests of the Party; let the professors engage in polemics if they care to do so, but *Vorwärts* is not the place in which to conduct them" (*Vorwärts*, No. 65, June 6, 1877). Here we have another example of the defence of "freedom of criticism", and our legal critics and illegal opportunists, who love so much to cite the example of the Germans, would do well to ponder it!

German party, whether diplomacy was appropriate and whether, in this case, a bad peace is better than a good quarrel; in short, opinions may differ as to the expediency of any one of the *methods* employed to reject Bernsteinism, but that the German party *did reject* Bernsteinism on two occasions is a fact no one can fail to see. Therefore, to think that the German example confirms the thesis that "The most pronounced Bernsteinians stand on the basis of the class struggle of the proletariat, for political and economic emancipation", means to fail completely to understand what is going on under our very eyes.*

Nor is that all. As we have seen, *Rabocheye Dyelo* demands "freedom of criticism" and defends Bernsteinism before *Russian* Social-Democracy. Apparently it convinced itself that we were unfair to our "Critics" and Bernsteinians. But to which ones? who? where? when? What did the unfairness represent? About this, not a word. *Rabocheye Dyelo* does not name a single Russian Critic or Bernsteinian! We are left with but one of two possible suppositions. *Either* the unfairly treated party is none other than *Rabocheye Dyelo* itself (this is confirmed by the fact that in the two articles in No. 10 reference is made only to the wrongs suffered by *Rabocheye Dyelo* at the hands of *Zarya* and *Iskra*). If that is the case, how

---

* It should be observed that *Rabocheye Dyelo* has always confined itself to a bare statement of facts concerning Bernsteinism in the German party and completely "refrained" from expressing its own opinion. See, for instance, the reports of the Stuttgart Congress[21] in No. 2-3 (p. 66), in which all the disagreements are reduced to "tactics" and the statement is merely made that the overwhelming majority remain true to the previous revolutionary tactics. Or, No. 4-5 (p. 25, *et seq.*), in which we have nothing but a paraphrasing of the speeches delivered at the Hanover Congress, with a reprint of Bebel's resolution. An exposition and a criticism of Bernstein's views are again put off (as was the case in No. 2-3) to be dealt with in a "special article". Curiously enough, in No. 4-5 (p. 33), we read the following: "...the views expounded by Bebel have the support of the vast majority of the Congress", and a few lines thereafter: "...David defended Bernstein's views.... First of all, he tried to show that ... Bernstein and his friends, after all is said and done [sic!], stand on the basis of the class struggle...." This was written in December 1899, and in September 1901 *Rabocheye Dyelo*, apparently no longer believing that Bebel was right, repeats David's views as its own!

is the strange fact to be explained that *Rabocheye Dyelo*, which always vehemently dissociates itself from all solidarity with Bernsteinism, could not defend itself without putting in a word in defence of the "most pronounced Bernsteinians" and of freedom of criticism? *Or* some third persons have been treated unfairly. If this is the case, then what reasons may there be for not naming them?

We see, therefore, that *Rabocheye Dyelo* is continuing to play the game of hide-and-seek it has played (as we shall show below) ever since its founding. And let us note further this *first* practical application of the vaunted "freedom of criticism". In actual fact, not only was it forthwith reduced to abstention from all criticism, but also to abstention from expressing independent views altogether. The very *Rabocheye Dyelo*, which avoids mentioning Russian Bernsteinism as if it were a shameful disease (to use Starover's[22] apt expression), proposes, for the treatment of this disease, *to copy word for word* the latest German prescription for the German variety of the malady! Instead of freedom of criticism—slavish (worse: apish) imitation! The very same social and political content of modern international opportunism reveals itself in a variety of ways according to national peculiarities. In one country the opportunists have long ago come out under a separate flag; in another, they have ignored theory and in fact pursued the policy of the Radicals-Socialists; in a third, some members of the revolutionary party have deserted to the camp of opportunism and strive to achieve their aims, not in open struggle for principles and for new tactics, but by gradual, imperceptible, and, if one may so put it, unpunishable corruption of their party; in a fourth country, similar deserters employ the same methods in the gloom of political slavery, and with a completely original combination of "legal" and "illegal" activity, etc. To talk of freedom of criticism and of Bernsteinism as a condition for uniting the *Russian* Social-Democrats and not to explain how *Russian* Bernsteinism has manifested itself and what particular fruits it has borne, amounts to talking with the aim of saying nothing.

Let us ourselves try, if only in a few words, to say what *Rabocheye Dyelo* did not want to say (or which was, perhaps, beyond its comprehension).

C. Criticism in Russia

The chief distinguishing feature of Russia in regard to the point we are examining is that *the very beginning* of the spontaneous working-class movement, on the one hand, and of the turn of progressive public opinion towards Marxism, on the other, was marked by the combination of manifestly heterogeneous elements under a common flag to fight the common enemy (the obsolete social and political world outlook). We refer to the heyday of "legal Marxism". Speaking generally, this was an altogether curious phenomenon that no one in the eighties or the beginning of the nineties would have believed possible. In a country ruled by an autocracy, with a completely enslaved press, in a period of desperate political reaction in which even the tiniest outgrowth of political discontent and protest is persecuted, the theory of revolutionary Marxism suddenly forces its way into the *censored* literature and, though expounded in Aesopian language, is understood by all the "interested". The government had accustomed itself to regarding only the theory of the (revolutionary) Narodnaya Volya as dangerous, without, as is usual, observing its internal evolution, and rejoicing at *any* criticism levelled against it. Quite a considerable time elapsed (by our Russian standards) before the government realised what had happened and the unwieldy army of censors and gendarmes discovered the new enemy and flung itself upon him. Meanwhile, Marxist books were published one after another, Marxist journals and newspapers were founded, nearly everyone became a Marxist, Marxists were flattered, Marxists were courted, and the book publishers rejoiced at the extraordinary, ready sale of Marxist literature. It was quite natural, therefore, that among the Marxian neophytes who were caught up in this atmosphere, there should be more than one "author who got a swelled head. . ."[23].

We can now speak calmly of this period as of an event of the past. It is no secret that the brief period in which Marxism blossomed on the surface of our literature was called forth by an alliance between people of extreme and of very moderate views. In point of fact, the latter were bourgeois democrats; this conclusion (so markedly confirmed by their subsequent "critical" development) suggested itself to some even when the "alliance" was still intact.*

That being the case, are not the revolutionary Social-Democrats who entered into the alliance with the future "Critics" mainly responsible for the subsequent "confusion"? This question, together with a reply in the affirmative, is sometimes heard from people with too rigid a view. But such people are entirely in the wrong. Only those who are not sure of themselves can fear to enter into temporary alliances even with unreliable people; not a single political party could exist without such alliances. The combination with the legal Marxists was in its way the first really political alliance entered into by Russian Social-Democrats. Thanks to this alliance, an astonishingly rapid victory was obtained over Narodism, and Marxist ideas (even though in a vulgarised form) became very widespread. Moreover, the alliance was not concluded altogether without "conditions". Evidence of this is the burning by the censor, in 1895, of the Marxist collection *Material on the Question of the Economic Development of Russia.*[24] If the literary agreement with the legal Marxists can be compared with a political alliance, then that book can be compared with a political treaty.

The rupture, of course, did not occur because the "allies" proved to be bourgeois democrats. On the contrary, the representatives of the latter trend are natural and desirable allies of Social-Democracy insofar as its democratic tasks, brought to the fore by the prevailing situation in Russia, are concerned. But an essential condition for such an alliance must be the full opportunity for the socialists to reveal to the working class that its interests are diametrically opposed to the interests of the bourgeoisie. However, the Bernsteinian and "critical" trend, to which the majority of the legal Marxists turned, deprived the socialists of this opportunity and demoralised the socialist consciousness by vulgarising Marxism, by advocating the theory of the blunting of social contradictions, by declaring

---

* The reference is to an article by K. Tulin directed against Struve. (See *Collected Works*, Vol. 1, pp. 333-507.—*Ed.*) The article was based on an essay entitled "The Reflection of Marxism in Bourgeois Literature". (Author's note to the 1907 edition.—*Ed.*)

the idea of the social revolution and of the dictatorship of the proletariat to be absurd, by reducing the working-class movement and the class struggle to narrow trade-unionism and to a "realistic" struggle for petty, gradual reforms. This was synonymous with bourgeois democracy's denial of socialism's right to independence and, consequently, of its right to existence; in practice it meant a striving to convert the nascent working-class movement into an appendage of the liberals.

Naturally, under such circumstances the rupture was necessary. But the "peculiar" feature of Russia manifested itself in the fact that this rupture simply meant the elimination of the Social-Democrats from the most accessible and widespread "legal" literature. The "ex-Marxists", who took up the flag of "criticism" and who obtained almost a monopoly to "demolish" Marxism, entrenched themselves in this literature. Catchwords like "Against orthodoxy" and "Long live freedom of criticism" (now repeated by *Rabocheye Dyelo*) forthwith became the vogue, and the fact that neither the censor nor the gendarmes could resist this vogue is apparent from the publication of *three* Russian editions of the work of the celebrated Bernstein (celebrated in the Herostratean sense) and from the fact that the works of Bernstein, Mr. Prokopovich, and others were recommended by Zubatov[25] (*Iskra*, No. 10). A task now devolved upon the Social-Democrats that was difficult in itself and was made incredibly more difficult by purely external obstacles—the task of combating the new trend. This trend did not confine itself to the sphere of literature. The turn towards "criticism" was accompanied by an infatuation for "Economism" among Social-Democratic practical workers.

The manner in which the connection between, and interdependence of, legal criticism and illegal Economism arose and grew is in itself an interesting subject, one that could serve as the theme of a special article. We need only note here that this connection undoubtedly existed. The notoriety deservedly acquired by the *Credo* was due precisely to the frankness with which it formulated this connection and blurted out the fundamental political tendency of "Economism"—let the workers carry on the economic struggle (it would be more correct to say the trade-unionist struggle, because the latter also embraces specifically working-class politics) and let the Marxist intelligentsia merge with the liberals for the political "struggle". Thus, trade-unionist work "among the people" meant fulfilling the first part of this task, while legal criticism meant fulfilling the second. This statement was such an excellent weapon against Economism that, had there been no *Credo*, it would have been worth inventing one.

The *Credo* was not invented, but it was published without the consent and perhaps even against the will of its authors. At all events, the present writer, who took part in dragging this new "programme" into the light of day,* has heard complaints and reproaches to the effect that copies of the résumé of the speakers' views were distributed, dubbed the *Credo*, and even published in the press together with the protest! We refer to this episode because it reveals a very peculiar feature of our Economism—fear of publicity. This is a feature of Economism generally, and not of the authors of the *Credo* alone. It was revealed by that most outspoken and honest advocate of Economism, *Rabochaya Mysl*,[27] and by *Rabocheye Dyelo* (which was indignant over the publication of "Economist" documents in the *Vademecum*[28]), as well as by the Kiev Committee, which two years ago refused to permit the publication of its *profession de foi*,[29] together with a repudiation of it,** and by many other individual representatives of Economism.

This fear of criticism displayed by the advocates of freedom of criticism cannot be attributed solely to craftiness (although, on occasion, no doubt craftiness is brought into play: it would be improvident to expose the young and as

---

* The reference is to the *Protest of the Seventeen* against the *Credo*. The present writer took part in drawing up this protest (the end of 1899).[26] The protest and the *Credo* were published abroad in the spring of 1900. (See "A Protest by Russian Social-Democrats", *Collected Works*, Vol. 4, pp. 167-82.—*Ed.*) It is now known from the article written by Madame Kuskova (I think in *Byloye*) that she was the author of the *Credo* and that Mr. Prokopovich was very prominent among the "Economists" abroad at the time. (Author's note to the 1907 edition.—*Ed.*)

** As far as our information goes, the composition of the Kiev Committee has changed since then.

yet frail shoots of the new trend to attacks by opponents). No, the majority of the Economists look with sincere resentment (as by the very nature of Economism they must) upon all theoretical controversies, factional disagreements, broad political questions, plans for organising revolutionaries, etc. "Leave all that to the people abroad!" said a fairly consistent Economist to me one day, thereby expressing a very widespread (and again purely trade-unionist) view; our concern is the working-class movement, the workers' organisations here, in our localities; all the rest is merely the invention of doctrinaires, "the overrating of ideology", as the authors of the letter, published in *Iskra*, No. 12, expressed it, in unison with *Rabocheye Dyelo*, No. 10.

The question now arises: such being the peculiar features of Russian "criticism" and Russian Bernsteinism, what should have been the task of those who sought to oppose opportunism in deeds and not merely in words? First, they should have made efforts to resume the theoretical work that had barely begun in the period of legal Marxism and that fell anew on the shoulders of the comrades working underground. Without such work the successful growth of the movement was impossible. Secondly, they should have actively combated the legal "criticism" that was perverting people's minds on a considerable scale. Thirdly, they should have actively opposed confusion and vacillation in the practical movement, exposing and repudiating every conscious or unconscious attempt to degrade our programme and our tactics.

That *Rabocheye Dyelo* did none of these things is well known; we shall have occasion below to deal with this well-known fact in detail and from various aspects. At the moment, however, we desire merely to show the glaring contradiction that exists between the demand for "freedom of criticism" and the specific features of our native criticism and Russian Economism. It suffices but to glance at the text of the resolution in which the Union of Russian Social-Democrats Abroad endorsed the point of view of *Rabocheye Dyelo*.

"In the interests of the further ideological development of Social-Democracy, we recognise the freedom of criticism of Social-Democratic theory in Party literature to be absolutely necessary insofar as the criticism does not run counter to the class and revolutionary character of this theory" (*Two Conferences*, p. 10).

And the motivation? The resolution "in its first part coincides with the resolution of the Lübeck Party Congress on Bernstein".... In the simplicity of their souls the "Unionists" failed to observe what a *testimonium paupertatis* (attestation of poverty) they betray with this copying.... "But ... in its second part, it restricts freedom of criticism much more than did the Lübeck Party Congress."

The resolution of the Union Abroad, then, is directed against the Russian Bernsteinians? If it is not, then the reference to Lübeck would be utterly absurd. But it is not true to say that it "restricts freedom of criticism". In adopting their Hanover resolution, the Germans, point by point, rejected *precisely* the amendments proposed by Bernstein, while in their Lübeck resolution they cautioned *Bernstein personally*, by naming him. Our "free" imitators, however, make *not a single allusion* to *a single* manifestation of specifically Russian "criticism" and Russian Economism. In view of this omission, the bare reference to the class and revolutionary character of the theory leaves far wider scope for misinterpretation, particularly when the Union Abroad refuses to identify "so-called Economism" with opportunism (*Two Conferences*, p. 8, Paragraph 1). But all this, in passing. The main thing to note is that the positions of the opportunists in relation to the revolutionary Social-Democrats in Russia are diametrically opposed to those in Germany. In that country, as we know, the revolutionary Social-Democrats are in favour of preserving that which exists—the old programme and the tactics, which are universally known and have been elucidated in all their details by many decades of experience. But the "Critics" desire to introduce changes, and since these Critics represent an insignificant minority, and since they are very timid in ther revisionist efforts, one can understand the motives of the majority in confining themselves to the dry rejection of "innovations". In Russia, however, it is the Critics and the Economists who are in favour of preserving that which exists: the "Critics" want us to go on regarding them as Marxists and to guarantee them the "freedom of criticism" they enjoyed to the full (for, in fact, they never recognised any kind of *party* ties,* and, moreover, we never had a generally recognised party body that could "restrict" freedom of criticism, if only by counsel); the Economists want the revolutionaries to recognise the "sovereign character of the present movement" (*Rabocheye Dyelo*, No. 10, p. 25), i.e., to recognise the "legitimacy" of that which exists; they want the "ideologists" not to try to "divert" the movement from the path that "is determined by the interaction of material elements and material environment" ("Letter" in *Iskra*, No. 12); they want to have that struggle recognised as desirable "which it is possible for the workers to wage under the present conditions", and as the only possible struggle, that "which they are actually waging at the present time" ("*Separate Supplement*" to *Rabochaya Mysl*,[30] p. 14). We revolutionary Social-Democrats, on the contrary, are dissatisfied with this worship of spontaneity, i.e., of that which exists "at the present moment". We demand that the tactics that have prevailed in recent years be changed; we declare that "before we can unite, and in order that we may unite, we must first of all draw firm and definite lines of demarcation" (see announcement of the publication of *Iskra*).** In a word, the Germans stand for that which exists and reject changes; we demand a

---

* The fact alone of the absence of public party ties and party traditions, representing as it does a cardinal difference between Russia and Germany, should have warned all sensible socialists against blind imitation. But here is an instance of the lengths to which "freedom of criticism" goes in Russia. Mr. Bulgakov, the Russian Critic, utters the following reprimand to the Austrian Critic, Hertz: "Notwithstanding the independence of his conclusions, Hertz, on this point [on the question of co-operative societies] apparently remains excessively bound by the opinions of his party, and although he disagrees with it in details, he dare not reject the common principle" (*Capitalism and Agriculture*, Vol. II, p. 287). The subject of a politically enslaved state, in which nine hundred and ninety-nine out of a thousand of the population are corrupted to the marrow by political subservience and completely lack the conception of party honour and party ties, superciliously reproves a citizen of a constitutional state for being excessively "bound by the opinions of his party"! Our illegal organisations have nothing else to do, of course, but draw up resolutions on freedom of criticism....

** See *Collected Works*, Vol. 4, p. 354.—*Ed.*

change of that which exists, and reject subservience thereto and reconciliation to it.

This "slight" difference our "free" copyists of German resolutions failed to notice.

D. Engels on the Importance of the Theoretical Struggle

"Dogmatism, doctrinairism", "ossification of the party—the inevitable retribution that follows the violent strait-lacing of thought"—these are the enemies against which the knightly champions of "freedom of criticism" in *Rabocheye Dyelo* rise up in arms. We are very glad that this question has been placed on the order of the day and we would only propose to add to it one other:

And who are the judges?

We have before us two publishers' announcements. One, "The Programme of the Periodical Organ of the Union of Russian Social-Democrats Abroad—*Rabocheye Dyelo*" (reprint from No. 1 of *Rabocheye Dyelo*), and the other, the "Announcement of the Resumption of the Publications of the Emancipation of Labour Group".[31] Both are dated 1899, when the "crisis of Marxism" had long been under discussion. And what do we find? We would seek in vain in the first announcement for any reference to this phenomenon, or a definite statement of the position the new organ intends to adopt on this question. Not a word is said about theoretical work and the urgent tasks that now confront it, either in this programme or in the supplements to it that were adopted by the Third Congress of the Union Abroad in 1901 (*Two Conferences*, pp. 15-18). During this entire time the Editorial Board of *Rabocheye Dyelo* ignored theoretical questions, in spite of the fact that these were questions that disturbed the minds of all Social-Democrats the world over.

The other announcement, on the contrary, points first of all to the declining interest in theory in recent years, imperatively demands "vigilant attention to the theoretical aspect of the revolutionary movement of the proletariat" and calls for "ruthless criticism of the Bernsteinian and other anti-revolutionary tendencies" in our movement. The issues of *Zarya* to date show how this programme has been carried out.

Thus, we see that high-sounding phrases against the ossification of thought, etc., conceal unconcern and help-lessness with regard to the development of theoretical thought. The case of the Russian Social-Democrats mani-festly illustrates the general European phenomenon (long ago noted also by the German Marxists) that the much vaunted freedom of criticism does not imply substitution of one theory for another, but freedom from all integral and pondered theory; it implies eclecticism and lack of principle. Those who have the slightest acquaintance with the actual state of our movement cannot but see that the wide spread of Marxism was accompanied by a certain lowering of the theoretical level. Quite a number of people with very little, and even a total lack of theoretical training joined the movement because of its practical significance and its practical successes. We can judge from that how tactless *Rabocheye Dyelo* is when, with an air of triumph, it quotes Marx's statement: "Every step of real movement is more important than a dozen programmes."[32] To repeat these words in a period of theoretical disorder is like wishing mourners at a funeral many happy returns of the day. More-over, these words of Marx are taken from his letter on the Gotha Programme, in which he *sharply condemns* eclec-ticism in the formulation of principles. If you must unite, Marx wrote to the party leaders, then enter into agree-ments to satisfy the practical aims of the movement, but do not allow any bargaining over principles, do not make theoretical "concessions". This was Marx's idea, and yet there are people among us who seek—in his name—to belittle the significance of theory!

Without revolutionary theory there can be no revolution-ary movement. This idea cannot be insisted upon too strongly at a time when the fashionable preaching of opportunism goes hand in hand with an infatuation for the narrowest forms of practical activity. Yet, for Russian Social-Democrats the importance of theory is enhanced by three other circumstances, which are often forgotten: first, by the fact that our Party is only in process of formation. its features are only just becoming defined, and it has as yet far from settled accounts with the other trends of revolutionary thought that threaten to divert the movement from the correct path. On the contrary, precisely the very recent past was marked by a revival of non-Social-Democratic revolutionary trends (an eventuation regarding which Axelrod long ago warned the Economists). Under these circumstances, what at first sight appears to be an "unimportant" error may lead to most deplorable consequences, and only short-sighted people can consider factional disputes and a strict differentiation between shades of opinion inopportune or superfluous. The fate of Russian Social-Democracy for very many years to come may depend on the strengthening of one or the other "shade".

Secondly, the Social-Democratic movement is in its very essence an international movement. This means, not only that we must combat national chauvinism, but that an incipient movement in a young country can be successful only if it makes use of the experiences of other countries. In order to make use of these experiences it is not enough merely to be acquainted with them, or simply to copy out the latest resolutions. What is required is the ability to treat these experiences critically and to test them independently. He who realises how enormously the modern working-class movement has grown and branched out will understand what a reserve of theoretical forces and political (as well as revolutionary) experience is required to carry out this task.

Thirdly, the national tasks of Russian Social-Democracy are such as have never confronted any other socialist party in the world. We shall have occasion further on to deal with the political and organisational duties which the task of emancipating the whole people from the yoke of autocracy imposes upon us. At this point, we wish to state only that the *role of vanguard fighter can be fulfilled only by a party that is guided by the most advanced theory*. To have a concrete understanding of what this means, let the reader recall such predecessors of Russian Social-Democracy as Herzen, Belinsky, Chernyshevsky, and the brilliant galaxy of revolutionaries of the seventies; let him ponder over the world significance which Russian literature is now acquiring; let him ... but be that enough!

Let us quote what Engels said in 1874 concerning the significance of theory in the Social-Democratic movement.

Engels recognises, *not two* forms of the great struggle of Social-Democracy (political and economic), as is the fashion among us, *but three, placing the theoretical struggle on a par with the first two.* His recommendations to the German working-class movement, which had become strong, practically and politically, are so instructive from the standpoint of present-day problems and controversies, that we hope the reader will not be vexed with us for quoting a long passage from his prefatory note to *Der deutsche Bauernkrieg,** which has long become a great bibliographical rarity:

"The German workers have two important advantages over those of the rest of Europe. First, they belong to the most theoretical people of Europe; and they have retained that sense of theory which the so-called 'educated' classes of Germany have almost completely lost. Without German philosophy, which preceded it, particularly that of Hegel, German scientific socialism—the only scientific socialism that has ever existed—would never have come into being. Without a sense of theory among the workers, this scientific socialism would never have entered their flesh and blood as much as is the case. What an immeasurable advantage this is may be seen, on the one hand, from the indifference towards all theory, which is one of the main reasons why the English working-class movement crawls along so slowly in spite of the splendid organisation of the individual unions; on the other hand, from the mischief and confusion wrought by Proudhonism, in its original form, among the French and Belgians, and, in the form further caricatured by Bakunin, among the Spaniards and Italians.

"The second advantage is that, chronologically speaking, the Germans were about the last to come into the workers' movement. Just as German theoretical socialism will never forget that it rests on the shoulders of Saint-Simon, Fourier, and Owen—three men who, in spite of all their fantastic notions and all their utopianism, have their place among the most eminent thinkers of all times, and whose genius anticipated innumerable things, the

---

* Dritter Abdruck. Leipzig, 1875. Verlag der Genossenschaftsbuchdruckerei. (*The Peasant War in Germany.* Third impression. Co-operative Publishers, Leipzig, 1875.—*Ed.*)

correctness of which is now being scientifically proved by us—so the practical workers' movement in Germany ought never to forget that it has developed on the shoulders of the English and French movements, that it was able simply to utilise their dearly bought experience, and could now avoid their mistakes, which in their time were mostly unavoidable. Without the precedent of the English trade unions and French workers' political struggles, without the gigantic impulse given especially by the Paris Commune, where would we be now?

"It must be said to the credit of the German workers that they have exploited the advantages of their situation with rare understanding. For the first time since a workers' movement has existed, the struggle is being conducted pursuant to its three sides—the theoretical, the political, and the practical-economic (resistance to the capitalists)—in harmony and in its interconnections, and in a systematic way. It is precisely in this, as it were, concentric attack, that the strength and invincibility of the German movement lies.

"Due to this advantageous situation, on the one hand, and to the insular peculiarities of the English and the forcible suppression of the French movement, on the other, the German workers have for the moment been placed in the vanguard of the proletarian struggle. How long events will allow them to occupy this post of honour cannot be foretold. But let us hope that as long as they occupy it, they will fill it fittingly. This demands redoubled efforts in every field of struggle and agitation. In particular, it will be the duty of the leaders to gain an ever clearer insight into all theoretical questions, to free themselves more and more from the influence of traditional phrases inherited from the old world outlook, and constantly to keep in mind that socialism, since it has become a science, demands that it be pursued as a science, i.e., that it be studied. The task will be to spread with increased zeal among the masses of the workers the ever more clarified understanding thus acquired, to knit together ever more firmly the organisation both of the party and of the trade unions....

"If the German workers progress in this way, they will not be marching exactly at the head of the movement—it is not at all in the interest of this movement that the workers of any particular country should march at its head—but they will occupy an honourable place in the battle line; and they will stand armed for battle when either unexpectedly grave trials or momentous events demand of them increased courage, increased determination and energy."[33]

Engels's words proved prophetic. Within a few years the German workers were subjected to unexpectedly grave trials in the form of the Exceptional Law Against the Socialists. And they met those trials armed for battle and succeeded in emerging from them victorious.

The Russian proletariat will have to undergo trials immeasurably graver; it will have to fight a monster compared with which an anti-socialist law in a constitutional country seems but a dwarf. History has now confronted us with an immediate task which is the *most revolutionary* of all the *immediate* tasks confronting the proletariat of any country. The fulfilment of this task, the destruction of the most powerful bulwark, not only of European, but (it may now be said) of Asiatic reaction, would make the Russian proletariat the vanguard of the international revolutionary proletariat. And we have the right to count upon acquiring this honourable title, already earned by our predecessors, the revolutionaries of the seventies, if we succeed in inspiring our movement, which is a thousand times broader and deeper, with the same devoted determination and vigour.

II

The Spontaneity of the Masses and the Consciousness of the Social-Democrats

We have said that our movement, much more extensive and deep than the movement of the seventies, must be inspired with the same devoted determination and energy that inspired the movement at that time. Indeed, no one, we think, has until now doubted that the strength of the present-day movement lies in the awakening of the masses (principally, the industrial proletariat) and that its weakness lies in the lack of consciousness and initiative among the revolutionary leaders.

However, of late a staggering discovery has been made, which threatens to disestablish all hitherto prevailing views on this question. This discovery was made by *Rabocheye Dyelo*, which in its polemic with *Iskra* and *Zarya* did not confine itself to making objections on separate points, but tried to ascribe "general disagreements" to a more profound cause—to the "different appraisals of the *relative* importance of the spontaneous and consciously 'methodical' element". *Rabocheye Dyelo* formulated its indictment as a *"belittling of the significance of the objective or the spontaneous element of development".** To this we say: Had the polemics with *Iskra* and *Zarya* resulted in nothing more than causing *Rabocheye Dyelo* to hit upon these "general disagreements", that alone would give us considerable satisfaction, so significant is this thesis and so clear is the light it sheds on the quintessence of the present-day theoretical and political differences that exist among Russian Social-Democrats.

For this reason the question of the relation between consciousness and spontaneity is of such enormous general interest, and for this reason the question must be dealt with in great detail.

A. The Beginning of the Spontaneous Upsurge

In the previous chapter we pointed out how *universally* absorbed the educated youth of Russia was in the theories of Marxism in the middle of the nineties. In the same period the strikes that followed the famous St. Petersburg industrial war of 1896 assumed a similar general character. Their spread over the whole of Russia clearly showed the depth of the newly awakening popular movement, and if we are to speak of the "spontaneous element" then, of course, it is this strike movement which, first and fore-

---

* *Rabocheye Dyelo*, No. 10, September 1901, pp. 17-18. *Rabocheye Dyelo*'s italics.

most, must be regarded as spontaneous. But there is spontaneity and spontaneity. Strikes occurred in Russia in the seventies and sixties (and even in the first half of the nineteenth century), and they were accompanied by the "spontaneous" destruction of machinery, etc. Compared with these "revolts", the strikes of the nineties might even be described as "conscious", to such an extent do they mark the progress which the working-class movement made in that period. This shows that the "spontaneous element", in essence, represents nothing more nor less than consciousness in an *embryonic form*. Even the primitive revolts expressed the awakening of consciousness to a certain extent. The workers were losing their age-long faith in the permanence of the system which oppressed them and began ... I shall not say to understand, but to sense the necessity for collective resistance, definitely abandoning their slavish submission to the authorities. But this was, nevertheless, more in the nature of outbursts of desperation and vengeance than of *struggle*. The strikes of the nineties revealed far greater flashes of consciousness; definite demands were advanced, the strike was carefully timed, known cases and instances in other places were discussed, etc. The revolts were simply the resistance of the oppressed, whereas the systematic strikes represented the class struggle in embryo, but only in embryo. Taken by themselves, these strikes were simply trade-union struggles, not yet Social-Democratic struggles. They marked the awakening antagonisms between workers and employers; but the workers were not, and could not be, conscious of the irreconcilable antagonism of their interests to the whole of the modern political and social system, i.e., theirs was not yet Social-Democratic consciousness. In this sense, the strikes of the nineties, despite the enormous progress they represented as compared with the "revolts", remained a purely spontaneous movement.

We have said that *there could not have been* Social-Democratic consciousness among the workers. It would have to be brought to them from without. The history of all countries shows that the working class, exclusively by its own effort, is able to develop only trade-union consciousness, i.e., the conviction that it is necessary to combine in unions, fight the employers, and strive to compel the government to pass necessary labour legislation, etc.* The theory of socialism, however, grew out of the philosophic, historical, and economic theories elaborated by educated representatives of the propertied classes, by intellectuals. By their social status, the founders of modern scientific socialism, Marx and Engels, themselves belonged to the bourgeois intelligentsia. In the very same way, in Russia, the theoretical doctrine of Social-Democracy arose altogether independently of the spontaneous growth of the working-class movement; it arose as a natural and inevitable outcome of the development of thought among the revolutionary socialist intelligentsia. In the period under discussion, the middle nineties, this doctrine not only represented the completely formulated programme of the Emancipation of Labour group, but had already won over to its side the majority of the revolutionary youth in Russia.

Hence, we had both the spontaneous awakening of the working masses, their awakening to conscious life and conscious struggle, and a revolutionary youth, armed with Social-Democratic theory and straining towards the workers. In this connection it is particularly important to state the oft-forgotten (and comparatively little-known) fact that, although the *early* Social-Democrats of that period *zealously carried on economic agitation* (being guided in this activity by the truly useful indications contained in the pamphlet *On Agitation*, then still in manuscript), they did not regard this as their sole task. On the contrary, *from the very beginning* they set for Russian Social-Democracy the most far-reaching historical tasks, in general, and the task of overthrowing the autocracy, in particular. Thus, towards the end of 1895, the St. Petersburg group of Social-Democrats, which founded the League of Struggle for the Emancipation of the Working Class,[34] prepared the first issue of a newspaper called *Rabocheye Dyelo*. This issue was ready to go to press when it was seized by the gendarmes, on the night of December 8, 1895, in a raid

* Trade-unionism does not exclude "politics" altogether, as some imagine. Trade unions have always conducted some political (but not Social-Democratic) agitation and struggle. We shall deal with the difference between trade-union politics and Social-Democratic politics in the next chapter.

on the house of one of the members of the group, Anatoly Alexeyevich Vaneyev,* so that the first edition of *Rabocheye Dyelo* was not destined to see the light of day. The leading article in this issue (which perhaps thirty years hence some *Russkaya Starina*[35] will unearth in the archives of the Department of Police) outlined the historical tasks of the working class in Russia and placed the achievement of political liberty at their head. The issue also contained an article entitled "What Are Our Ministers Thinking About?"** which dealt with the crushing of the elementary education committees by the police. In addition, there was some correspondence from St. Petersburg, and from other parts of Russia (e.g., a letter on the massacre of the workers in Yaroslavl Gubernia). This, "first effort", if we are not mistaken, of the Russian Social-Democrats of the nineties was not a purely local, or less still, "Economic", newspaper, but one that aimed to unite the strike movement with the revolutionary movement against the autocracy, and to win over to the side of Social-Democracy all who were oppressed by the policy of reactionary obscurantism. No one in the slightes degree acquainted with the state of the movement at that ɪeriod could doubt that such a paper would have met with warm response among the workers of the capital and the revolutionary intelligentsia and would have had a wide circulation. The failure of the enterprise merely showed that the Social-Democrats of that period were unable to meet the immediate requirements of the time owing to their lack of revolutionary experience and practical training. This must be said, too, with regard to the *S. Peterburgsky Rabochy Listok*[36] and particularly with regard to *Rabochaya Gazeta* and the *Manifesto* of the Russian Social-Democratic Labour Party, founded in the spring of 1898. Of course, we would not dream of blaming the Social-Democrats of that time for this unpreparedness.

---

* A. A. Vaneyev died in Eastern Siberia in 1899 from consumption, which he contracted during solitary confinement in prison prior to his banishment. That is why we considered it possible to publish the above information, the authenticity of which we guarantee, for it comes from persons who were closely and directly acquainted with A. A. Vaneyev.

** See *Collected Works*, Vol. 2, pp. 87-92.—*Ed.*

But in order to profit from the experience of that movement, and to draw practical lessons from it, we must
thoroughly understand the causes and significance of this
or that shortcoming. It is therefore highly important to
establish the fact that a part (perhaps even a majority)
of the Social-Democrats, active in the period of 1895-98,
justly considered it possible even then, at the very beginning of the "spontaneous" movement, to come forward
with a most extensive programme and a militant tactical
line.* Lack of training of the majority of the revolutionaries, an entirely natural phenomenon, could not have
roused any particular fears. Once the tasks were correctly
defined, once the energy existed for repeated attempts to
fulfil them, temporary failures represented only part misfortune. Revolutionary experience and organisational skill
are things that can be acquired, provided the desire is there
to acquire them, provided the shortcomings are recognised,
which in revolutionary activity is more than half-way towards their removal.

But what was only part misfortune became full misfortune when this consciousness began to grow dim (it was
very much alive among the members of the groups mentioned), when there appeared people—and even Social-
Democratic organs—that were prepared to regard shortcomings as virtues, that even tried to invent a *theoretical*
basis for their *slavish cringing before spontaneity*. It is
time to draw conclusions from this trend, the content of
which is incorrectly and too narrowly characterised as
"Economism".

* "In adopting a hostile attitude towards the activities of the
Social-Democrats of the late nineties, *Iskra* ignores the absence at
that time of conditions for any work other than the struggle for
petty demands," declare the Economists in their "Letter to Russian
Social-Democratic Organs" (*Iskra*, No. 12). The facts given above
show that the assertion about "absence of conditions" *is diametrically opposed to the truth.* Not only at the end, but even in the mid-
nineties, all the conditions existed for *other* work, besides the struggle
for petty demands—all the conditions except adequate training of
leaders. Instead of frankly admitting that we, the ideologists, the
leaders, lacked sufficient training—the "Economists" seek to shift
the blame entirely upon the "absence of conditions", upon the effect
of material environment that determines the road from which no
ideologist will be able to divert the movement. What is this but
slavish cringing before spontaneity, what but the infatuation of the
"ideologists" with their own shortcomings?

B. Bowing to Spontaneity.
Rabochaya Mysl

Before dealing with the literary manifestation of this subservience to spontaneity, we should like to note the following characteristic fact (communicated to us from the above-mentioned source), which throws light on the conditions in which the two future conflicting trends in Russian Social-Democracy arose and grew among the comrades working in St. Petersburg. In the beginning of 1897, just prior to their banishment, A. A. Vaneyev and several of his comrades attended a private meeting[37] at which "old" and "young" members of the League of Struggle for the Emancipation of the Working Class gathered. The conversation centred chiefly about the question of organisation, particularly about the "rules for the workers' mutual benefit fund", which, in their final form, were published in *"Listok" Rabotnika*,[38] No. 9-10, p. 46. Sharp differences immediately showed themselves between the "old" members ("Decembrists", as the St. Petersburg Social-Democrats jestingly called them) and several of the "young" members (who subsequently took an active part in the work of *Rabochaya Mysl*), with a heated discussion ensuing. The "young" members defended the main principles of the rules in the form in which they were published. The "old" members contended that the prime necessity was not this, but the consolidation of the League of Struggle into an organisation of revolutionaries to which all the various workers' mutual benefit funds, students' propaganda circles, etc., should be subordinated. It goes without saying that the disputing sides far from realised at the time that these disagreements were the beginning of a cleavage; on the contrary, they regarded them as something isolated and casual. But this fact shows that in Russia, too, "Economism" did not arise and spread without a struggle against the "old" Social-Democrats (which the Economists of today are apt to forget). And if, in the main, this struggle has not left "documentary" traces behind it, it is *solely* because the membership of the circles then functioning underwent such constant change that no continuity was established and, consequently, differences in point of view were not recorded in any documents.

The founding of *Rabochaya Mysl* brought Economism to the light of day, but not at one stroke. We must picture to ourselves concretely the conditions for activity and the short-lived character of the majority of the Russian study circles (a thing that is possible only for those who have themselves experienced it) in order to understand how much there was of the fortuitous in the successes and failures of the new trend in various towns, and the length of time during which neither the advocates nor the opponents of the "new" could make up their minds—and literally had no opportunity of so doing—as to whether this really expressed a distinct trend or merely the lack of training of certain individuals. For example, the first mimeographed copies of *Rabochaya Mysl* never reached the great majority of Social-Democrats, and if we are able to refer to the leading article in the first number, it is only because it was reproduced in an article by V. I.[39] (*"Listok" Rabotnika*, No. 9-10, p. 47, et seq.), who, of course, did not fail to extol with more zeal than reason the new paper, which was so different from the papers and projects for papers mentioned above.* It is well worth dwelling on this leading article because it brings out in bold relief *the entire spirit of Rabochaya Mysl* and Economism generally.

After stating that the arm of the "blue-coats"[40] could never halt the progress of the working-class movement, the leading article goes on to say: "...The virility of the working-class movement is due to the fact that the workers themselves are at last taking their fate into their own hands, and out of the hands of the leaders"; this fundamental thesis is then developed in greater detail. Actually, the leaders (i.e., the Social-Democrats, the organisers of the League of Struggle) were, one might say, torn out of the hands of the workers** by the police; yet it is made

---

* It should be stated in passing that the praise of *Rabochaya Mysl* in November 1898, when Economism had become fully defined, especially abroad, emanated from the selfsame V. I., who very soon after became one of the editors of *Rabocheye Dyelo*. And yet *Rabocheye Dyelo* denied that there were two trends in Russian Social-Democracy, and continues to deny it to this day!

** That this simile is a correct one is shown by the following characteristic fact. When, after the arrest of the "Decembrists", the news spread among the workers of the Schlüsselburg Highway that the discovery and arrest were facilitated by an *agent-provocateur,*

to appear that the workers were fighting against the leaders and liberated themselves from their yoke! Instead of sounding the call to go forward towards the consolidation of the revolutionary organisation and the expansion of political activity, the call was issued for a *retreat* to the purely trade-union struggle. It was announced that "the economic basis of the movement is eclipsed by the effort never to forget the political ideal", and that the watchword for the working-class movement was "Struggle for economic conditions" (!) or, better still, "The workers for the workers". It was declared that strike funds "are more valuable to the movement than a hundred other organisations" (compare this statement made in October 1897, with the polemic between the "Decembrists" and the young members in the beginning of 1897), etc. Catchwords like "We must concentrate, not on the 'cream' of the workers, but on the 'average', mass worker"; "Politics always obediently follows economics",* etc., etc., became the fashion, exercising an irresistible influence upon the masses of the youth who were attracted to the movement but who, in the majority of cases, were acquainted only with such fragments of Marxism as were expounded in legally appearing publications.

Political consciousness was completely overwhelmed by spontaneity—the spontaneity of the "Social-Democrats" who repeated Mr. V. V.'s "ideas", the spontaneity of those workers who were carried away by the arguments that a kopek added to a ruble was worth more than any socialism or politics, and that they must "fight, knowing that they are fighting, not for the sake of some future generation, but for themselves and their children" (leader in *Rabochaya Mysl*, No. 1). Phrases like these have always

---

N. N. Mikhailov, a dentist, who had been in contact with a group associated with the "Decembrists", the workers were so enraged that they decided to kill him.

* These quotations are taken from the same leading article in the first number of *Rabochaya Mysl*. One can judge from this the degree of theoretical training possessed by these "V.V.'s of Russian Social-Democracy",[41] who kept repeating the crude vulgarisation of "economic materialism" at a time when the Marxists were carrying on a literary war against the real Mr. V. V., who had long ago been dubbed "a past master of reactionary deeds", for holding *similar* views on the relations between politics and economics!

been a favourite weapon of the West-European bourgeois, who, in their hatred for socialism, strove (like the German "*Sozial-Politiker*" Hirsch) to transplant English trade-unionism to their native soil and to preach to the workers that by engaging in the purely trade-union struggle* they would be fighting for themselves and for their children, and not for some future generations with some future socialism. And now the "V. V.'s of Russian Social-Democracy" have set about repeating these bourgeois phrases. It is important at this point to note three circumstances that will be useful to our further analysis of *contemporary* differences.**

In the first place, the overwhelming of political consciousness by spontaneity, to which we referred above, also took place *spontaneously*. This may sound like a pun, but, alas, it is the bitter truth. It did not take place as a result of an open struggle between two diametrically opposed points of view, in which one triumphed over the other; it occurred because of the fact that an increasing number of "old" revolutionaries were "torn away" by the gendarmes and increasing numbers of "young" "V. V.'s of Russian Social-Democracy" appeared on the scene. Everyone, who has, I shall not say participated in, but at least breathed the atmosphere of, the *present-day* Russian movement, knows perfectly well that this is precisely the case. And if, nevertheless, we insist strongly that the reader be fully clear on this generally known fact, if we cite, for explicitness, as it were, the facts of the first edition of *Rabocheye Dyelo* and of the polemic between the "old" and the "young" at the beginning of 1897, we do this because the people who vaunt their "democracy" speculate on the ignorance of these facts on the part of the broad public (or of the very young generation). We shall return to this point further on.

---

* The Germans even have a special expression, *Nur-Gewerkschaftler*, which means an advocate of the "pure trade-union" struggle.

** We emphasise the word *contemporary* for the benefit of those who may pharisaically shrug their shoulders and say: It is easy enough to attack *Rabochaya Mysl* now, but is not all this ancient history? *Mutato nomine de te fabula narratur* (change the name and the tale is about you.—*Ed.*) is our answer to such contemporary Pharisees, whose complete subjection to the ideas of *Rabochaya Mysl* will be *proved* further on.

Secondly, in the very first literary expression of Economism we observe the exceedingly curious phenomenon—highly characteristic for an understanding of all the differences prevailing among present-day Social-Democrats—that the adherents of the "labour movement pure and simple", worshippers of the closest "organic" contacts (*Rabocheye Dyelo's* term) with the proletarian struggle, opponents of any non-worker intelligentsia (even a socialist intelligentsia), are compelled, in order to defend their positions, to resort to the arguments of the *bourgeois* "pure trade-unionists". This shows that from the very outset *Rabochaya Mysl* began—unconsciously—to implement the programme of the *Credo*. This shows (something *Rabocheye Dyelo* cannot grasp) that *all* worship of the spontaneity of the working-class movement, all belittling of the role of "the conscious element", of the role of Social-Democracy, *means, quite independently of whether he who belittles that role desires it or not, a strengthening of the influence of bourgeois ideology upon the workers.* All those who talk about "overrating the importance of ideology",* about exaggerating the role of the conscious element,** etc., imagine that the labour movement pure and simple can elaborate, and will elaborate, an independent ideology for itself, if only the workers "wrest their fate from the hands of the leaders". But this is a profound mistake. To supplement what has been said above, we shall quote the following profoundly true and important words of Karl Kautsky on the new draft programme of the Austrian Social-Democratic Party:***

"Many of our revisionist critics believe that Marx asserted that economic development and the class struggle create, not only the conditions for socialist production, but also, and directly, the *consciousness* [K. K.'s italics] of its necessity. And these critics assert that England, the country most highly developed capitalistically, is more remote than any other from this consciousness. Judging by the draft, one might assume that this allegedly orthodox-Marxist view, which is thus refuted, was shared by the committee that drafted the Austrian programme. In the draft programme it is stated: 'The

---

* Letter of the "Economists", in *Iskra*, No. 12.
** *Rabocheye Dyelo*, No. 10.
*** *Neue Zeit*, 1901-02, XX, I, No. 3, p. 79. The committee's draft to which Kautsky refers was adopted by the Vienna Congress (at the end of last year) in a slightly amended form.

more capitalist development increases the numbers of the proletariat, the more the proletariat is compelled and becomes fit to fight against capitalism. The proletariat becomes conscious' of the possibility and of the necessity for socialism. In this connection socialist consciousness appears to be a necessary and direct result of the proletarian class struggle. But this is absolutely untrue. Of course, socialism, as a doctrine, has its roots in modern economic relationships just as the class struggle of the proletariat has, and, like the latter, emerges from the struggle against the capitalist-created poverty and misery of the masses. But socialism and the class struggle arise side by side and not one out of the other; each arises under different conditions. Modern socialist consciousness can arise only on the basis of profound scientific knowledge. Indeed, modern economic science is as much a condition for socialist production as, say, modern technology, and the proletariat can create neither the one nor the other, no matter how much it may desire to do so; both arise out of the modern social process. The vehicle of science is not the proletariat, but the *bourgeois intelligentsia* [K. K.'s italics]: it was in the minds of individual members of this stratum that modern socialism originated, and it was they who communicated it to the more intellectually developed proletarians who, in their turn, introduce it into the proletarian class struggle where conditions allow that to be done. Thus, socialist consciousness is something introduced into the proletarian class struggle from without [*von Aussen Hineingetragenes*] and not something that arose within it spontaneously [*urwüchsig*]. Accordingly, the old Hainfeld programme quite rightly stated that the task of Social-Democracy is to imbue the proletariat [literally: saturate the proletariat] with the *consciousness* of its position and the consciousness of its task. There would be no need for this if consciousness arose of itself from the class struggle. The new draft copied this proposition from the old programme, and attached it to the proposition mentioned above. But this completely broke the line of thought...."

Since there can be no talk of an independent ideology formulated by the working masses themselves in the process of their movement,* the *only* choice is—either

* This does not mean, of course, that the workers have no part in creating such an ideology. They take part, however, not as workers, but as socialist theoreticians, as Proudhons and Weitlings; in other words, they take part only when they are able, and to the extent that they are able, more or less, to acquire the knowledge of their age and develop that knowledge. But in order that working men *may succeed in this more often*, every effort must be made to raise the level of the consciousness of the workers in general; it is necessary that the workers do not confine themselves to the artificially restricted limits of "*literature for workers*" but that they learn to an increasing degree to master *general literature*. It would be even truer to say "are not confined", instead of "do not confine themselves", because the workers themselves wish to read and do

bourgeois or socialist ideology. There is no middle course (for mankind has not created a "third" ideology, and, moreover, in a society torn by class antagonisms there can never be a non-class or an above-class ideology). Hence, to belittle the socialist ideology *in any way, to turn aside from it in the slightest degree* means to strengthen bourgeois ideology. There is much talk of spontaneity. But the *spontaneous* development of the working-class movement leads to its subordination to bourgeois ideology, *to its development along the lines of the Credo programme*; for the spontaneous working-class movement is trade-unionism, is *Nur-Gewerkschaftlerei*, and trade-unionism means the ideological enslavement of the workers by the bourgeoisie. Hence, our task, the task of Social-Democracy, is *to combat spontaneity, to divert* the working-class movement from this spontaneous, trade-unionist striving to come under the wing of the bourgeoisie, and to bring it under the wing of revolutionary Social-Democracy. The sentence employed by the authors of the "Economist" letter published in *Iskra*, No. 12, that the efforts of the most inspired ideologists fail to divert the working-class movement from the path that is determined by the interaction of the material elements and the material environment *is* therefore *tantamount to renouncing socialism*. If these authors were capable of fearlessly, consistently, and thoroughly considering what they say, as everyone who enters the arena of literary and public activity should be, there would be nothing left for them but to "fold their useless arms over their empty breasts" and—surrender the field of action to the Struves and Prokopoviches, who are dragging the working-class movement "along the line of least resistance", i.e., along the line of bourgeois trade-unionism, or to the Zubatovs, who are dragging it along the line of clerical and gendarme "ideology".

Let us recall the example of Germany. What was the historic service Lassalle rendered to the German working-class movement? It was that he *diverted* that movement from the path of progressionist trade-unionism and co-

---

read all that is written for the intelligentsia, and only a few (bad) intellectuals believe that it is enough "for workers" to be told a few things about factory conditions and to have repeated to them over and over again what has long been known.

operativism towards which it had been spontaneously moving (*with the benign assistance of Schulze-Delitzsch and his like*). To fulfil such a task it was necessary to do something quite different from talking of underrating the spontaneous element, of tactics-as-process, of the interaction between elements and environment, etc. *A fierce struggle against spontaneity* was necessary, and only after such a struggle, extending over many years, was it possible, for instance, to convert the working population of Berlin from a bulwark of the progressionist party into one of the finest strongholds of Social-Democracy. This struggle is by no means over even today (as might seem to those who learn the history of the German movement from Prokopovich, and its philosophy from Struve). Even now the German working class is, so to speak, split up among a number of ideologies. A section of the workers is organised in Catholic and monarchist trade unions; another section is organised in the Hirsch-Duncker unions,[42] founded by the bourgeois worshippers of English trade-unionism; the third is organised in Social-Democratic trade unions. The last-named group is immeasurably more numerous than the rest, but the Social-Democratic ideology was able to achieve this superiority, and will be able to maintain it, only in an unswerving struggle against all other ideologies.

But why, the reader will ask, does the spontaneous movement, the movement along the line of least resistance, lead to the domination of bourgeois ideology? For the simple reason that bourgeois ideology is far older in origin than socialist ideology, that it is more fully developed, and that it has at its disposal *immeasurably* more means of dissemination.* And the younger the socialist movement in any

---

* It is often said that the working class *spontaneously* gravitates towards socialism. This is perfectly true in the sense that socialist theory reveals the causes of the misery of the working class more profoundly and more correctly than any other theory, and for that reason the workers are able to assimilate it so easily, *provided*, however, this theory does not itself yield to spontaneity, *provided* it subordinates spontaneity to itself. Usually this is taken for granted, but it is precisely this which *Rabocheye Dyelo* forgets or distorts. The working class spontaneously gravitates towards socialism; nevertheless, most widespread (and continuously and diversely revived) bourgeois ideology spontaneously imposes itself upon the working class to a still greater degree.

given country, the more vigorously it must struggle against all attempts to entrench non-socialist ideology, and the more resolutely the workers must be warned against the bad counsellors who shout against "overrating the conscious element", etc. The authors of the Economist letter, in unison with *Rabocheye Dyelo*, inveigh against the intolerance that is characteristic of the infancy of the movement. To this we reply: Yes, our movement is indeed in its infancy, and in order that it may grow up faster, it must become imbued with intolerance against those who retard its growth by their subservience to spontaneity. Nothing is so ridiculous and harmful as pretending that we are "old hands" who have long ago experienced all the decisive stages of the struggle.

Thirdly, the first issue of *Rabochaya Mysl* shows that the term "Economism" (which, of course, we do not propose to abandon, since, in one way or another, this designation has already established itself) does not adequately convey the real character of the new trend. *Rabochaya Mysl* does not altogether repudiate the political struggle; the rules for a workers' mutual benefit fund published in its first issue contain a reference to combating the government. *Rabochaya Mysl* believes, however, that "politics always obediently follows economics" (*Rabocheye Dyelo* varies this thesis when it asserts in its programme that "in Russia more than in any other country, the economic struggle is *inseparable* from the political struggle"). *If by politics is meant Social-Democratic politics*, then the theses of *Rabochaya Mysl* and *Rabocheye Dyelo* are utterly incorrect. The economic struggle of the workers is very often connected (although not inseparably) with bourgeois politics, clerical politics, etc., as we have seen. *Rabocheye Dyelo*'s theses are correct, if by politics is meant trade-union politics, viz., the common striving of all workers to secure from the government measures for alleviating the distress to which their condition gives rise, but which do not abolish that condition, i.e., which do not remove the subjection of labour to capital. That striving indeed is common to the English trade-unionists, who are hostile to socialism, to the Catholic workers, to the "Zubatov" workers, etc. There is politics and politics. Thus, we see that *Rabochaya Mysl* does not so much deny the political struggle as it bows to its *spontaneity*, to its unconsciousness. While fully recognising the political struggle (better: the political desires and demands of the workers), which arises spontaneously from the working-class movement itself, it absolutely refuses *independently to work out* a specifically *Social-Democratic politics* corresponding to the general tasks of socialism and to present-day conditions in Russia. Further on we shall show that *Rabocheye Dyelo* commits the same error.

C. The Self-Emancipation Group[43] and *Rabocheye Dyelo*

We have dealt at such length with the little-known and now almost forgotten leading article in the first issue of *Rabochaya Mysl* because it was the first and most striking expression of that general stream of thought which afterwards emerged into the light of day in innumerable streamlets. V. I. was perfectly right when, in praising the first issue and the leading article of *Rabochaya Mysl*, he said that the article had been written in a "sharp and fervent" manner ("*Listok*" *Rabotnika*, No. 9-10, p. 49). Every man with convictions who thinks he has something new to say writes "fervently" and in such a way as to make his views stand out in bold relief. Only those who are accustomed to sitting between two stools lack "fervour"; only such people are able to praise the fervour of *Rabochaya Mysl* one day and attack the "fervent polemics" of its opponents the next.

We shall not dwell on the "*Separate Supplement*" to *Rabochaya Mysl* (below we shall have occasion, on various points, to refer to this work, which expresses the ideas of the Economists more consistently than any other) but shall briefly mention the "Appeal of the Self-Emancipation of the Workers Group" (March 1899, reprinted in the London *Nakanune*,[44] No. 7, July 1899). The authors of the "Appeal" rightly say that "the workers of Russia are *only just awakening*, are just beginning to look about them, and are *instinctively clutching at the first available* means of struggle". Yet they draw from this the same false conclusion as that drawn by *Rabochaya Mysl*, forgetting that the instinctive is the unconscious (the spontaneous) to the aid of which socialists must come; that the "first available means of struggle" will always be, in modern society, the trade-union means of struggle, and the "first available" ideology the bourgeois (trade-union) ideology. Similarly, these authors do not "repudiate" politics, they merely (merely!) echo Mr. V. V. that politics is the superstructure, and therefore, "political agitation must be the superstructure to the agitation carried on in favour of the economic struggle; it must arise on the basis of this struggle and follow in its wake."

As for *Rabocheye Dyelo*, it began its activity with the "defence" of the Economists. It stated a *downright untruth* in its opening issue (No. 1, pp. 141-42) in claiming that it "does not know to which young comrades Axelrod referred" when he warned the Economists in his well-known pamphlet.* In the polemic that flared up with Axelrod and Plekhanov over this untruth, *Rabocheye Dyelo* had to admit that "in form of perplexity, it sought *to defend* all the younger Social-Democrats abroad from this unjust accusation" (the charge of narrowness levelled by Axelrod at the Economists). In reality this accusation was completely justified, and *Rabocheye Dyelo* knew perfectly well that, among others, it applied also to V. I., a member of its Editorial Board. Let me note in passing that in this polemic Axelrod was entirely right and *Rabocheye Dyelo* entirely wrong in their respective interpretations of my pamphlet *The Tasks of the Russian Social-Democrats*.** The pamphlet was written in 1897, before the appearance of *Rabochaya Mysl*, when I thought, rightly, that the *original* tendency of the St. Petersburg League of Struggle, which I characterised above, was dominant. And this tendency was dominant at least until the middle of 1898. Consequently, *Rabocheye Dyelo* had no right whatever, in its attempt to deny the existence and danger of Economism, to refer to a pamphlet that expressed views *forced out* by "Economist" views in St. Petersburg in 1897-98.***

---

* *Present Tasks and Tactics of the Russian Social-Democracy*, Geneva, 1898. Two letters to *Rabochaya Gazeta*, written in 1897.

** See *Collected Works*, Vol. 2, pp. 323-51.—*Ed.*

*** In defending its first untruth ("we do not know to which young comrades Axelrod referred"), *Rabocheye Dyelo* added a second, when it wrote in its *Reply*: "Since the review of *The Tasks* was

But *Rabocheye Dyelo* not only "defended" the Economists, it itself constantly fell into their fundamental errors. The source of this confusion is to be found in the ambiguity of the interpretation given to the following thesis of the *Rabocheye Dyelo* programme: "We consider that the most important phenomenon of Russian life, the one that will mainly *determine the tasks* [our italics] and the character of the publication activity of the Union, is the *mass working-class movement* [*Rabocheye Dyelo*'s italics] which has arisen in recent years." That the mass movement is a most important phenomenon is a fact not to be disputed. But the crux of the matter is, how is one to understand the statement that the mass working-class movement will "determine the tasks"? It may be interpreted in one of two ways. *Either* it means bowing to the spontaneity of this movement, i.e., reducing the role of Social-Democracy to mere subservience to the working-class movement as such (the interpretation of *Rabochaya Mysl*, the Self-Emancipation Group, and other Economists), *or* it means that the mass movement places before us *new* theoretical, political, and organisational tasks, far more complicated than those that might have satisfied us in the period before the rise of the mass movement. *Rabocheye Dyelo* inclined and still inclines towards the first interpretation, for it has said nothing definite about any new tasks, but has argued constantly as though the "mass movement" *relieves* us of the necessity of clearly understanding and fulfilling the tasks it sets before us. We need only point out that *Rabocheye Dyelo* considered that it was impossible to set the overthrow of the autocracy as the *first* task of the mass working-class movement, and that it degraded this task (in the name of the mass move-

---

published, tendencies have arisen, or become more or less clearly defined, among certain Russian Social-Democrats, towards economic one-sidedness, which represent a step backwards from the state of our movement as described in *The Tasks*" (p. 9). This, in the *Reply*, published *in 1900*. But the first issue of *Rabocheye Dyelo* (containing the review) appeared *in April 1899*. Did Economism really arise only in 1899? No. The year 1899 saw the first protest of the *Russian* Social-Democrats against Economism (the protest against the *Credo*). Economism arose in 1897, as *Rabocheye Dyelo* very well knows, for already *in November 1898, V. I.* was praising *Rabochaya Mysl* (see "*Listok*" *Rabotnika*, No. 9-10).

ment) to that of a struggle for immediate political demands (*Reply*, p. 25).

We shall pass over the article by B. Krichevsky, editor of *Rabocheye Dyelo*, entitled "The Economic and the Political Struggle in the Russian Movement", published in No. 7 of that paper, in which these very mistakes* are repeated, and proceed directly to *Rabocheye Dyelo*, No. 10. We shall not, of course, enter in detail into the various objections raised by Krichevsky and Martynov against *Zarya* and *Iskra*. We are here interested solely in the basis of principles on which *Rabocheye Dyelo*, in its tenth issue, took its stand. Thus, we shall not examine the strange fact that *Rabocheye Dyelo* saw a "diametrical contradiction" between the proposition:

"Social-Democracy does not tie its hands, it does not restrict its activities to some one preconceived plan or method of political struggle; it recognises all means of struggle, as long as they correspond to the forces at the disposal of the Party," etc. (*Iskra*, No. 1)**

---

* The "stages theory", or the theory of "timid zigzags", in the political struggle is expressed, for example, in this article, in the following way: "Political demands, which in their character are common to the whole of Russia, should, however, at first [this was written in August 1900!] correspond to the experience gained by the given stratum [*sic!*] of workers in the economic struggle. Only [!] on the basis of this experience can and should political agitation be taken up," etc. (p. 11). On page 4, the author, protesting against what he regards as the absolutely unfounded charge of Economist heresy, pathetically exclaims: "What Social-Democrat does not know that according to the theories of Marx and Engels the economic interests of certain classes play a decisive role in history, and, *consequently*, that particularly the proletariat's struggle for its economic interests must be of paramount importance in its class development and struggle for emancipation?" (Our italics.) The word "consequently" is completely irrelevant. The fact that economic interests play a decisive role *does not in the least imply* that the economic (i.e., trade-union) struggle is of prime importance; for the most essential, the "decisive" interests of classes can be satisfied *only* by radical *political* changes in general. In particular the fundamental economic interests of the proletariat can be satisfied only by a political revolution that will replace the dictatorship of the bourgeoisie by the dictatorship of the proletariat. Krichevsky repeats the arguments of the "V.V.'s of Russian Social-Democracy" (viz., that politics follows economics, etc.) and of the Bernsteinians of German Social-Democracy (e.g., by similar arguments Woltmann sought to prove that the workers must first of all acquire "economic power" before they can think about political revolution).

** See *Collected Works*, Vol. 4, pp. 370-71.—*Ed.*

and the proposition:

"Without a strong organisation skilled in waging political struggle under all circumstances and at all times, there can be no question of that systematic plan of action, illumined by firm principles and steadfastly carried out, which alone is worthy of the name of tactics" (*Iskra*, No. 4).*

To confound recognition, *in principle*, of all means of struggle, of all plans and methods, provided they are expedient, with the demand *at a given political moment* to be guided by a strictly observed plan is tantamount, if we are to talk of tactics, to confounding the recognition by medical science of various methods of treating diseases with the necessity for adopting a certain definite method of treatment for a given disease. The point is, however, that *Rabocheye Dyelo*, itself the victim of a disease which we have called bowing to spontaneity, refuses to recognise any "method of treatment" for *that* disease. Hence, it has made the remarkable discovery that "tactics-as-plan contradicts the fundamental spirit of Marxism" (No. 10, p. 18), that tactics are "*a process of growth of Party tasks, which grow together with the Party*" (p. 11, *Rabocheye Dyelo*'s italics). This remark has every chance of becoming a celebrated maxim, a permanent monument to the *Rabocheye Dyelo* "trend". To the question, *whither*? the leading organ replies: Movement is a process of changing the distance between the starting-point and subsequent points of the movement. This matchless example of profundity is not merely a curiosity (were it that, it would not be worth dealing with at length), but *the programme of a whole trend*, the very programme which R. M. (in the "*Separate Supplement*" *to Rabochaya Mysl*) expressed in the words: That struggle is desirable which is possible, and the struggle which is possible is that which is going on at the given moment. This is precisely the trend of unbounded opportunism, which passively adapts itself to spontaneity.

"Tactics-as-plan contradicts the essence of Marxism!" But this is a slander of Marxism; it means turning Marxism into the caricature held up by the Narodniks in their struggle against us. It means belittling the initiative and energy of class-conscious fighters, whereas Marxism, on

---

* See *Collected Works*, Vol. 5, p. 18.—*Ed.*

the contrary, gives a gigantic impetus to the initiative and energy of the Social-Democrat, opens up for him the widest perspectives, and (if one may so express it) places at his disposal the mighty force of many millions of workers "spontaneously" rising for the struggle. The entire history of international Social-Democracy teems with plans advanced now by one, now by another, political leader, some confirming the far-sightedness and the correct political and organisational views of their authors and others revealing their short-sightedness and their political errors. At the time when Germany was at one of the crucial turning-points in its history—the formation of the Empire, the opening of the Reichstag, and the granting of universal suffrage—Liebknecht had one plan for Social-Democratic politics and work in general, and Schweitzer had another. When the anti-socialist law came down on the heads of the German socialists, Most and Hasselmann had one plan—they were prepared then and there to call for violence and terror; Höchberg, Schramm, and (partly) Bernstein had another—they began to preach to the Social-Democrats that they themselves had provoked the enactment of the law by being unreasonably bitter and revolutionary, and must now earn forgiveness by their exemplary conduct. There was yet a third plan proposed by those who prepared and carried out the publication of an illegal organ. It is easy, of course, with hindsight, many years after the struggle over the selection of the path to be followed, and after history has pronounced its verdict as to the expediency of the path selected, to utter profound maxims about the growth of Party tasks, which grow together with the Party. But at a time of confusion,* when the Russian "Critics" and Economists are degrading Social-Democracy to the level of trade-unionism, and when the terrorists are strongly advocating the adoption of "tactics-as-plan" that repeats the old mistakes, at such a time, to confine oneself to profundities of this kind, means simply to issue to oneself a "certificate of poverty". At a time when many Rus-

---

* "*Ein Jahr der Verwirrung*" ("A Year of Confusion") is the title Mehring gave to the chapter of his *History of German Social-Democracy* in which he describes the hesitancy and lack of determination displayed at first by the socialists in selecting the "tactics-as-plan" for the new situation.

sian Social-Democrats suffer from a lack of initiative and energy, from an inadequate "scope of political propaganda, agitation, and organisation,"* from a lack of "plans" for a broader organisation of revolutionary work, at such a time, to declare that "tactics-as-plan contradicts the essence of Marxism" means not only to vulgarise Marxism in the realm of theory, but *to drag the Party backward* in practice.

Rabocheye Dyelo goes on to sermonise:

"The task of the revolutionary Social-Democrat is only to accelerate objective development by his conscious work, not to obviate it or substitute his own subjective plans for this development. *Iskra* knows all this in theory; but the enormous importance which Marxism justly attaches to conscious revolutionary work causes it in practice, owing to its doctrinaire view of tactics, *to belittle the significance of the objective or the spontaneous element of development*" (p. 18).

Another example of the extraordinary theoretical confusion worthy of Mr. V. V. and his fraternity. We would ask our philosopher: how may a designer of subjective plans "belittle" objective development? Obviously by losing sight of the fact that this objective development creates or strengthens, destroys or weakens certain classes, strata, or groups, certain nations or groups of nations, etc., and in this way serves to determine a given international political alignment of forces, or the position adopted by revolutionary parties, etc. If the designer of plans did that, his guilt would not be that he belittled the spontaneous element, but, on the contrary, that he belittled the *conscious* element, for he would then show that he lacked the "consciousness" properly to understand objective development. Hence, the very talk of "estimating the *relative* significance" (*Rabocheye Dyelo's* italics) of spontaneity and consciousness itself reveals a complete lack of "consciousness". If certain "spontaneous elements of development" can be grasped at all by human understanding, then an incorrect estimation of them will be tantamount to "belittling the conscious element". But if they cannot be grasped, then we do not know them, and therefore cannot speak of them. What then is Krichevsky discussing? If he thinks

---

* Leading article in *Iskra*, No. 1. (See *Collected Works*, Vol. 4, p. 369.—*Ed.*)

that *Iskra*'s "subjective plans" are erroneous (as he in fact declares them to be), he should have shown what objective facts they ignore, and only then charged *Iskra* with *lacking political consciousness* for ignoring them, with "belittling the conscious element", to use his own words. If, however, displeased with subjective plans, he can bring forward no argument other than that of "belittling the spontaneous element" (!), he merely shows: (1) that, theoretically, he understands Marxism *à la* Kareyev and Mikhailovsky, who have been sufficiently ridiculed by Beltov[45]; and (2) that, practically, he is quite satisfied with the "spontaneous elements of development" that have drawn our legal Marxists towards Bernsteinism and our Social-Democrats towards Economism, and that he is "full of wrath" against those who have determined at all costs *to divert* Russian Social-Democracy from the path of "spontaneous" development.

Further, there follow things that are positively droll. "Just as human beings will reproduce in the old-fashioned way despite all the discoveries of natural science, so the birth of a new social order will come about, in the future too, *mainly* as a result of elemental outbursts, despite all the discoveries of social science and the increase in the number of conscious fighters" (p. 19). Just as our grandfathers in their old-fashioned wisdom used to say, Anyone can bring children into the world, so today the "modern socialists" (*à la* Nartsis Tuporylov)[46] say in their wisdom, Anyone can participate in the spontaneous birth of a new social order. We too hold that anyone can. All that is required for participation of that kind is *to yield* to Economism when Economism reigns and to terrorism when terrorism arises. Thus, in the spring of this year, when it was so important to utter a note of warning against infatuation with terrorism, *Rabocheye Dyelo* stood in amazement, confronted by a problem that was "new" to it. And now, six months after, when the problem has become less topical, it presents us at one and the same time with the declaration: "We think that it is not and should not be the task of Social-Democracy to counteract the rise of terroristic sentiments" (*Rabocheye Dyelo*, No. 10, p. 23), and with the Conference resolution: "The Conference regards systematic and aggressive terror as being inopportune" (*Two Conferences*, p. 18). How beautifully clear and coherent this is! Not to counteract, but to declare inopportune, and to declare it in such a way that unsystematic and defensive terror does not¹ come within the scope of the "resolution". It must be admitted that such a resolution is extremely safe and is fully insured against error, just as a man who talks, but says nothing, insures himself against error. All that is needed to frame such a resolution is an ability to keep *at the tail-end* of the movement. When *Iskra* ridiculed *Rabocheye Dyelo* for declaring the question of terror to be new,* the latter angrily accused *Iskra* of "having the incredible effrontery to impose upon the Party organisation solutions of tactical questions proposed by a group of emigrant writers more than fifteen years ago" (p. 24). Effrontery indeed, and what an overestimation of the conscious element—first to resolve questions theoretically beforehand, and then to try to convince the organisation, the Party, and the masses of the correctness of this solution!** How much better it would be to repeat the elements and, without "imposing" anything upon anybody, swing with every "turn"— whether in the direction of Economism or in the direction of terrorism. *Rabocheye Dyelo* even generalises this great precept of wordly wisdom and accuses *Iskra* and *Zarya* of "setting up their programme against the movement, like a spirit hovering over the formless chaos" (p. 29). But what else is the function of Social-Democracy if not to be a "spirit" that not only hovers over the spontaneous movement, but also *raises* this movement *to the level of "its programme"*? Surely, it is not its function to drag at the *tail* of the movement. At best, this would be of no service to the movement; at worst, it would be exceedingly harmful. *Rabocheye Dyelo*, however, not only follows this "tactics-as-process", but elevates it to a principle, so that it would be more correct to describe its tendency not as opportunism, but as *tail-ism* (from the word *tail*). And it must be admitted that those who are determined always to

---

* See *Collected Works*, Vol. 5, pp. 18-20.—*Ed.*
** Nor must it be forgotten that in solving "theoretically" the problem of terror, the Emancipation of Labour Group *generalised* the experience of the antecedent revolutionary movement.

follow behind the movement and be its tail are absolutely and forever guaranteed against "belittling the spontaneous element of development".

*　*　*

And so, we have become convinced that the fundamental error committed by the "new trend" in Russian Social-Democracy is its bowing to spontaneity and its failure to understand that the spontaneity of the masses demands a high degree of consciousness from us Social-Democrats. The greater the spontaneous upsurge of the masses and the more widespread the movement, the more rapid, incomparably so, the demand for greater consciousness in the theoretical, political, and organisational work of Social-Democracy.

The spontaneous upsurge of the masses in Russia proceeded (and continues) with such rapidity that the young Social-Democrats proved unprepared to meet these gigantic tasks. This unpreparedness is our common misfortune, the misfortune of *all* Russian Social-Democrats. The upsurge of the masses proceeded and spread with uninterrupted continuity; it not only continued in the places where it began, but spread to new localities and to new strata of the population (under the influence of the working-class movement, there was a renewed ferment among the student youth, among the intellectuals generally, and even among the peasantry). Revolutionaries, however, *lagged behind* this upsurge, both in their "theories" and in their activity; they failed to establish a constant and continuous organisation capable of *leading* the whole movement.

In Chapter I, we established that *Rabocheye Dyelo* belittled our theoretical tasks and that it "spontaneously" repeated the fashionable catchword "freedom of criticism"; those who repeated this catchword lacked the "consciousness" to understand that the positions of the opportunist "Critics" and those of the revolutionaries in Germany and in Russia are diametrically opposed.

In the following chapters, we shall show how this bowing to spontaneity found expression in the sphere of the political tasks and in the organisational work of Social-Democracy.

III

Trade-unionist Politics and Social-Democratic Politics

We shall again begin by praising *Rabocheye Dyelo*. "Literature of Exposure and the Proletarian Struggle" is the title Martynov gave the article on his differences with *Iskra* published in *Rabocheye Dyelo*, No. 10. He formulated the substance of the differences as follows: "We cannot confine ourselves solely to exposing the system that stands in its [the working-class party's] path of development. We must also react to the immediate and current interests of the proletariat.... *Iskra* ... is in fact an organ of revolutionary opposition that exposes the state of affairs in our country, particularly the political state of affairs.... We, however, work and shall continue to work for the cause of the working class in close organic contact with the proletarian struggle" (p. 63). One cannot help being grateful to Martynov for this formula. It is of outstanding general interest, because substantially it embraces not only our disagreements with *Rabocheye Dyelo*, but the general disagreement between ourselves and the "Economists" on the political struggle. We have shown that the "Economists" do not altogether repudiate "politics", but that they are constantly straying from the Social-Democratic to the trade-unionist conception of politics. Martynov strays in precisely this way, and we shall therefore take his views as a *model* of Economist error on this question. As we shall endeavour to prove, neither the authors of the "*Separate Supplement*" to *Rabochaya Mysl* nor the authors of the manifesto issued by the Self-Emancipation Group, nor the authors of the Economist letter published in *Iskra*, No. 12, will have any right to complain against this choice.

A. Political Agitation and Its Restriction by the Economists

Everyone knows that the economic* struggle of the Russian workers underwent widespread development and con-

* To avoid misunderstanding, we must point out that here, and throughout this pamphlet, by economic struggle, we imply (in keep-

solidation simultaneously with the production of "literature" exposing economic (factory and occupational) conditions. The "leaflets" were devoted mainly to the exposure of the factory system, and very soon a veritable passion for exposures was roused among the workers. As soon as the workers realised that the Social-Democratic study circles desired to, and could, supply them with a new kind of leaflet that told the whole truth about their miserable existence, about their unbearably hard toil, and their lack of rights, they began to send in, actually flood us with, correspondence from the factories and workshops. This "exposure literature" created a tremendous sensation, not only in the particular factory exposed in the given leaflet, but in all the factories to which news of the revealed facts spread. And since the poverty and want among the workers in the various enterprises and in the various trades are much the same, the "truth about the life of the workers" stirred *everyone*. Even among the most backward workers, a veritable passion arose to "get into print"—a noble passion for this rudimentary form of war against the whole of the present social system which is based upon robbery and oppression. And in the overwhelming majority of cases these "leaflets" were in truth a declaration of war, because the exposures served greatly to agitate the workers; they evoked among them common demands for the removal of the most glaring outrages and roused in them a readiness to support the demands with strikes. Finally, the employers themselves were compelled to recognise the significance of these leaflets as a declaration of war, so much so that in a large number of cases they did not even wait for the outbreak of hostilities. As is always the case, the mere publication of these exposures made them effective, and they acquired the significance of a strong moral influence. On more than one occasion, the mere appearance of a leaflet proved sufficient to secure the satisfaction of all or part of the demands put forward. In a word, economic (factory) exposures were and remain an important lever in the economic struggle. And they will continue to

---

ing with the accepted usage among us) the "practical economic struggle", which Engels, in the passage quoted above, described as "resistance to the capitalists", and which in free countries is known as the organised-labour, syndical, or trade-union struggle.

retain this significance as long as there is capitalism, which makes it necessary for the workers to defend themselves. Even in the most advanced countries of Europe it can still be seen that the exposure of abuses in some backward trade, or in some forgotten branch of domestic industry, serves as a starting-point for the awakening of class-consciousness, for the beginning of a trade-union struggle, and for the spread of socialism.*

The overwhelming majority of Russian Social-Democrats have of late been almost entirely absorbed by this work of organising the exposure of factory conditions. Suffice it to recall *Rabochaya Mysl* to see the extent to which they have been absorbed by it—so much so, indeed, that they have lost sight of the fact that this, *taken by itself*, is in essence still not Social-Democratic work, but merely trade-union work. As a matter of fact, the exposures merely dealt with the relations between the workers *in a given trade* and their employers, and all they achieved was that the sellers of labour-power learned to sell their "commodity" on better terms and to fight the purchasers over a purely commercial deal. These exposures could have served (if properly utilised by an organisation of revolutionaries) as a beginning and a component part of Social-Democratic activity; but they could also have led (and, given a worshipful attitude towards spontaneity, were bound to lead) to a "purely trade-union" struggle and to a non-Social-Democratic working-class movement. Social-

---

* In the present chapter we deal only with the *political* struggle, in its broader or narrower meaning. Therefore, we note only in passing, merely as a curiosity, *Rabocheye Dyelo's* charge that *Iskra* is "too restrained" in regard to the economic struggle (*Two Conferences*, p. 27, rehashed by Martynov in his pamphlet, *Social-Democracy and the Working Class*). If the accusers computed by the hundredweights or reams (as they are so fond of doing) any given year's discussion of the economic struggle in the industrial section of *Iskra*, in comparison with the corresponding sections of *Rabocheye Dyelo* and *Rabochaya Mysl* combined, they would easily see that the latter lag behind even in this respect. Apparently, the realisation of this simple truth compels them to resort to arguments that clearly reveal their confusion. "*Iskra*", they write, "willy-nilly [!] is compelled [!] to reckon with the imperative demands of life and to publish at least [!!] correspondence about the working-class movement" (*Two Conferences*, p. 27). Now this is really a crushing argument!

Democracy leads the struggle of the working class, not only for better terms for the sale of labour-power, but for the abolition of the social system that compels the propertyless to sell themselves to the rich. Social-Democracy represents the working class, not in its relation to a given group of employers alone, but in its relation to all classes of modern society and to the state as an organised political force. Hence, it follows that not only must Social-Democrats not confine themselves exclusively to the economic struggle, but that they must not allow the organisation of economic exposures to become the predominant part of their activities. We must take up actively the political education of the working class and the development of its political consciousness. *Now* that *Zarya* and *Iskra* have made the first attack upon Economism, "all are agreed" on this (although some agree only in words, as we shall soon see).

The question arises, what should political education consist in? Can it be confined to the propaganda of working-class hostility to the autocracy? Of course not. It is not enough *to explain* to the workers that they are politically oppressed (any more than it is *to explain* to them that their interests are antagonistic to the interests of the employers). Agitation must be conducted with regard to every concrete example of this oppression (as we have begun to carry on agitation round concrete examples of economic oppression). Inasmuch as *this* oppression affects the most divers classes of society, inasmuch as it manifests itself in the most varied spheres of life and activity—vocational, civic, personal, family, religious, scientific, etc., etc.—is it not evident that *we shall not be fulfilling our task* of developing the political consciousness of the workers if we do not *undertake* the organisation of the *political exposure* of the autocracy *in all its aspects*? In order to carry on agitation round concrete instances of oppression, these instances must be exposed (as it is necessary to expose factory abuses in order to carry on economic agitation).

One might think this to be clear enough. It turns out, however, that it is only in words that "all" are agreed on the need to develop political consciousness, *in all its aspects*. It turns out that *Rabocheye Dyelo*, for example, far from tackling the task of organising (or making a start in organising) comprehensive political exposure, is even trying *to drag Iskra*, which has undertaken this task, *away from it*. Listen to the following: "The political struggle of the working class is merely [it is certainly not "merely"] the most developed, wide, and effective form of economic struggle" (programme of *Rabocheye Dyelo*, published in issue No. 1, p. 3). "The Social-Democrats are now confronted with the task of lending the economic struggle itself, as far as possible, a political character" (Martynov, *Rabocheye Dyelo*, No. 10, p. 42). "The economic struggle is the most widely applicable means of drawing the masses into active political struggle" (resolution adopted by the Conference of the Union Abroad[47] and "amendments" thereto, *Two Conferences*, pp. 11 and 17). As the reader will observe, all these theses permeate *Rabocheye Dyelo* from its very first number to the latest "Instructions to the Editors", and all of them evidently express a single view regarding political agitation and struggle. Let us examine this view from the standpoint of the opinion prevailing among all Economists, that political agitation must *follow* economic agitation. Is it true that, in general,* the economic struggle "is the most widely applicable means" of drawing the masses into the political struggle? It is entirely untrue. *Any and every* manifestation of police tyranny and autocratic outrage, not only in connection with the economic struggle, is not one whit less "widely applicable" as a means of "drawing in" the masses. The rural superintendents[48] and the flogging of peasants, the corruption of the officials and the police treatment of the

---

* We say "in general", because *Rabocheye Dyelo* speaks of general principles and of the general tasks of the Party as a whole. Undoubtedly, cases occur in practice when politics really *must* follow economics, but only Economists can speak of this in a resolution intended to apply to the whole of Russia. Cases do occur when *it is possible* "right from the beginning" to carry on political agitation "exclusively on an economic basis"; yet *Rabocheye Dyelo* came in the end to the conclusion that "there is no need for this whatever" (*Two Conferences*, p. 11). In the following chapter, we shall show that the tactics of the "politicians" and revolutionaries not only do not ignore the trade-union tasks of Social-Democracy, but that, on the contrary, they alone *can secure* their consistent fulfilment.

"common people" in the cities, the fight against the famine-stricken and the suppression of the popular striving towards enlightenment and knowledge, the extortion of taxes and the persecution of the religious sects, the humiliating treatment of soldiers and the barrack methods in the treatment of the students and liberal intellectuals— do all these and a thousand other similar manifestations of tyranny, though not directly connected with the "economic" struggle, represent, in general, *less* "widely applicable" means and occasions for political agitation and for drawing the masses into the political struggle? The very opposite is true. Of the sum total of cases in which the workers suffer (either on their own account or on account of those closely connected with them) from tyranny, violence, and the lack of rights, undoubtedly only a small minority represent cases of police tyranny in the trade-union struggle as such. Why then should we, beforehand, *restrict* the scope of political agitation by declaring only *one* of the means to be "the most widely applicable", when Social-Democrats must have, in addition, other, generally speaking, no less "widely applicable" means?

In the dim and distant past (a full year ago!...) *Rabocheye Dyelo* wrote: "The masses begin to understand immediate political demands after one strike, or at all events, after several", "as soon as the government sets the police and gendarmerie against them" [*August* (No. 7) 1900, p. 15]. This opportunist theory of stages has now been rejected by the Union Abroad, which makes a concession to us by declaring: "There is no need whatever to conduct political agitation right from the beginning, exclusively on an economic basis" (*Two Conferences*, p. 11). The Union's repudiation of part of its former errors will show the future historian of Russian Social-Democracy better than any number of lengthy arguments the depths to which our Economists have degraded socialism! But the Union Abroad must be very naïve indeed to imagine that the abandonment of one form of restricting politics will induce us to agree to another form. Would it not be more logical to say, in this case too, that the economic struggle should be conducted on the widest possible basis, that it should always be utilised for political agitation, but that "there is no need whatever" to regard the economic struggle as the *most* widely applicable means of drawing the masses into active political struggle?

The Union Abroad attaches significance to the fact that it has substituted the phrase "most widely applicable means" for the phrase "the best means" contained in one of the resolutions of the Fourth Congress of the Jewish Workers' Union (Bund).[49] We confess that we find it difficult to say which of these resolutions is the better one. In our opinion they are *both worse.* Both the Union Abroad and the Bund fall into the error (partly, perhaps, unconsciously, under the influence of tradition) of giving an Economist, trade-unionist interpretation to politics. Whether this is done by employing the word "best" or the words "most widely applicable" makes no essential difference whatever. Had the Union Abroad said that "political agitation on an economic basis" is the most widely applied (not "applicable") means, it would have been right in regard to a certain period in the development of our Social-Democratic movement. It would have been right in regard to the *Economists* and to many (if not the majority) of the practical workers of 1898-1901; for these practical Economists *applied* political agitation (to the extent that they applied it at all) *almost exclusively on an economic basis.* Political agitation on *such* lines was recognised and, as we have seen, even recommended by *Rabochaya Mysl* and the Self-Emancipation Group. *Rabocheye Dyelo* should have *strongly condemned* the fact that the useful work of economic agitation was accompanied by the harmful restriction of the political struggle; instead, it declares the means most widely *applied (by the Economists)* to be the most widely *applicable*! It is not surprising that when we call these people Economists, they can do nothing but pour every manner of abuse upon us; call us "mystifiers", "disrupters", "papal nuncios", and "slanderers"*; go complaining to the whole world that we have mortally offended them; and declare almost on oath that "not a single Social-Democratic organisation is now tinged with Economism".** Oh, those evil, slanderous politicians!

---

* These are the precise expressions used in *Two Conferences,* pp. 31, 32, 28, and 30.

** *Two Conferences,* p. 32.

They must have deliberately invented this Economism, out of sheer hatred of mankind, in order mortally to offend other people.

What concrete, real meaning attaches to Martynov's words when he sets before Social-Democracy the task of "lending the economic struggle itself a political character"? The economic struggle is the collective struggle of the workers against their employers for better terms *in the sale of their labour-power*, for better living and working conditions. This struggle is necessarily a trade-union struggle, because working conditions differ greatly in different trades, and, consequently, the struggle *to improve* them can only be conducted on the basis of trade organisations (in the Western countries, through trade unions; in Russia, through temporary trade associations and through leaflets, etc.). Lending "the economic struggle itself a political character" means, therefore, striving to secure satisfaction of these trade demands, the improvement of working conditions in each separate trade by means of "legislative and administrative measures" (as Martynov puts it on the ensuing page of his article, p. 43). This is precisely what all workers' trade unions do and always have done. Read the works of the soundly scientific (and "soundly" opportunist) Mr. and Mrs. Webb and you will see that the British trade unions long ago recognised, and have long been carrying out, the task of "lending the economic struggle itself a political character"; they have long been fighting for the right to strike, for the removal of all legal hindrances to the co-operative and trade-union movements, for laws to protect women and children, for the improvement of labour conditions by means of health and factory legislation, etc.

Thus, the pompous phrase about "lending the economic struggle *itself* a political character", which sounds so "terrifically" profound and revolutionary, serves as a screen to conceal what is in fact the traditional striving *to degrade* Social-Democratic politics to the level of trade-union politics. Under the guise of rectifying the one-sidedness of *Iskra*, which, it is alleged, places "the revolutionising of dogma higher than the revolutionising of life",* we are

---

* *Rabocheye Dyelo*, No. 10, p. 60. This is the Martynov variation of the application, which we have characterised above, of the thesis

presented with the *struggle for economic reforms* as if it were something entirely new. In point of fact, the phrase "lending the economic struggle itself a political character" means nothing more than the struggle for economic reforms. Martynov himself might have come to this simple conclusion, had he pondered over the significance of his own words. "Our Party," he says, training his heaviest guns on *Iskra*, "could and should have presented concrete demands to the government for legislative and administrative measures against economic exploitation, unemployment, famine, etc." (*Rabocheye Dyelo*, No. 10, pp. 42-43). Concrete demands for measures—does not this mean demands for social reforms? Again we ask the impartial reader: Are we slandering the *Rabocheye Dyelo*ites (may I be forgiven for this awkward, currently used designation!) by calling them concealed Bernsteinians when, as their point of *disagreement* with *Iskra*, they advance their thesis on the necessity of struggling for economic reforms?

Revolutionary Social-Democracy has always included the struggle for reforms as part of its activities. But it utilises "economic" agitation for the purpose of presenting to the government, not only demands for all sorts of measures, but also (and primarily) the demand that it cease to be an autocratic government. Moreover, it considers it its duty to present this demand to the government on the basis, not of the economic struggle *alone*, but of all manifestations in general of public and political life. In a word, it subordinates the struggle for reforms, as the part to the whole, to the revolutionary struggle for freedom and for socialism. Martynov, however, resuscitates the theory of stages in a new form and strives to prescribe, as it were, an exclusively economic path of development for the political struggle. By advancing at this moment, when the revolutionary movement is on the upgrade, an alleged special "task" of struggling for reforms, he is dragging the party backwards and is playing into the hands of both "Economist" and liberal opportunism.

"Every step of real movement is more important than a dozen programmes" to the present chaotic state of our movement. In fact, this is merely a translation into Russian of the notorious Bernsteinian sentence: "The movement is everything, the final aim is nothing."

To proceed. Shamefacedly hiding the struggle for reforms behind the pompous thesis of "lending the economic struggle itself a political character", Martynov advanced, as if it were a special point, *exclusively economic* (indeed, exclusively factory) *reforms*. As to the reason for his doing that, we do not know it. Carelessness, perhaps? Yet if he had in mind something else besides "factory" reforms, then the whole of his thesis, which we have cited, loses all sense. Perhaps he did it because he considers it possible and probable that the government will make "concessions" only in the economic sphere?* If so, then it is a strange delusion. Concessions are also possible and are made in the sphere of legislation concerning flogging, passports, land redemption payments,[50] religious sects, the censorship, etc., etc. "Economic" concessions (or pseudo-concessions) are, of course, the cheapest and most advantageous from the government's point of view, because by these means it hopes to win the confidence of the working masses. For this very reason, we Social-Democrats *must not* under any circumstances or in any way whatever create grounds for the belief (or the misunderstanding) that we attach greater value to economic reforms, or that we regard them as being particularly important, etc. "Such demands," writes Martynov, speaking of the concrete demands for legislative and administrative measures referred to above, "would not be merely a hollow sound, because, promising certain palpable results, they might be actively supported by the working masses...." We are not Economists, oh no! We only cringe as slavishly before the "palpableness" of concrete results as do the Bernsteins, the Prokopoviches, the Struves, the R. M.'s, and *tutti quanti*! We only wish to make it understood (together with Nartsis Tuporylov) that all which "does not promise palpable results" is merely a "hollow sound"! We are only trying to argue as if the working masses were incapable (and had not already proved their capabilities, notwithstanding those who ascribe their own philistinism to them) of actively supporting *every* protest against the autocracy,

---

* P. 43. "Of course, when we advise the workers to present certain economic demands to the government, we do so because in the *economic* sphere the autocratic government is, of necessity, prepared to make certain concessions."

even if it *promises absolutely no palpable results whatever*!

Let us take, for example, the very "measures" for the relief of unemployment and the famine that Martynov himself advances. *Rabocheye Dyelo* is engaged, judging by what it has promised, in drawing up and elaborating a programme of "concrete [in the form of bills?] demands for legislative and administrative measures", "promising palpable results", while *Iskra,* which "constantly places the revolutionising of dogma higher than the revolutionising of life", has tried to explain the inseparable connection between unemployment and the whole capitalist system, has given warning that "famine is coming", has exposed the police "fight against the famine-stricken", and the outrageous "provisional penal servitude regulations"; and *Zarya* has published a special reprint, in the form of an agitational pamphlet, of a section of its "Review of Home Affairs", dealing with the famine.* But good God! How "one-sided" were these incorrigibly narrow and orthodox doctrinaires, how deaf to the calls of "life itself"! Their articles contained—oh horror!—*not a single*, can you imagine it?—not a single "concrete demand" "promising palpable results"! Poor doctrinaires! They ought to be sent to Krichevsky and Martynov to be taught that tactics are a process of growth, of that which grows, etc., and that the economic struggle *itself* should be given a political character!

"In addition to its immediate revolutionary significance, the economic struggle of the workers against the employers and the government ["*economic* struggle against the government"!] has also this significance: it constantly brings home to the workers the fact that they have no political rights" (Martynov, p. 44). We quote this passage, not in order to repeat for the hundredth and thousandth time what has been said above, but in order to express particular thanks to Martynov for this excellent new formula: "the economic struggle of the workers against the employers and the government." What a pearl! With what inimitable skill and mastery in eliminating all partial disagreements and shades of differences among Economists

---

* See *Collected Works*, Vol. 5, pp. 253-74.—*Ed.*

this clear and concise proposition expresses the *quintes-sence of Economism*, from summoning the workers "to the political struggle, which they carry on in the general interest, for the improvement of the conditions of all the workers",* continuing through the theory of stages, and ending in the resolution of the Conference on the "most widely applicable", etc. "Economic struggle against the government" is precisely trade-unionist politics, which is still very far from being Social-Democratic politics.

B. How Martynov Rendered Plekhanov More Profound

"What a large number of Social-Democratic Lomonosovs have appeared among us lately!" observed a comrade one day, having in mind the astonishing propensity of many who are inclined toward Economism to arrive, "neces-sarily, by their own understanding", at great truths (e.g., that the economic struggle stimulates the workers to ponder over their lack of rights) and in doing so to ignore, with the supreme contempt of born geniuses, all that has been produced by the antecedent development of revolu-tionary thought and of the revolutionary movement. Lomonosov-Martynov is precisely such a born genius. We need but glance at his article "Urgent Questions" to see how by "his own understanding" he *arrives at* what was long ago said by Axelrod (of whom our Lomonosov, naturally, says not a word); how, for instance, he *is be-ginning* to understand that we cannot ignore the opposi-tion of such or such strata of the bourgeoisie (*Rabocheye Dyelo*, No. 9, pp. 61, 62, 71; compare this with *Rabocheye Dyelo*'s *Reply* to Axelrod, pp. 22, 23-24), etc. But alas, he is only "arriving" and is only "beginning", not more than that, for so little has he understood Axelrod's ideas, that he talks about "the economic struggle against the em-ployers and the government". For three years (1898-1901) *Rabocheye Dyelo* has tried hard to understand Axelrod, but has so far not understood him! Can one of the reasons be that Social-Democracy, "like mankind", always sets itself only tasks that can be achieved?

---

* *Rabochaya Mysl, "Separate Supplement,"* p. 14.

But the Lomonosovs are distinguished not only by their ignorance of many things (that would be but half misfortune!), but also by their unawareness of their own ignorance. Now this is a real misfortune; and it is this misfortune that prompts them without further ado to attempt to render Plekhanov "more profound".

"Much water," Lomonosov-Martynov says, "has flowed under the bridge since Plekhanov wrote this book [*Tasks of the Socialists in the Fight Against the Famine in Russia*]. The Social-Democrats who for a decade led the economic struggle of the working class... have failed as yet to lay down a broad theoretical basis for Party tactics. This question has now come to a head, and if we should wish to lay down such a theoretical basis, we should certainly have to deepen considerably the principles of tactics developed at one time by Plekhanov.... Our present definition of the distinction between propaganda and agitation would have to be different from Plekhanov's. [Martynov has just quoted Plekhanov's words: "A propagandist presents many ideas to one or a few persons; an agitator presents only one or a few ideas, but he presents them to a mass of people."] By propaganda we would understand the revolutionary explanation of the present social system, entire or in its partial manifestations, whether that be done in a form intelligible to individuals or to broad masses. By agitation, in the strict sense of the word [*sic!*], we would understand the call upon the masses to undertake definite, concrete actions and the promotion of the direct revolutionary intervention of the proletariat in social life."

We congratulate Russian—and international—Social-Democracy on having found, thanks to Martynov, a new terminology, more strict and more profound. Hitherto we thought (with Plekhanov, and with all the leaders of the international working-class movement) that the propagandist, dealing with, say, the question of unemployment, must explain the capitalistic nature of crises, the cause of their inevitability in modern society, the necessity for the transformation of this society into a socialist society, etc. In a word, he must present "many ideas", so many, indeed, that they will be understood as an integral whole only by a (comparatively) few persons. The agitator, however, speaking on the same subject, will take as an illustration a fact that is most glaring and most widely known to his audience, say, the death of an unemployed worker's family from starvation, the growing impoverishment, etc., and, utilising this fact, known to all, will direct his efforts to presenting *a single idea* to the "masses", e.g., the senselessness of the contradiction between the increase of wealth and the increase of poverty; he will strive *to rouse* discontent and indignation among the masses against this crying injustice, leaving a more complete explanation of this contradiction to the propagandist. Consequently, the propagandist operates chiefly by means of the *printed* word; the agitator by means of the *spoken* word. The propagandist requires qualities different from those of the agitator. Kautsky and Lafargue, for example, we term propagandists; Bebel and Guesde we term agitators. To single out a third sphere, or third function, of practical activity, and to include in this function "the call upon the masses to undertake definite concrete actions", is sheer nonsense, because the "call", as a single act, either naturally and inevitably supplements the theoretical treatise, propagandist pamphlet, and agitational speech, or represents a purely executive function. Let us take, for example, the struggle the German Social-Democrats are now waging against the corn duties. The theoreticians write research works on tariff policy, with the "call", say, to struggle for commercial treaties and for Free Trade. The propagandist does the same thing in the periodical press, and the agitator in public speeches. At the present time, the "concrete action" of the masses takes the form of signing petitions to the Reichstag against raising the corn duties. The call for this action comes indirectly from the theoreticians, the propagandists, and the agitators, and, directly, from the workers who take the petition lists to the factories and to private homes for the gathering of signatures. According to the "Martynov terminology", Kautsky and Bebel are both propagandists, while those who solicit the signatures are agitators. Isn't it clear?

The German example recalled to my mind the German word "Verballhornung", which, literally translated, means "Ballhorning". Johann Ballhorn, a Leipzig publisher of the sixteenth century, published a child's reader in which, as was the custom, he introduced a drawing of a cock, but a cock without spurs and with a couple of eggs lying near it. On the cover he printed the legend, "*Revised* edition by Johann Ballhorn". Ever since then, the Germans describe any "revision" that is really a worsening as "Ballhorning". And one cannot help recalling Ballhorn upon seeing how the Martynovs try to render Plekhanov "more profound".

Why did our Lomonosov "invent" this confusion? In order to illustrate how *Iskra* "devotes attention only to one side of the case, just as Plekhanov did a decade and a half ago" (39). "With *Iskra*, propagandist tasks force agitational tasks into the background, at least for the present" (52). If we translate this last proposition from the language of Martynov into ordinary human language (because mankind has not yet managed to learn the newly-invented terminology), we shall get the following: with *Iskra*, the tasks of political propaganda and political agitation force into the background the task of "presenting to the government concrete demands for legislative and administrative measures" that "promise certain palpable results" (or demands for social reforms, that is, if we are permitted once again to employ the old terminology of the old mankind not yet grown to Martynov's level). We suggest that the reader compare this thesis with the following tirade:

> "What also astonishes us in these programmes [the programmes advanced by revolutionary Social-Democrats] is their constant stress upon the benefits of workers' activity in parliament [non-existent in Russia], though they completely ignore [thanks to their revolutionary nihilism] the importance of workers' participation in the legislative manufacturers' assemblies on factory affairs [which do exist in Russia]... or at least the importance of workers' participation in municipal bodies. ..."

The author of this tirade expresses in a somewhat more forthright and clearer manner the very idea which Lomonosov-Martynov discovered by his own understanding. The author is R. M., in the *"Separate Supplement" to Rabochaya Mysl* (p. 15).

C. Political Exposures and "Training in Revolutionary Activity"

In advancing against *Iskra* his theory of "raising the activity of the working masses", Martynov actually betrayed an urge *to belittle* that activity, for he declared the very economic struggle before which all economists grovel to be the preferable, particularly important, and "most widely applicable" means of rousing this activity and its broadest field. This error is characteristic, precisely in that it is by no means peculiar to Martynov. In reality, it is possible to "raise the activity of the working masses" *only* when this activity *is not restricted* to "political agitation on an economic basis". A basic condition for the necessary expansion of political agitation is the organisation of *comprehensive* political exposure. *In no way* except by means of such exposures *can* the masses be trained in political consciousness and revolutionary activity. Hence, activity of this kind is one of the most important functions of international Social-Democracy as a whole, for even political freedom does not in any way eliminate exposures; it merely shifts somewhat their sphere of direction. Thus, the German party is especially strengthening its positions and spreading its influence, thanks particularly to the untiring energy with which it is conducting its campaign of political exposure. Working-class consciousness cannot be genuine political consciousness unless the workers are trained to respond to *all* cases of tyranny, oppression, violence, and abuse, no matter *what class* is affected—unless they are trained, moreover, to respond from a Social-Democratic point of view and no other. The consciousness of the working masses cannot be genuine class-consciousness, unless the workers learn, from concrete, and above all from topical, political facts and events to observe *every* other social class in *all* the manifestations of its intellectual, ethical, and political life; unless they learn to apply in practice the materialist analysis and the materialist estimate of *all* aspects of the life and activity of *all* classes, strata, and groups of the population. Those who concentrate the attention, observation, and consciousness of the working class exclusively, or even mainly, upon itself alone are not Social-Democrats; for the self-knowledge of the working class is indissolubly bound up, not solely with a fully clear theoretical understanding or rather, not so much with the theoretical, as with the practical, understanding—of the relationships between *all* the various classes of modern society, acquired through the experience of political life. For this reason the conception of the economic struggle as the most widely applicable means of drawing the masses into the political movement, which our Economists preach, is so extremely harmful and reactionary in its practical significance. In order to become a Social-Democrat, the worker must have a clear picture in his mind of the economic nature and the social and political features of the landlord and the priest, the high state official and the peasant, the student and the vagabond; he must know their strong and weak points; he must grasp the meaning of all the catchwords and sophisms by which each class and each stratum *camouflages* its selfish strivings and its real "inner workings"; he must understand what interests are reflected by certain institutions and certain laws and how they are reflected. But this "clear picture" cannot be obtained from any book. It can be obtained only from living examples and from exposures that follow close upon what is going on about us at a given moment; upon what is being discussed, in whispers perhaps, by each one in his own way; upon what finds expression in such and such events, in such and such statistics, in such and such court sentences, etc., etc. These comprehensive political exposures are an essential and *fundamental* condition for training the masses in revolutionary activity.

Why do the Russian workers still manifest little revolutionary activity in response to the brutal treatment of the people by the police, the persecution of religious sects, the flogging of peasants, the outrageous censorship, the torture of soldiers, the persecution of the most innocent cultural undertakings, etc.? Is it because the "economic struggle" does not "stimulate" them to this, because such activity does not "promise palpable results", because it produces little that is "positive"? To adopt such an opinion, we repeat, is merely to direct the charge where it does not belong, to blame the working masses for one's own philistinism (or Bernsteinism). We must blame ourselves, our lagging behind the mass movement, for still being unable to organise sufficiently wide, striking, and rapid exposures of all the shameful outrages. When we do that (and we must and can do it), the most backward worker will understand, *or will feel*, that the students and religious sects, the peasants and the authors are being abused and outraged by those same dark forces that are oppressing and crushing him at every step of his life. Feeling that, he himself will be filled with an irresistible desire to react, and he will know how to hoot the censors one day, on another day to demonstrate outside the house of a governor who has brutally suppressed a peasant uprising, on still another day to teach a lesson to the gendarmes in surplices who are doing the work of the Holy Inquisition, etc. As yet we have done very little, almost nothing, *to bring* before the working masses prompt exposures on all possible issues. Many of us as yet do not recognise this as our *bounden duty* but trail spontaneously in the wake of the "drab everyday struggle", in the narrow confines of factory life. Under such circumstances to say that "*Iskra* displays a tendency to minimise the significance of the forward march of the drab everyday struggle in comparison with the propaganda of brilliant and complete ideas" (Martynov, op. cit., p. 61), means to drag the Party back, to defend and glorify our unpreparedness and backwardness.

As·for calling the masses to action, that will come of itself as soon as energetic political agitation, live and striking exposures come into play. To catch some criminal red-handed and immediately to brand him publicly in all places is of itself far more effective than any number of "calls"; the effect very often is such as will make it impossible to tell exactly who it was that "called" upon the masses and who suggested this or that plan of demonstration, etc. Calls for action, not in the general, but in the concrete, sense of the term can be made only at the place of action; only those who themselves go into action, and do so immediately, can sound such calls. Our business as Social-Democratic publicists is to deepen, expand, and intensify political exposures and political agitation.

A word in passing about "calls to action". *The only newspaper* which *prior to* the spring events *called upon* the workers to intervene actively in a matter that certainly did not *promise* any *palpable results* whatever for the workers, i.e., the drafting of the students into the army, *was Iskra.* Immediately after the publication of the order of January 11, on "drafting the 183 students into the army", *Iskra* published an article on the matter (in its February issue, No. 2),* and, *before* any demonstration was begun, forthwith *called upon* "the workers to go to the aid of the students", called upon the "people" openly to take up the government's arrogant challenge. We ask:

---

* See *Collected Works*, Vol. 4, pp. 414-19.—*Ed.*

how is the remarkable fact to be explained that although Martynov talks so much about "calls to action", and even suggests "calls to action" as a special form of activity, he said not a word about *this* call? After this, was it not sheer philistinism on Martynov's part to allege that *Iskra* was *one-sided* because it did not issue sufficient "calls" to struggle for demands "promising palpable results"?

Our Economists, including *Rabocheye Dyelo*, were successful because they adapted themselves to the backward workers. But the Social-Democratic worker, the revolutionary worker (and the number of such workers is growing) will indignantly reject all this talk about struggle for demands "promising palpable results", etc., because he will understand that this is only a variation of the old song about adding a kopek to the ruble. Such a worker will say to his counsellors from *Rabochaya Mysl* and *Rabocheye Dyelo*: you are busying yourselves in vain, gentlemen, and shirking your proper duties, by meddling with such excessive zeal in a job that we can very well manage ourselves. There is nothing clever in your assertion that the Social-Democrats' task is to lend the economic struggle itself a political character; that is only the beginning, it is not the main task of the Social-Democrats. For all over the world, including Russia, *the police themselves often take the initiative in lending* the economic struggle a political character, and the workers themselves learn to understand whom the government supports.* The

---

* The demand "to lend the economic struggle itself a political character" most strikingly expresses *subservience to spontaneity* in the sphere of political activity. Very often the economic struggle *spontaneously* assumes a political character, that is to say, without the intervention of the "revolutionary bacilli—the intelligentsia", without the intervention of the class-conscious Social-Democrats. The economic struggle of the English workers, for instance, also assumed a political character without any intervention on the part of the socialists. The task of the Social-Democrats, however, is not exhausted by political agitation on an economic basis; their task is *to convert* trade-unionist politics into Social-Democratic political struggle, *to utilise* the sparks of political consciousness which the economic struggle generates among the workers, for the purpose of *raising* the workers to the level of *Social-Democratic* political consciousness. The Martynovs, however, instead of raising and stimulating the spontaneously awakening political consciousness of the workers, *bow to spontaneity* and repeat over and over *ad nauseam*, that the eco-

"economic struggle of the workers against the employers and the government", about which you make as much fuss as if you had discovered a new America, is being waged in all parts of Russia, even the most remote, by the workers themselves who have heard about strikes, but who have heard almost nothing about socialism. The "activity" you want to stimulate among us workers, by advancing concrete demands that promise palpable results, we are already displaying and in our everyday, limited trade-union work we put forward these concrete demands, very often without any assistance whatever from the intellectuals. But *such* activity is not enough for us; we are not children to be fed on the thin gruel of "economic" politics alone; we want to know everything that others know, we want to learn the details of *all* aspects of political life and to take part *actively* in every single political event. In order that we may do this, the intellectuals must talk to us less of what we already know* and tell us more about

nomic struggle "impels" the workers to realise their own lack of political rights. It is unfortunate, gentlemen, that the spontaneously awakening trade-unionist political consciousness does not *"impel"* you to an understanding of your Social-Democratic tasks.

* To prove that this imaginary speech of a worker to an Economist is based on fact, we shall refer to two witnesses who undoubtedly have direct knowledge of the working-class movement and who are least of all inclined to be partial towards us "doctrinaires"; for one witness is an Economist (who regards even *Rabocheye Dyelo* as a political organ!), and the other is a terrorist. The first witness is the author of a remarkably truthful and vivid article entitled "The St. Petersburg Working-Class Movement and the Practical Tasks of Social-Democracy", published in *Rabocheye Dyelo*, No. 6. He divides the workers into the following categories: (1) class-conscious revolutionaries; (2) intermediate stratum; (3) the remaining masses. The intermediate stratum, he says, "is often more interested in questions of political life than in its own immediate economic interests, the connection between which and the general social conditions it has long understood".... *Rabochaya Mysl* "is sharply criticised": "It keeps on repeating the same thing over and over again, things we have long known, read long ago." "Again nothing in the political review!" (pp. 30-31). But even the third stratum, "the younger and more sensitive section of the workers, less corrupted by the tavern and the church, who hardly ever have the opportunity of getting hold of political literature, discuss political events in a rambling way and ponder over the fragmentary news they get about student riots", etc. The terrorist writes as follows: "...They read over once or twice the petty details of factory life in other towns, not their own, and then they read no more ... dull, they find it.... To say what we do not yet know and what we can never learn from our factory and "economic" experience, namely, political knowledge. You intellectuals can acquire this knowledge, and it is your *duty* to bring it to us in a hundred- and a thousand-fold greater measure than you have done up to now; and you must bring it to us, not only in the form of discussions, pamphlets, and articles (which very often—pardon our frankness—are rather dull), but precisely in the form of vivid *exposures* of what our government and our governing classes are doing at this very moment in all spheres of life. Devote more zeal to carrying out this duty and *talk less about "raising the activity of the working masses"*. We are far more active than you think, and we are quite able to support, by open street fighting, even demands that do not promise any "palpable results" whatever. It is not for you to "raise" our activity. because *activity is precisely the thing you yourselves lack*. Bow less in subservience to spontaneity, and think more about raising *your own* activity, gentlemen!

D. What Is There in Common Between Economism and Terrorism?

In the last footnote we cited the opinion of an Economist and of a non-Social-Democratic terrorist, who showed themselves to be accidentally in agreement. Speaking generally, however, there is not an accidental, but a necessary, inherent connection between the two, of which we shall have need to speak later, and which must be mentioned here in connection with the question of education for revolutionary activity. The Economists and the present-day terrorists have one common root, namely, *subservience to spontaneity*, with which we dealt in the preceding chapter as a general phenomenon and which we shall now examine in relation to its effect upon political activity and the political struggle. At first sight, our assertion may appear paradoxical, so great is the difference between those who stress the "drab everyday struggle" and those

nothing in a workers' paper about the government ... is to regard the workers as being little children.... The workers are not little children" (*Svoboda*, published by the Revolutionary-Socialist Group, pp. 69-70).

who call for the most self-sacrificing struggle of individuals. But this is no paradox. The Economists and the terrorists merely bow to different poles of spontaneity; the Economists bow to the spontaneity of "the labour movement pure and simple", while the terrorists bow to the spontaneity of the passionate indignation of intellectuals, who lack the ability or opportunity to connect the revolutionary struggle and the working-class movement into an integral whole. It is difficult indeed for those who have lost their belief, or who have never believed, that this is possible, to find some outlet for their indignation and revolutionary energy other than terror. Thus, both forms of subservience to spontaneity we have mentioned are nothing but *the beginning of the implementation* of the notorious *Credo* programme: Let the workers wage their "economic struggle against the employers and the government" (we apologise to the author of the *Credo* for expressing her views in Martynov's words. We think we have a right to do so since the *Credo,* too, says that in the economic struggle the workers "come up against the political régime"), and let the intellectuals conduct the political struggle by their own efforts—with the aid of terror, of course! This is an absolutely logical and inevitable *conclusion* which must be insisted on—*even though those* who are beginning to carry out this programme *do not themselves realise* that it is inevitable. Political activity has its logic quite apart from the consciousness of those who, with the best intentions, call either for terror or for lending the economic struggle itself a political character. The road to hell is paved with good intentions, and, in this case, good intentions cannot save one from being spontaneously drawn "along the line of least resistance", along the line of the *purely bourgeois Credo* programme. Surely it is no accident either that many Russian liberals—avowed liberals and liberals that wear the mask of Marxism— whole-heartedly sympathise with terror and try to foster the terrorist moods that have surged up in the present time.

The formation of the Revolutionary-Socialist *Svoboda* Group—which set itself the aim of helping the working-class movement in every possible way, but which included in its *programme* terror, and emancipation, so to speak, from Social-Democracy—once again confirmed the remarkable perspicacity of P. B. Axelrod, who *literally foretold* these results of Social-Democratic waverings *as far back as the end of 1897* (*Present Tasks and Tactics*), when he outlined his famous "two perspectives". All the subsequent disputes and disagreements among Russian Social-Democrats are contained, like a plant in the seed, in these two perspectives.*

From this point of view it also becomes clear why *Rabocheye Dyelo*, unable to withstand the spontaneity of Economism, has likewise been unable to withstand the spontaneity of terrorism. It is highly interesting to note here the specific arguments that *Svoboda* has advanced in defence of terrorism. It "completely denies" the deterrent role of terrorism (*The Regeneration of Revolutionism*, p. 64), but instead stresses its "excitative significance". This is characteristic, first, as representing one of the stages of the break-up and decline of the traditional (pre-Social-Democratic) cycle of ideas which insisted upon terrorism. The admission that the government cannot now be "terrified", and hence disrupted, by terror, is tantamount to a complete condemnation of terror as a system of struggle, as a sphere of activity sanctioned by the programme. Secondly, it is still more characteristic as an example of the failure to understand our immediate tasks in regard to "education for revolutionary activity". *Svoboda* advocates terror as a means of "exciting" the work-

---

* Martynov "conceives of another, more realistic [?] dilemma" (*Social-Democracy and the Working Class*, p. 19): "Either Social-Democracy takes over the direct leadership of the economic struggle of the proletariat and by that [!] transforms it into a revolutionary class struggle...." "By that", i.e., apparently by the direct leadership of the economic struggle. Can Martynov cite an instance in which leading the trade-union struggle *alone* has succeeded in transforming a trade-unionist movement into a revolutionary class movement? Can he not understand that in order to bring about this "transformation" we must actively take up the "direct leadership" of *all-sided* political agitation?... "Or the other perspective: Social-Democracy refrains from assuming the leadership of the economic struggle of the workers and so ... clips its own wings...." In *Rabocheye Dyelo*'s opinion, quoted above, it is *Iskra* that "refrains". We have seen, however, that the latter *does far more than Rabocheye Dyelo* to lead the economic struggle, but that, moreover, it does not confine itself thereto and *does not narrow down* its political tasks for its sake.

ing-class movement and of giving it a "strong impetus". It is difficult to imagine an argument that more thoroughly disproves itself. Are there not enough outrages committed in Russian life without special "excitants" having to be invented? On the other hand, is it not obvious that those who are not, and cannot be, roused to excitement even by Russian tyranny will stand by "twiddling their thumbs" and watch a handful of terrorists engaged in single combat with the government? The fact is that the working masses are roused to a high pitch of excitement by the social evils in Russian life, but we are unable to gather, if one may so put it, and concentrate all these drops and streamlets of popular resentment that are brought forth to a far larger extent than we imagine by the conditions of Russian life, and that must be combined into a *single* gigantic torrent. That this can be accomplished is irrefutably proved by the enormous growth of the working-class movement and the eagerness, noted above, with which the workers clamour for political literature. On the other hand, calls for terror and calls to lend the economic struggle itself a political character are merely two different forms of *evading* the most pressing duty now resting upon Russian revolution-aries, namely, the organisation of comprehensive political agitation. *Svoboda* desires *to substitute* terror for agita-tion, openly admitting that "as soon as intensified and strenuous agitation is begun among the masses the excita-tive function of terror will be ended" (*The Regeneration of Revolutionism*, p. 68). This proves precisely that both the terrorists and the Economists *underestimate* the revolu-tionary activity of the masses, despite the striking evidence of the events that took place in the spring,* and whereas the one group goes out in search of artificial "excitants", the other talks about "concrete demands". But both fail to devote sufficient attention to the development of *their own activity* in political agitation and in the organisation of political exposures. And no other work can serve as a *substitute* for this task either at the present time or at any other.

---

* The big street demonstrations which began in the spring of 1901. (Author's note to the 1907 edition.—*Ed.*)

E. The Working Class as Vanguard Fighter for Democracy

We have seen that the conduct of the broadest political agitation and, consequently, of all-sided political exposures is an absolutely necessary and a *paramount* task of our activity, if this activity is to be truly Social-Democratic. However, we arrived at this conclusion *solely* on the grounds of the pressing needs of the working class for political knowledge and political training. But such a presentation of the question is too narrow, for it ignores the general democratic tasks of Social-Democracy, in particular of present-day Russian Social-Democracy. In order to explain the point more concretely we shall approach the subject from an aspect that is "nearest" to the Economist, namely, from the practical aspect. "Everyone agrees" that it is necessary to develop the political consciousness of the working class. The question is, *how* that is to be done and what is required to do it. The economic struggle merely "impels" the workers to realise the government's attitude towards the working class. Consequently, *however much we may try* to "lend the economic struggle itself a political character", we *shall never be able* to develop the political consciousness of the workers (to the level of Social-Democratic political consciousness) by keeping within the framework of the economic struggle, for *that framework is too narrow*. The Martynov formula has some value for us, not because it illustrates Martynov's aptitude for confusing things, but because it pointedly expresses the basic error that all the Economists commit, namely, their conviction that it is possible to develop the class political consciousness of the workers *from within*, so to speak, from their economic struggle, i.e., by making this struggle the exclusive (or, at least, the main) starting-point, by making it the exclusive (or, at least, the main) basis. Such a view is radically wrong. Piqued by our polemics against them, the Economists refuse to ponder deeply over the origins of these disagreements, with the result that we simply cannot understand one another. It is as if we spoke in different tongues.

Class political consciousness can be brought to the workers *only from without*, that is, only from outside the economic struggle, from outside the sphere of relations between workers and employers. The sphere from which alone it is possible to obtain this knowledge is the sphere of relationships of *all* classes and strata to the state and the government, the sphere of the interrelations between *all* classes. For that reason, the reply to the question as to what must be done to bring political knowledge to the workers cannot be merely the answer with which, in the majority of cases, the practical workers, especially those inclined towards Economism, mostly content themselves, namely: "To go among the workers." To bring political knowledge to the *workers* the Social-Democrats must *go among all classes of the population*; they must dispatch units of their army *in all directions*.

We deliberately select this blunt formula, we deliberately express ourselves in this sharply simplified manner, not because we desire to indulge in paradoxes, but in order to "impel" the Economists to a realisation of their tasks which they unpardonably ignore, to suggest to them strongly the difference between trade-unionist and Social-Democratic politics, which they refuse to understand. We therefore beg the reader not to get wrought up, but to hear us patiently to the end.

Let us take the type of Social-Democratic study circle that has become most widespread in the past few years and examine its work. It has "contacts with the workers" and rests content with this, issuing leaflets in which abuses in the factories, the government's partiality towards the capitalists, and the tyranny of the police are strongly condemned. At workers' meetings the discussions never, or rarely ever, go beyond the limits of these subjects. Extremely rare are the lectures and discussions held on the history of the revolutionary movement, on questions of the government's home and foreign policy, on questions of the economic evolution of Russia and of Europe, on the position of the various classes in modern society, etc. As to systematically acquiring and extending contact with other classes of society, no one even dreams of that. In fact, the ideal leader, as the majority of the members of such circles picture him, is something far more in the nature of a trade-union secretary than a socialist political leader. For the secretary of any, say English, trade union always helps the workers to carry on the economic struggle, he helps them to expose factory abuses, explains the injustice of the laws and of measures that hamper the freedom to strike and to picket (i.e., to warn all and sundry that a strike is proceeding at a certain factory), explains the partiality of arbitration court judges who belong to the bourgeois classes, etc., etc. In a word, every trade-union secretary conducts and helps to conduct "the economic struggle against the employers and the government". It cannot be too strongly maintained that *this is still not* Social-Democracy, that the Social-Democrat's ideal should not be the trade-union secretary, but *the tribune of the people*, who is able to react to every manifestation of tyranny and oppression, no matter where it appears, no matter what stratum or class of the people it affects; who is able to generalise all these manifestations and produce a single picture of police violence and capitalist exploitation; who is able to take advantage of every event, however small, in order to set forth *before all* his socialist convictions and his democratic demands, in order to clarify for *all* and everyone the world-historic significance of the struggle for the emancipation of the proletariat. Compare, for example, a leader like Robert Knight (the well-known secretary and leader of the Boiler-Makers' Society, one of the most powerful trade unions in England), with Wilhelm Liebknecht, and try to apply to them the contrasts that Martynov draws in his controversy with *Iskra*. You will see—I am running through Martynov's article—that Robert Knight engaged more in "calling the masses to certain concrete actions" (Martynov, op. cit., p. 39), while Wilhelm Liebknecht engaged more in "the revolutionary elucidation of the whole of the present system or partial manifestations of it" (38-39); that Robert Knight "formulated the immediate demands of the proletariat and indicated the means by which they can be achieved" (41), whereas Wilhelm Liebknecht, while doing this, did not hold back from "simultaneously guiding the activities of various opposition strata", "dictating a positive programme of action for them"* (41); that Robert Knight strove "as

---

* For example, during the Franco-Prussian War, Liebknecht dictated a programme of action *for the whole of democracy;* to an even greater extent Marx and Engels did this in 1848.

far as possible to lend the economic struggle itself a political character" (42) and was excellently able "to submit to the government concrete demands promising certain palpable results" (43), whereas Liebknecht engaged to a much greater degree in "one-sided" "exposures" (40); that Robert Knight attached more significance to the "forward march of the drab everyday struggle" (61), whereas Liebknecht attached more significance to the "propaganda of brilliant and completed ideas" (61); that Liebknecht converted the paper he was directing into "an organ of revolutionary opposition that exposed the state of affairs in our country, particularly the political state of affairs, insofar as it affected the interests of the most varied strata of the population" (63), whereas Robert Knight "worked for the cause of the working class in close organic connection with the proletarian struggle" (63)—if by "close and organic connection" is meant the subservience to spontaneity which we examined above, by taking the examples of Krichevsky and Martynov—and "restricted the sphere of his influence", convinced, of course, as is Martynov, that "by doing so he deepened that influence" (63). In a word, you will see that *de facto* Martynov reduces Social-Democracy to the level of trade-unionism, though he does so, of course, not because he does not desire the good of Social-Democracy, but simply because he is a little too much in a hurry to render Plekhanov more profound, instead of taking the trouble to understand him.

Let us return, however, to our thesis. We said that a Social-Democrat, if he really believes it necessary to develop comprehensively the political consciousness of the proletariat, must "go among all classes of the population". This gives rise to the questions: how is this to be done? have we enough forces to do this? is there a basis for such work among all the other classes? will this not mean a retreat, or lead to a retreat, from the class point of view? Let us deal with these questions.

We must "go among all classes of the population" as theoreticians, as propagandists, as agitators, and as organisers. No one doubts that the theoretical work of Social-Democrats should aim at studying all the specific features of the social and political condition of the various classes.

But extremely little is done in this direction, as compared with the work that is done in studying the specific features of factory life. In the committees and study circles, one can meet people who are immersed in the study even of some special branch of the metal industry; but one can hardly ever find members of organisations (obliged, as often happens, for some reason or other to give up practical work) who are especially engaged in gathering material on some pressing question of social and political life in our country which could serve as a means for conducting Social-Democratic work among other strata of the population. In dwelling upon the fact that the majority of the present-day leaders of the working-class movement lack training, we cannot refrain from mentioning training in this respect also, for it too is bound up with the "Economist" conception of "close organic connection with the proletarian struggle". The principal thing, of course, is *propaganda* and *agitation* among all strata of the people. The work of the West-European Social-Democrat is in this respect facilitated by the public meetings and rallies which *all* are free to attend, and by the fact that in parliament he addresses the representatives of *all* classes. We have neither a parliament nor freedom of assembly; nevertheless, we are able to arrange meetings of workers who desire to listen to *a Social-Democrat*. We must also find ways and means of calling meetings of representatives of all social classes that desire to listen to *a democrat*; for he is no Social-Democrat who forgets in practice that "the Communists support every revolutionary movement", that we are obliged for that reason to expound and emphasise *general democratic tasks before the whole people*, without for a moment concealing our socialist convictions. He is no Social-Democrat who forgets in practice his obligation to be *ahead of all* in raising, accentuating, and solving *every* general democratic question.

"But everyone agrees with this!" the impatient reader will exclaim, and the new instructions adopted by the last conference of the Union Abroad for the Editorial Board of *Rabocheye Dyelo* definitely say: "All events of social and political life that affect the proletariat either directly as a special class or as *the vanguard of all the revolutionary forces in the struggle for freedom* should serve as subjects for political propaganda and agitation" (*Two Conferences,* p. 17, our italics). Yes, these are very true and very good words, and we would be fully satisfied if *Rabocheye Dyelo understood* them *and if it refrained from saying in the next breath things that contradict them.* For it is not enough to call ourselves the "vanguard", the advanced contingent; we must act in such a way that *all* the other contingents recognise and are obliged to admit that we are marching in the vanguard. And we ask the reader: Are the representatives of the other "contingents" such fools as to take our word for it when we say that we are the "vanguard"? Just picture to yourselves the following: a Social-Democrat comes to the "contingent" of Russian educated radicals, or liberal constitutionalists, and says, We are the vanguard; "the task confronting us now is, as far as possible, to lend the economic struggle itself a political character." The radical, or constitutionalist, if he is at all intelligent (and there are many intelligent men among Russian radicals and constitutionalists), would only smile at such a speech and would say (to himself, of course, for in the majority of cases he is an experienced diplomat): "Your 'vanguard' must be made up of simpletons. They do not even understand that it is our task, the task of the progressive representatives of bourgeois democracy to lend the workers' economic struggle *itself* a political character. Why, we too, like the West-European bourgeois, want to draw the workers into politics, *but only into trade-unionist, not into Social-Democratic politics.* Trade-unionist politics of the working class is precisely *bourgeois politics* of the working class, and this 'vanguard's' formulation of its task is the formulation of trade-unionist politics! Let them call themselves Social-Democrats to their heart's content, I am not a child to get excited over a label. But they must not fall under the influence of those pernicious orthodox doctrinaires, let them allow 'freedom of criticism' to those who unconsciously are driving Social-Democracy into trade-unionist channels."

And the faint smile of our constitutionalist will turn into Homeric laughter when he learns that the Social-Democrats who talk of Social-Democracy as the vanguard, today, when spontaneity almost completely dominates our movement, fear nothing so much as "belittling the spontaneous element", as "underestimating the significance of the forward movement of the drab everyday struggle, as compared with the propaganda of brilliant and completed ideas", etc., etc.! A "vanguard" which fears that consciousness will outstrip spontaneity, which fears to put forward a bold "plan" that would compel general recognition even among those who differ with us. Are they not confusing "vanguard" with "rearguard"?

Indeed, let us examine the following piece of reasoning by Martynov. On page 40 he says that *Iskra* is one-sided in its tactics of exposing abuses, that "however much we may spread distrust and hatred of the government, we shall not achieve our aim until we have succeeded in developing sufficient active social energy for its overthrow". This, it may be said parenthetically, is the familiar solicitude for the activation of the masses, with a simultaneous striving to restrict one's own activity. But that is not the main point at the moment. Martynov speaks here, accordingly, of *revolutionary* energy ("for overthrowing"). And what conclusion does he arrive at? Since in ordinary times various social strata inevitably march separately, "it is, therefore, clear that we Social-Democrats cannot simultaneously guide the activities of various opposition strata, we cannot dictate to them a positive programme of action, we cannot point out to them in what manner they should wage a day-to-day struggle for their interests.... The liberal strata will themselves take care of the active struggle for their immediate interests, the struggle that will bring them face to face with our political regime" (p. 41). Thus, having begun with talk about revolutionary energy, about the active struggle for the overthrow of the autocracy, Martynov immediately turns towards trade-union energy and active struggle for immediate interests! It goes without saying that we cannot guide the struggle of the students, liberals, etc., for their "immediate interests"; but this was not the point at issue, most worthy Economist! The point we were discussing was the possible and necessary participation of various social strata in the overthrow of the autocracy; and not only are we *able*, but it is our bounden duty, to guide *these* "activities of the various opposition strata", if we desire to be the "vanguard". Not only will our students and liberals, etc., themselves take care of "the struggle that brings them face to face with our political regime"; the police and the officials of the autocratic government will see to this first and foremost. But if "we" desire to be front-rank democrats, we must make it our concern *to direct* the thoughts of those who are dissatisfied only with conditions at the university, or in the Zemstvo, etc., to the idea that the entire political system is worthless. *We* must take upon ourselves the task of organising an all-round political struggle under the leadership of *our* Party in such a manner as to make it possible for all oppositional strata to render their fullest support to the struggle and to our Party. *We* must train our Social-Democratic practical workers to become political leaders, able to guide all the manifestations of this all-round struggle, able at the right time to "dictate a positive programme of action" for the aroused students, the discontented Zemstvo people, the incensed religious sects, the offended elementary schoolteachers, etc., etc. For that reason, Martynov's assertion that "with regard to these, we can function *merely in the negative* role of exposers of abuses ... we can *only* dissipate their hopes in various government commissions" *is completely false* (our italics). By saying this, Martynov shows that he *absolutely fails to understand* the role that the revolutionary "vanguard" must really play. If the reader bears this in mind, he will be clear as to *the real meaning* of Martynov's concluding remarks: "*Iskra* is the organ of the revolutionary opposition which exposes the state of affairs in our country, particularly the political state of affairs, insofar as it affects the interests of the most varied strata of the population. We, however, work and will continue to work for the cause of the working class in close organic contact with the proletarian struggle. By restricting the sphere of our active influence we deepen that influence" (63). The true sense of this conclusion is as follows: *Iskra* desires *to elevate* the trade-unionist politics of the working class (to which, through misconception, through lack of training, or through conviction, our practical workers frequently confine themselves) to the level of Social-Democratic politics. *Rabocheye Dyelo*, however, desires to *degrade* Social-Democratic politics to trade-unionist politics. Moreover, it assures the world that the two positions are "entirely compatible within the common cause" (63). *O, sancta simplicitas!*

To proceed. Have we sufficient forces to direct our propaganda and agitation among *all* social classes? Most certainly. Our Economists, who are frequently inclined to deny this, lose sight of the gigantic progress our movement has made from (approximately) 1894 to 1901. Like real "tailenders", they often go on living in the bygone stages of the movement's inception. In the earlier period, indeed, we had astonishingly few forces, and it was perfectly natural and legitimate then to devote ourselves exclusively to activities among the workers and to condemn severely any deviation from this course. The entire task then was to consolidate our position in the working class. At the present time, however, gigantic forces have been attracted to the movement. The best representatives of the younger generation of the educated classes are coming over to us. Everywhere in the provinces there are people, resident there by dint of circumstance, who have taken part in the movement in the past or who desire to do so now and who are gravitating towards Social-Democracy (whereas in 1894 one could count the Social-Democrats on the fingers of one's hand). A basic political and organisational shortcoming of our movement is our *inability* to utilise all these forces and give them appropriate work (we shall deal with this more fully in the next chapter). The overwhelming majority of these forces entirely lack the opportunity of "going among the workers", so that there are no grounds for fearing that we shall divert forces from our main work. In order to be able to provide the workers with real, comprehensive, and live political knowledge, we must have "our own people", Social-Democrats, everywhere, among all social strata, and in all positions from which we can learn the inner springs of our state mechanism. Such people are required, not only for propaganda and agitation, but in a still larger measure for organisation.

Is there a basis for activity among all classes of the population? Whoever doubts this lags in his consciousness behind the spontaneous awakening of the masses. The working-class movement has aroused and is continuing to arouse discontent in some, hopes of support for the opposition in others, and in still others the realisation that the autocracy is unbearable and must inevitably fall. We would be "politicians" and Social-Democrats in name only (as all too often happens in reality), if we failed to realise that our task is to utilise every manifestation of discontent, and to gather and turn to the best account every protest, however small. This is quite apart from the fact that the millions of the labouring peasantry, handicraftsmen, petty artisans, etc., would always listen eagerly to the speech of any Social-Democrat who is at all qualified. Indeed, is there a single social class in which there are no individuals, groups, or circles that are discontented with the lack of rights and with tyranny and, therefore, accessible to the propaganda of Social-Democrats as the spokesmen of the most pressing general democratic needs? To those who desire to have a clear idea of what the political agitation of a Social-Democrat among *all* classes and strata of the population should be like, we would point to *political exposures* in the broad sense of the word as the principal (but, of course, not the sole) form of this agitation.

"We must arouse in every section of the population that is at all politically conscious a passion for *political* exposure," I wrote in my article "Where To Begin" [*Iskra*, May (No. 4) 1901], with which I shall deal in greater detail later. "We must not be discouraged by the fact that the voice of political exposure is today so feeble, timid, and infrequent. This is not because of a wholesale submission to police despotism, but because those who are able and ready to make exposures have no tribune from which to speak, no eager and encouraging audience, they do not see anywhere among the people that force to which it would be worth while directing their complaint against the 'omnipotent' Russian Government.... We are now in a position to provide a tribune for the nation-wide exposure of the tsarist government, and it is our duty to do this. That tribune must be a Social-Democratic newspaper."*

The ideal audience for political exposure is the working class, which is first and foremost in need of all-round and live political knowledge, and is most capable of converting this knowledge into active struggle, even when that struggle does not promise "palpable results". A tribune for *nation-wide* exposures can be only an All-Russian news-

---

* See *Collected Works*, Vol. 5, pp. 21-22.—*Ed.*

paper. "Without a political organ, a political movement deserving that name is inconceivable in the Europe of today"; in this respect Russia must undoubtedly be included in present-day Europe. The press long ago became a power in our country, otherwise the government would not spend tens of thousands of rubles to bribe it and to subsidise the Katkovs and Meshcherskys. And it is no novelty in autocratic Russia for the underground press to break through the wall of censorship and *compel* the legal and conservative press to speak openly of it. This was the case in the seventies and even in the fifties. How much broader and deeper are now the sections of the people willing to read the illegal underground press, and to learn from it "how to live and how to die", to use the expression of a worker who sent a letter to *Iskra* (No. 7).[51] Political exposures are as much a declaration of war against the *government* as economic exposures are a declaration of war against the factory owners. The moral significance of this declaration of war will be all the greater, the wider and more powerful the campaign of exposure will be and the more numerous and determined the social *class* that has *declared war in order to begin the war*. Hence, political exposures in themselves serve as a powerful instrument for *disintegrating* the system we oppose, as a means for diverting from the enemy his casual or temporary allies, as a means for spreading hostility and distrust among the permanent partners of the autocracy.

In our time only a party that will *organise* really *nation-wide* exposures can become the vanguard of the revolutionary forces. The word "nation-wide" has a very profound meaning. The overwhelming majority of the non-working-class exposers (be it remembered that in order to become the vanguard, we must attract other classes) are sober politicians and level-headed men of affairs. They know perfectly well how dangerous it is to "complain" even against a minor official, let alone against the "omnipotent" Russian Government. And they will come *to us* with their complaints only when they see that these complaints can really have effect, and that we represent *a political force*. In order to become such a force in the eyes of outsiders, much persistent and stubborn work is required *to raise* our own consciousness, initiative, and energy. To accomplish this it is not enough to attach a "vanguard" label to rearguard theory and practice.

But if we have to undertake the organisation of a really nation-wide exposure of the government, in what way will then the class character of our movement be expressed?— the overzealous advocate of "close organic contact with the proletarian struggle" will ask us, as indeed he does. The reply is manifold: we Social-Democrats will organise these nation-wide exposures; all questions raised by the agitation will be explained in a consistently Social-Democratic spirit, without any concessions to deliberate or undeliberate distortions of Marxism; the all-round political agitation will be conducted by a party which unites into one inseparable whole the assault on the government in the name of the entire people, the revolutionary training of the proletariat, and the safeguarding of its political independence, the guidance of the economic struggle of the working class, and the utilisation of all its spontaneous conflicts with its exploiters which rouse and bring into our camp increasing numbers of the proletariat.

But a most characteristic feature of Economism is its failure to understand this connection, more, this identity of the most pressing need of the proletariat (a comprehensive political education through the medium of political agitation and political exposures) with the need of the general democratic movement. This lack of understanding is expressed, not only in "Martynovite" phrases, but in the references to a supposedly class point of view identical in meaning with these phrases. Thus, the authors of the "Economist" letter in *Iskra*, No. 12, state*: "This basic drawback of *Iskra* [overestimation of ideology] is also the cause of its inconsistency on the question of the attitude of Social-Democracy to the various social classes and tendencies. By theoretical reasoning [not by "the growth of Party tasks, which grow together with the Party"],

* Lack of space has prevented us from replying in detail, in *Iskra,* to this letter, which is highly characteristic of the Economists. We were very glad at its appearance, for the allegations that *Iskra* did not maintain a consistent class point of view had reached us long before that from various sources, and we were waiting for an appropriate occasion, or for a formulated expression of this fashionable charge, to give our reply. Moreover, it is our habit to reply to attacks, not by defence, but by counter-attack.

Iskra solved the problem of the immediate transition to the struggle against absolutism. In all probability it senses the difficulty of such a task for the workers under the present state of affairs [not only senses, but knows fully well that this task appears less difficult to the workers than to the "Economist" intellectuals with their nursemaid concern, for the workers are prepared to fight even for demands which, to use the language of the never-to-be-forgotten Martynov, do not "promise palpable results"] but lacking the patience to wait until the workers will have gathered sufficient forces for this struggle, *Iskra* begins to seek allies in the ranks of the liberals and intellectuals"....

Yes, we have indeed lost all "patience" "waiting" for the blessed time, long promised us by divers "conciliators", when the Economists will have stopped charging the workers with *their own* backwardness and justifying their own lack of energy with allegations that the workers lack strength. We ask our Economists: What do they mean by "the gathering of working-class strength for the struggle"? Is it not evident that this means the political training of the workers, so that *all* the aspects of our vile autocracy are revealed to them? And is it not clear that *precisely for this work* we need "allies in the ranks of the liberals and intellectuals", who are prepared to join us in the exposure of the political attack on the Zemstvos, on the teachers, on the statisticians, on the students, etc.? Is this surprisingly "intricate mechanism" really so difficult to understand? Has not P. B. Axelrod constantly repeated since 1897 that "the task before the Russian Social-Democrats of acquiring adherents and direct and indirect allies among the non-proletarian classes will be solved principally and primarily by the character of the propagandist activities conducted among the proletariat itself"? But the Martynovs and the other Economists continue to imagine that "by economic struggle against the employers and the government" the workers must *first* gather strength (for trade-unionist politics) and *then* "go over"—we presume from trade-unionist "training for activity"—to Social-Democratic activity!

"...In this quest," continue the Economists, "*Iskra* not infrequently departs from the class point of view, obscures class antagonisms, and puts into the forefront the common nature of the discontent with the government, although the causes and the degree of the discontent vary considerably among the 'allies'. Such, for example, is *Iskra*'s attitude towards the Zemstvo...." *Iskra*, it is alleged, "promises the nobles that are dissatisfied with the government's sops the assistance of the working class, but it does not say a word about the class antagonism that exists between these social strata". If the reader will turn to the article "The Autocracy and the Zemstvo" (*Iskra*, Nos. 2 and 4), to which, *in all probability*, the authors of the letter refer, he will find that they* deal with the attitude of the *government* towards the "mild agitation of the bureaucratic Zemstvo, which is based on the social-estates", and towards the "independent activity of even the propertied classes". The article states that the workers cannot look on indifferently while the government is waging a struggle against the Zemstvo, and the Zemstvos are called upon to stop making mild speeches and to speak firmly and resolutely when revolutionary Social-Democracy confronts the government in all its strength. What the authors of the letter do not agree with here is not clear. Do they think that the workers will "not understand" the phrases "propertied classes" and "bureaucratic Zemstvo based on the social-estates"? Do they think that *urging* the Zemstvo to abandon mild speeches and to speak firmly is "overestimating ideology"? Do they imagine the workers can "gather strength" for the struggle against the autocracy if they know nothing about the attitude of the autocracy towards the Zemstvo *as well*? All this too remains unknown. One thing alone is clear and that is that the authors of the letter have a very vague idea of what the political tasks of Social-Democracy are. This is revealed still more clearly by their remark: "Such, too, is *Iskra*'s attitude towards the student movement" (i.e., it also "obscures the class antagonisms"). Instead of calling on the workers to declare by means of public demonstrations that the real breeding-place of unbridled violence, disorder, and outrage is not the university youth but the

---

* In the interval *between* these articles there was one (*Iskra*, No. 3), which dealt especially with class antagonisms in the countryside. See *Collected Works*, Vol. 4, pp. 420-28.—*Ed.*)

Russian Government (*Iskra*, No. 2*), we ought probably to have inserted arguments in the spirit of *Rabochaya Mysl*! Such ideas were expressed by Social-Democrats in the autumn of 1901, after the events of February and March, on the eve òf a fresh upsurge of the student movement, which reveals that even in this sphere the "spontaneous" protest against the autocracy is *outstripping* the conscious Social-Democratic leadership of the movement. The spontaneous striving of the workers to defend the students who are being assaulted by the police and the Cossacks surpasses the conscious activity of the Social-Democratic organisation!

"And yet in other articles," continue the authors of the letter, "*Iskra* sharply condemns all compromise and defends, for instance, the intolerant conduct of the Guesdists." We would advise those who are wont so conceitedly and frivolously to declare that the present disagreements among the Social-Democrats are unessential and do not justify a split, to ponder these words. Is it possible for people to work together in the same organisation, when some among them contend that we have done extremely little to explain the hostility of the autocracy to the various classes and to inform the workers of the opposition displayed by the various social strata to the autocracy, while others among them see in this clarification a "compromise"—evidently a compromise with the theory of "economic struggle against the employers and the government"?

We urged the necessity of carrying the class struggle into the rural districts in connection with the fortieth anniversary of the emancipation of the peasantry (issue No. 3**), and spoke of the irreconcilability of the local government bodies and the autocracy in relation to Witte's secret Memorandum (No. 4). In connection with the new law we attacked the feudal landlords and the government which serves them (No. 8***) and we welcomed the illegal Zemstvo congress. We urged the Zemstvo to pass over from abject petitions (No. 8****) to struggle. We encouraged the

---

* See *Collected Works*, Vol. 4, pp. 414-19.—*Ed.*
** See *Collected Works*, Vol. 4, pp. 420-28.—*Ed.*
*** See *Collected Works*, Vol. 5, pp. 95-100.—*Ed.*
**** See *Collected Works*, Vol. 5, pp. 101-02.—*Ed.*

students, who had begun to understand the need for the political struggle, and to undertake this struggle (No. 3), while, at the same time, we lashed out at the "outrageous incomprehension" revealed by the adherents of the "purely student" movement, who called upon the students to abstain from participating in the street demonstrations (No. 3, in connection with the manifesto issued by the Executive Committee of the Moscow students on February 25). We exposed the "senseless dreams" and the "lying hypocrisy" of the cunning liberals of *Rossiya*[52] (No. 5), while pointing to the violent fury with which the government-gaoler persecuted "peaceful writers, aged professors, scientists, and well-known liberal Zemstvo members" (No. 5, "Police Raid on Literature"). We exposed the real significance of the programme of "state protection for the welfare of the workers" and welcomed the "valuable admission" that "it is better, by granting reforms from above, to forestall the demand for such reforms from below than to wait for those demands to be put forward" (No. 6*). We encouraged the protesting statisticians (No. 7) and censured the strike-breaking statisticians (No. 9). He who sees in these tactics an obscuring of the class-consciousness of the proletariat and *a compromise with liberalism* reveals his utter failure to understand the true significance of the programme of the *Credo* and *carries out that programme de facto*, however much he may repudiate it. For by *such an approach* he drags Social-Democracy towards the "economic struggle against the employers and the government" and *yields to liberalism*, abandons the task of actively intervening in *every* "liberal" issue and of determining *his own*, Social-Democratic, attitude towards this question.

F. Once More "Slanderers", Once More "Mystifiers"

These polite expressions, as the reader will recall, belong to *Rabocheye Dyelo,* which in this way answers our charge that it "is indirectly preparing the ground for converting the working-class movement into an instrument of bourgeois democracy". In its simplicity of heart *Rabocheye*

---

* See *Collected Works*, Vol. 5, pp. 87-88.—*Ed.*

Dyelo decided that this accusation was nothing more than a polemical sally: these malicious doctrinaires are bent on saying all sorts of unpleasant things about us, and, what can be more unpleasant than being an instrument of bourgeois democracy? And so they print in bold type a "refutation": "Nothing but downright slander", "mystification", "mummery" (*Two Conferences*, pp. 30, 31, 33). Like Jove, *Rabocheye Dyelo* (although bearing little resemblance to that deity) is wrathful because it is wrong, and proves by its hasty abuse that it is incapable of understanding its opponents' mode of reasoning. And yet, with only a little reflection it would have understood why *any* subservience to the spontaneity of the mass movement and *any* degrading of Social-Democratic politics to the level of trade-unionist politics mean preparing the ground for converting the working-class movement into an instrument of bourgeois democracy. The spontaneous working-class movement is by itself able to create (and inevitably does create) only trade-unionism, and working-class trade-unionist politics is precisely working-class bourgeois politics. The fact that the working class participates in the political struggle, and even in the political revolution, does not in itself make its politics Social-Democratic politics. Will *Rabocheye Dyelo* make bold to deny this? Will it, at long last, publicly, plainly, and without equivocation explain how it understands the urgent questions of international and of Russian Social-Democracy? Hardly. It will never do anything of the kind, because it holds fast to the trick, which might be described as the "not here" method—"It's not me, it's not my horse, I'm not the driver. We are not Economists; *Rabochaya Mysl* does not stand for Economism; there is no Economism at all in Russia." This is a remarkably adroit and "political" trick, which suffers from the slight defect, however, that the publications practising it are usually nicknamed, "At your service, sir".

Rabocheye Dyelo imagines that bourgeois democracy in Russia is, in general, merely a "phantom" (*Two Conferences*, p. 32).* Happy people! Ostrich-like, they bury

---

* There follows a reference to the "concrete Russian conditions which fatalistically impel the working-class movement on to the revolutionary path". But these people refuse to understand that the revolutionary path of the working-class movement might not be a

their heads in the sand and imagine that everything around has disappeared. Liberal publicists who month after month proclaim to the world their triumph over the collapse and even the disappearance of Marxism; liberal newspapers (*S. Petersburgskiye Vedomosti*, *Russkiye Vedomosti*, and many others) which encourage the liberals who bring to the workers the Brentano[53] conception of the class struggle and the trade-unionist conception of politics; the galaxy of critics of Marxism, whose real tendencies were so very well disclosed by the *Credo* and whose literary products alone circulate in Russia without let or hindrance; the revival of revolutionary *non*-Social-Democratic tendencies, particularly after the February and March events—all these, apparently, are just phantoms! All these have nothing at all to do with bourgeois democracy!

Rabocheye Dyelo and the authors of the Economist letter published in *Iskra*, No. 12, should "ponder over the reason why the events of the spring brought about such a revival of revolutionary non-Social-Democratic tendencies instead of increasing the authority and the prestige of Social-Democracy".

The reason lies in the fact that we failed to cope with our tasks. The masses of the workers proved to be more active than we. We lacked adequately trained revolutionary leaders and organisers possessed of a thorough knowledge of the mood prevailing among all the opposition strata and able to head the movement, to turn a spontaneous demonstration into a political one, broaden its political character, etc. Under such circumstances, our backwardness will inevitably be utilised by the more mobile and more energetic non-Social-Democratic revolutionaries, and the workers, however energetically and self-sacrificingly they may fight the police and the troops, however revolutionary their actions may be, will prove to be merely a force supporting those revolutionaries, the rearguard of bourgeois democracy, and not the Social-Democratic van-

---

Social-Democratic path. When absolutism reigned, the entire West-European bourgeoisie "impelled", deliberately impelled, the workers on to the path of revolution. We Social-Democrats, however, cannot be satisfied with that. And if we, by any means whatever, degrade Social-Democratic politics to the level of spontaneous trade-unionist politics, we thereby play into the hands of bourgeois democracy.

guard. Let us take, for example, the German Social-Democrats, whose weak aspects alone our Economists desire to emulate. Why is there *not a single* political event in Germany that does not add to the authority and prestige of Social-Democracy? Because Social-Democracy is always found to be in advance of all others in furnishing the most revolutionary appraisal of every given event and in championing every protest against tyranny. It does not lull itself with arguments that the economic struggle brings the workers to realise that they have no political rights and that the concrete conditions unavoidably impel the working-class movement on to the path of revolution. It intervenes in every sphere and in every question of social and political life; in the matter of Wilhelm's refusal to endorse a bourgeois progressist as city mayor (our Economists have not yet managed to educate the Germans to the understanding that such an act is, in fact, a compromise with liberalism!); in the matter of the law against "obscene" publications and pictures; in the matter of governmental influence on the election of professors, etc., etc. Everywhere the Social-Democrats are found in the forefront, rousing political discontent among all classes, rousing the sluggards, stimulating the laggards, and providing a wealth of material for the development of the political consciousness and the political activity of the proletariat. As a result, even the avowed enemies of socialism are filled with respect for this advanced political fighter, and not infrequently an important document from bourgeois, and even from bureaucratic and Court circles, makes its way by some miraculous means into the editorial office of *Vorwärts*.

This, then, is the resolution of the seeming "contradiction" that surpasses *Rabocheye Dyelo*'s powers of understanding to such an extent that it can only throw up its hands and cry, "Mummery!" Indeed, just think of it: We, *Rabocheye Dyelo*, regard the *mass* working-class movement as the *cornerstone* (and say so in bold type!); we warn all and sundry against belittling the significance of the element of spontaneity; we desire to lend the economic struggle itself—*itself*—a political character; we desire to maintain close and organic contact with the proletarian struggle. And yet we are told that we are preparing the ground for the conversion of the working-class movement into an instrument of bourgeois democracy! And who are they that presume to say this? People who "compromise" with liberalism by intervening in every "liberal" issue (what a gross misunderstanding of "organic contact with the proletarian struggle"!), by devoting so much attention to the students and even (oh horror!) to the Zemstvos! People who in general wish to devote a greater percentage (compared with the Economists) of their efforts to activity among non-proletarian classes of the population! What is this but "mummery"?

Poor *Rabocheye Dyelo*! Will it ever find the solution to this perplexing puzzle?

IV

The Primitiveness of the Economists and the Organisation of the Revolutionaries

Rabocheye Dyelo's assertions, which we have analysed, that the economic struggle is the most widely applicable means of political agitation and that our task now is to lend the economic struggle itself a political character, etc., express a narrow view, not only of our political, but also of our *organisational* tasks. The "economic struggle against the employers and the government" does not at all require an All-Russian centralised organisation, and hence this struggle can never give rise to such an organisation as will combine, in one general assault, all the manifestations of political opposition, protest, and indignation, an organisation that will consist of professional revolutionaries and be led by the real political leaders of the entire people. This stands to reason. The character of any organisation is naturally and inevitably determined by the content of its activity. Consequently, *Rabocheye Dyelo,* by the assertions analysed above, sanctifies and legitimises not only narrow ness of political activity, but also of organisational work In this case, too, *Rabocheye Dyelo*, as always, proves itself an organ whose consciousness yields to spontaneity. Yet subservience to spontaneously developing forms of organisation, failure to realise the narrowness and primitiveness of our organisational work, of our "handicraft" methods in this most important sphere, failure to realise this, I say, is a veritable ailment from which our movement suffers. It is not an ailment that comes with decline, but one, of course, that comes with growth. It is however at the present time, when the wave of spontaneous indignation, as it were, is sweeping over us, leaders and organisers of the movement, that an irreconcilable struggle must be waged against all defence of backwardness, against any legitimation of narrowness in this matter. It is particularly necessary to arouse in all who participate in practical work, or are preparing to take up that work, discontent with the *amateurism* prevailing among us and an unshakable determination to rid ourselves of it.

A. What Is Primitiveness?

We shall try to answer this question by giving a brief description of the activity of a typical Social-Democratic study circle of the period 1894-1901. We have noted that the entire student youth of the period was absorbed in Marxism. Of course, these students were not only, or even not so much, interested in Marxism as a theory; they were interested in it as an answer to the question, "What is to be done?", as a call to take the field against the enemy. These new warriors marched to battle with astonishingly primitive equipment and training. In a vast number of cases they had almost no equipment and absolutely no training. They marched to war like peasants from the plough, armed only with clubs. A students' circle establishes contacts with workers and sets to work, without any connection with the old members of the movement, without any connection with study circles in other districts, or even in other parts of the same city (or in other educational institutions), without any organisation of the various divisions of revolutionary work, without any systematic plan of activity covering any length of time. The circle gradually expands its propaganda and agitation; by its activities it wins the sympathies of fairly large sections of workers and of a certain section of the educated strata, which provide it with money and from among whom the "committee" recruits new groups of young people. The attractive power of the committee (or League of Struggle) grows, its sphere of activity becomes wider, and the committee expands this activity quite spontaneously; the very people who a year or a few months previously spoke at the students' circle gatherings and discussed the question, "Whither?", who established and maintained contacts with the workers and wrote and published leaflets, now establish contacts with other groups of revolutionaries, procure literature, set to work to publish a local newspaper, begin to talk of organising a demonstration, and finally turn to open warfare (which may, according to circumstances, take the form of issuing the first agitational leaflet or the first issue of a newspaper, or of organising the first demonstration). Usually the initiation of such actions ends in an immediate and complete fiasco. Immediate and complete, because this open warfare was not the result of a systematic and carefully thought-out and gradually prepared plan for a prolonged and stubborn struggle, but simply the result of the spontaneous growth of traditional study circle work; because, naturally, the police, in almost every case, knew the principal leaders of the local movement, since they had already "gained a reputation" for themselves in their student days, and the police waited only for the right moment to make their raid. They deliberately allowed the study circle sufficient time to develop its work so that they might obtain a palpable *corpus delicti*, and they always permitted several of the persons known to them to remain at liberty "for breeding" (which, as far as I know, is the technical term used both by our people and by the gendarmes). One cannot help comparing this kind of warfare with that conducted by a mass of peasants, armed with clubs, against modern troops. And one can only wonder at the vitality of the movement which expanded, grew, and scored victories despite the total lack of training on the part of the fighters. True, from the historical point of view, the primitiveness of equipment was not only inevitable at first, but *even legitimate* as one of the conditions for the wide recruiting of fighters, but as soon as serious war operations began (and they began in fact with the strikes in the summer of 1896), the defects in our fighting organisations made themselves felt to an ever-increasing degree. The government, at first thrown into confusion and committing a number of blunders (e.g., its appeal to the public describing the misdeeds of the socialists, or the banishment of workers from the capitals to provincial industrial centres), very soon adapted itself to the new conditions of the struggle and managed to deploy well its perfectly equipped detachments of *agents provocateurs*, spies, and gendarmes. Raids became so frequent, affected such a vast number of people, and cleared out the local study circles so thoroughly that the masses of the workers lost literally all their leaders, the movement assumed an amazingly sporadic character, and it became utterly impossible to establish continuity and coherence in the work. The terrible dispersion of the local leaders; the fortuitous character of the study circle memberships; the lack of training in, and the narrow outlook on, theoretical, political, and organisational questions were all the inevitable result of the conditions described above. Things have reached such a pass that in several places the workers, because of our lack of self-restraint and the ability to maintain secrecy, begin to lose faith in the intellectuals and to avoid them; the intellectuals, they say, are much too careless and cause police raids!

Anyone who has the slightest knowledge of the movement is aware that all thinking Social-Democrats have at last begun to regard these amateurish methods as a disease. In order that the reader who is not acquainted with the movement may have no grounds for thinking that we are "inventing" a special stage or special disease of the movement, we shall refer once again to the witness we have quoted. We trust we shall be forgiven for the length of the passage:

"While the gradual transition to more extensive practical activity," writes B—v in *Rabocheye Dyelo*, No. 6, "a transition that is directly dependent on the general transitional period through which the Russian working-class movement is now passing, is a characteristic feature,... there is, however, another, no less interesting, feature in the general mechanism of the Russian workers' revolution. We refer to *the general lack of revolutionary forces fit for action*,* which is felt not only in St. Petersburg, but throughout Russia. With the general revival of the working-class movement, with the general development of the working masses, with the growing frequency of

---

* All italics ours.

strikes, with the increasingly open mass struggle of the workers, and with the intensified government persecution, arrests, deportation, and exile, this *lack of highly skilled revolutionary forces is becoming more and more marked* and, without a doubt, *cannot but affect the depth and the general character of the movement.* Many strikes take place without any strong and direct influence upon them by the revolutionary organisations.... A shortage of agitational leaflets and illegal literature is felt.... The workers' study circles are left without agitators.... In addition, there is a constant dearth of funds. In a word, *the growth of the working-class movement is outstripping the growth and development of the revolutionary organisations.* The numerical strength of the active revolutionaries is too small to enable them to concentrate in their own hands the influence exercised upon the whole mass of discontented workers, or to give this discontent even a shadow of coherence and organisation.... The separate study circles, the separate revolutionaries, scattered, uncombined, do not represent a single, strong, and disciplined organisation with proportionately developed parts...." Admitting that the immediate organisation of fresh study circles to replace those that have been broken up "merely proves the vitality of the movement ... but does not prove the existence of an adequate number of adequately prepared revolutionary workers", the author concludes: "The lack of practical training among the St. Petersburg revolutionaries is seen in the results of their work. The recent trials, especially that of the Self-Emancipation group and the Labour-against-Capital group,[54] clearly showed that the young agitator, lacking a detailed knowledge of working-class conditions and, consequently, of the conditions under which agitation can be carried on in a given factory, ignorant of the principles of secrecy, and understanding only the general principles of Social-Democracy [if he does] is able to carry on his work for perhaps four, five, or six months. Then come arrests, which frequently lead to the break-up of the entire organisation, or at all events, of part of it. The question arises, therefore, can the group conduct successful activity if its existence is measured by months? Obviously, the defects of the existing organisations cannot be wholly ascribed to the transitional period.... Obviously, the numerical, and above all the qualitative, make-up of the functioning organisations is no small factor, and the first task our Social-Democrats must undertake... is that of *effectively combining the organisations and making a strict selection of their membership.*"

B. Primitiveness and Economism

We must now deal with a question that has undoubtedly come to the mind of every reader. Can a connection be established between primitiveness as growing pains that affect the *whole* movement, and Economism, which is *one* of the currents in Russian Social-Democracy? We think that it can. Lack of practical training, of ability to carry on organisational work is certainly common *to us all,*

including those who have from the very outset unswervingly stood for revolutionary Marxism. Of course, were
it only lack of practical training, no one could blame the
practical workers. But the term "primitiveness" embraces
something more than lack of training; it denotes a narrow
scope of revolutionary work generally, failure to understand that a good organisation of revolutionaries cannot
be built on the basis of such narrow activity, and lastly—
and this is the main thing—attempts to justify this narrowness and to elevate it to a special "theory", i.e., subservience to spontaneity on this question too. Once such
attempts were revealed, it became clear that primitiveness
is connected with Economism and that we shall never rid
ourselves of this narrowness of our organisational activity
until we rid ourselves of Economism generally (i.e., the
narrow conception of Marxist theory, as well as of the role
of Social-Democracy and of its political tasks). These
attempts manifested themselves in a twofold direction.
Some began to say that the working masses themselves
have not yet advanced the broad and militant political
tasks which the revolutionaries are attempting to "impose"
on them; that they must continue to struggle for *immediate* political demands, to conduct "the economic struggle
against the employers and the government"* (and, naturally, corresponding to this struggle which is "accessible"
to the mass movement there must be an organisation that
will be "accessible" to the most untrained youth). Others,
far removed from any theory of "gradualness", said that
it is possible and necessary to "bring about a political
revolution", but that this does not require building a strong
organisation of revolutionaries to train the proletariat in
steadfast and stubborn struggle. All we need do is to snatch
up our old friend, the "accessible" cudgel. To drop meta-
phor, it means that we must organise a general strike,** or
that we must stimulate the "spiritless" progress of the
working-class movement by means of "excitative terror".***

---

* *Rabochaya Mysl* and *Rabocheye Dyelo*, especially the *Reply*
to Plekhanov.
** See "Who Will Bring About the Political Revolution?" in the
collection published in Russia, entitled *The Proletarian Struggle*. Re-
issued by the Kiev Committee.
*** *Regeneration of Revolutionism* and the journal *Svoboda*.

Both these trends, the opportunists and the "revolutionists", bow to the prevailing amateurism; neither believes that it can be eliminated, neither understands our primary and imperative practical task to establish *an organisation of revolutionaries* capable of lending energy, stability, and continuity to the political struggle.

We have quoted the words of B—v: "The growth of the working-class movement is outstripping the growth and development of the revolutionary organisations." This "valuable remark of a close observer" (*Rabocheye Dyelo's* comment on B—v's article) has a twofold value for us. It shows that we were right in our opinion that the principal cause of the present crisis in Russian Social-Democracy is *the lag of the leaders* ("ideologists", revolutionaries, Social-Democrats) behind *the spontaneous upsurge of the masses*. It shows that all the arguments advanced by the authors of the Economist letter (in *Iskra*, No. 12), by Krichevsky and by Martynov, as to the danger of belittling the significance of the spontaneous element, of the drab everyday struggle, as to tactics-as-process, etc., are nothing more than a glorification and a defence of primitiveness. These people who cannot pronounce the word "theoretician" without a sneer, who describe their genuflections to common lack of training and backwardness as a "sense for the realities of life", reveal in practice a failure to understand our most imperative *practical* tasks. To laggards they shout: Keep in step! Don't run ahead! To people suffering from a lack of energy and initiative in organisational work, from a lack of "plans" for wide and bold activity, they prate about "tactics-as-process"! The worst sin we commit is that we *degrade* our political *and organisational* tasks to the level of the immediate, "palpable", "concrete" interests of the everyday economic struggle; yet they keep singing to us the same refrain: Lend the economic struggle itself a political character! We repeat: this kind of thing displays as much "sense for the realities of life" as was displayed by the hero in the popular fable who cried out to a passing funeral procession, "Many happy returns of the day!"

Recall the matchless, truly "Nartsis-like" superciliousness with which these wiseacres lectured Plekhanov on the "workers' *circles* generally" (*sic*!) being "unable to cope with political tasks in the real and *practical* sense of the word, i.e., in the sense of the expedient and successful *practical* struggle for political demands" (*Rabocheye Dyelo's Reply*, p. 24). There are circles and circles, gentlemen! Circles of "amateurs" are not, of course, capable of coping with political tasks so long as they have not become aware of their amateurism and do not abandon it. If, besides this, these amateurs are enamoured of their primitive methods, and insist on writing the word "practical" in italics, and imagine that being practical demands that one's tasks be reduced to the level of understandng of the most backward strata of the masses, then they are hopeless amateurs and, of course, certainly cannot *in general cope with any political tasks.* But a circle of leaders, of the type of Alexeyev and Myshkin, of Khalturin and Zhelyabov, is capable of coping with political tasks in the genuine and most practical sense of the term, for the reason and to the extent that their impassioned propaganda meets with response among the spontaneously awakening masses, and their sparkling energy is answered and supported by the energy of the revolutionary class. Plekhanov was profoundly right, not only in pointing to this revolutionary class and proving that its spontaneous awakening was inevitable, but in setting even the "workers' circles" a great and lofty political task. But you refer to the mass movement that has sprung up since that time in order *to degrade* this task, *to curtail* the energy and scope of activity of the "workers' circles". If you are not amateurs enamoured of your primitive methods, what are you then? You boast that you are practical, but you fail to see what every Russian practical worker knows, namely, the miracles that the energy, not only of a circle, but even of an individual person is able to perform in the revolutionary cause. Or do you think that our movement cannot produce leaders like those of the seventies? If so, why do you think so? Because we lack training? But we are training ourselves, we will go on training ourselves, and we will be trained! Unfortunately it is true that the surface of the stagnant waters of the "economic struggle against the employers and the government" is overgrown with fungus; people have appeared among us who kneel in prayer to spontaneity, gazing with awe (to take an expression from Plekhanov) upon the "posterior" of the Russian proletariat. But we will get rid of this fungus. The time has come when Russian revolutionaries, guided by a genuinely revolutionary theory, relying upon the genuinely revolutionary and spontaneously awakening class, can at last—at long last!—rise to full stature in all their giant strength. All that is required is for the masses of our practical workers, and still larger masses of those who dreamed of practical work when they were still at school, to pour scorn and ridicule upon any suggestion that may be made to degrade our political tasks and to restrict the scope of our organisational work. And we will achieve that, rest assured, gentlemen!

In the article "Where To Begin", I wrote in opposition to *Rabocheye Dyelo*: "The tactics of agitation in relation to some special question, or the tactics with regard to some detail of party organisation may be changed in twenty-four hours; but only people devoid of all principle are capable of changing, in twenty-four hours, or, for that matter, in twenty-four months, their view on the necessity—in general, constantly, and absolutely—of an organisation of struggle and of political agitation among the masses."* To this *Rabocheye Dyelo* replied: "This, the only one of *Iskra*'s charges that makes a pretence of being based on facts, is totally without foundation. Readers of *Rabocheye Dyelo* know very well that from the outset we not only called for political agitation, without waiting for the appearance of *Iskra*... [saying at the same time that not only the workers' study circles, "but also the mass working-class movement could not regard as its first political task the overthrow of absolutism", but only the struggle for immediate political demands, and that "the masses begin to understand immediate political demands after one, or at all events, after several strikes"],... but that with our publications which we furnished from abroad for the comrades working in Russia, we provided the *only* Social-Democratic political and agitational material... [and in this sole material you not only based the widest political agitation exclusively on the economic struggle, but you even went to the extent of claiming that this restrict-

---

* See *Collected Works*, Vol. 5, p. 18.—*Ed.*

ed agitation was the "most widely applicable". And do you not observe, gentlemen, that your own argument—that this was the *only* material provided—proves the necessity for *Iskra*'s appearance, and its struggle against *Rabocheye Dyelo*?].... On the other hand, our publishing activity actually prepared the ground for the tactical unity of the Party ... [unity in the conviction that tactics is a process of growth of Party tasks that grow together with the Party? A precious unity indeed!]... and by that rendered possible the creation of a 'militant organisation' for which the Union Abroad did all that an organisation abroad could do" (*Rabocheye Dyelo*, No. 10, p. 15). A vain attempt at evasion! I would never dream of denying that you did all you possibly could. I have asserted and assert now that the *limits* of what is "possible" for you to do are restricted by the narrowness of your outlook. It is ridiculous to talk of a "militant organisation" to fight for "immediate political demands", or to conduct "the economic struggle against the employers and the government".

But if the reader wishes to see the pearls of "Economist" infatuation with amateurism, he must, of course, turn from the eclectic and vacillating *Rabocheye Dyelo* to the consistent and determined *Rabochaya Mysl*. In its *Separate Supplement,* p. 13, R. M. wrote: "Now two words about the so-called revolutionary intelligentsia proper. True, on more than one occasion it has proved itself prepared 'to enter into determined battle with tsarism'. The unfortunate thing, however, is that our revolutionary intelligentsia, ruthlessly persecuted by the political police, imagined the struggle against the political police to be the political struggle against the autocracy. That is why, to this day, it cannot understand 'where the forces for the struggle against the autocracy are to be obtained'."

Truly matchless is the lofty contempt for the struggle against the police displayed by this worshipper (in the worst sense of the word) of the *spontaneous* movement! He is prepared to *justify* our inability to organise secret activity by the argument that with the spontaneous mass movement it is not at all important for us to struggle against the political police! Very few people indeed would subscribe to this appalling conclusion; to such an extent have our deficiencies in revolutionary organisations become a matter of acute importance. But if Martynov, for example, refuses to subscribe to this, it will only be because he is unable, or lacks the courage, to think out his ideas to their logical conclusion. Indeed, does the "task" of advancing concrete demands by the masses, demands that promise palpable results, call for special efforts to create a stable, centralised, militant organisation of revolutionaries? Cannot such a "task" be carried out even by masses that do not "struggle against the political police" at all? Could this task, moreover, be fulfilled if, in addition to the few leaders, it were not undertaken by such workers (the overwhelming majority) as are quite *incapable* of "struggling against the political police"? Such workers, average people of the masses, are capable of displaying enormous energy and self-sacrifice in strikes and in street battles with the police and the troops, and are capable (in fact, are alone capable) of *determining* the outcome of our entire movement—but the struggle against the *political* police requires special qualities; it requires *professional* revolutionaries. And we must see to it, not only that the masses "advance" concrete demands, but that the masses of the workers "advance" an increasing number of such professional revolutionaries. Thus, we have reached the question of the relation between an organisation of professional revolutionaries and the labour movement pure and simple. Although this question has found little reflection in literature, it has greatly engaged us "politicians" in conversations and polemics with comrades who gravitate more or less towards Economism. It is a question meriting special treatment. But before taking it up, let us offer one further quotation by way of illustrating our thesis on the connection between primitiveness and Economism.

In his *Reply*, Mr. N. N.[55] wrote: "The Emancipation of Labour group demands direct struggle against the government without first considering where the material forces for this struggle are to be obtained, and without indicating *the path of the struggle*." Emphasising the last words, the author adds the following footnote to the word "path": "This cannot be explained by purposes of secrecy, because the programme does not refer to a plot but to *a mass movement*. And the masses cannot proceed by secret paths. Can we conceive of a secret strike? Can we conceive of secret demonstrations and petitions?" (*Vademecum*, p. 59.) Thus, the author comes quite close to the question of the "material forces" (organisers of strikes and demonstrations) and to the "paths" of the struggle, but, nevertheless, is still in a state of consternation, because he "worships" the mass movement, i.e., he regards it as something that *relieves* us of the necessity of conducting revolutionary activity and not as something that should encourage us and *stimulate* our revolutionary activity. It is impossible for a strike to remain a secret to those participating in it and to those immediately associated with it, but it may (and in the majority of cases does) remain a "secret" to the masses of the Russian workers, because the government takes care to cut all communication with the strikers, to prevent all news of strikes from spreading. Here indeed is where a special "struggle against the political police" is required, a struggle that can never be conducted actively by such large masses as take part in strikes. This struggle must be organised, according to "all the rules of the art", by people who are professionally engaged in revolutionary activity. The fact that the masses are spontaneously being drawn into the movement does not make the organisation of this struggle *less necessary*. On the contrary, it makes it *more necessary;* for we socialists would be failing in our direct duty to the masses if we did not prevent the police from making a secret of every strike and every demonstration (and if we did not ourselves from time to time secretly prepare strikes and demonstrations). And we *will succeed in doing this,* because the spontaneously awakening masses will *also produce* increasing numbers of "professional revolutionaries" *from their own ranks* (that is, if we do not take it into our heads to advise the workers to keep on marking time).

C. Organisation of Workers and Organisation of Revolutionaries

It is only natural to expect that for a Social-Democrat whose conception of the political struggle coincides with the conception of the "economic struggle against the employers and the government", the "organisation of revolutionaries" will more or less coincide with the "organisation of workers". This, in fact, is what actually happens; so that when we speak of organisation, we literally speak in different tongues. I vividly recall, for example, a conversation I once had with a fairly consistent Economist, with whom I had not been previously acquainted. We were discussing the pamphlet, *Who Will Bring About the Political Revolution?* and were soon of a mind that its principal defect was its ignoring of the question of organisation. We had begun to assume full agreement between us; but, as the conversation proceeded, it became evident that we were talking of different things. My interlocutor accused the author of ignoring strike funds, mutual benefit societies, etc., whereas I had in mind an organisation of revolutionaries as an essential factor in "bringing about" the political revolution. As soon as the disagreement became clear, there was, hardly, as I remember, a single question of principle upon which I was in agreement with the Economist!

What was the source of our disagreement? It was the fact that on questions both of organisation and of politics the Economists are forever lapsing from Social-Democracy into trade-unionism. The political struggle of Social-Democracy is far more extensive and complex than the economic struggle of the workers against the employers and the government. Similarly (indeed for that reason), the organisation of the revolutionary Social-Democratic Party must inevitably be of *a kind different* from the organisation of the workers designed for this struggle. The workers' organisation must in the first place be a trade-union organisation; secondly, it must be as broad as possible; and thirdly, it must be as public as conditions will allow (here, and further on, of course, I refer only to absolutist Russia). On the other hand, the organisation of the revolutionaries must consist first and foremost of people who make revolutionary activity their profession (for which reason I speak of the organisation of *revolutionaries,* meaning revolutionary Social-Democrats). In view of this common characteristic of the members of such an organisation, *all distinctions as between workers and intellectuals,* not to speak of distinctions of trade and profession, in both categories, *must be effaced.* Such an organisation must perforce not be very extensive and must be as secret as possible. Let us examine this threefold distinction.

In countries where political liberty exists the distinction between a trade-union and a political organisation is clear enough, as is the distinction between trade unions and Social-Democracy. The relations between the latter and the former will naturally vary in each country according to historical, legal, and other conditions; they may be more or less close, complex, etc. (in our opinion they should be as close and as little complicated as possible); but there can be no question in free countries of the organisation of trade unions coinciding with the organisation of the Social-Democratic Party. In Russia, however, the yoke of the autocracy appears at first glance to obliterate all distinctions between the Social-Democratic organisation and the workers' associations, since *all* workers' associations and *all* study circles are prohibited, and since the principal manifestation and weapon of the workers' economic struggle—the strike—is regarded as a criminal (and sometimes even as a political!) offence. Conditions in our country, therefore, on the one hand, strongly "impel" the workers engaged in economic struggle to concern themselves with political questions, and, on the other, they "impel" Social-Democrats to confound trade-unionism with Social-Democracy (and our Krichevskys, Martynovs, and Co., while diligently discussing the first kind of "impulsion", fail to notice the second). Indeed, picture to yourselves people who are immersed ninety-nine per cent in "the economic struggle against the employers and the government". Some of them will never, during the *entire* course of their activity (from four to six months), be impelled to think of the need for a more complex organisation of revolutionaries. Others, perhaps, will come across the fairly widely distributed Bernsteinian literature, from which they will become convinced of the profound importance of the forward movement of "the drab everyday struggle". Still others will be carried away, perhaps, by the seductive idea of showing the world a new example of "close and organic contact with the proletarian struggle"—contact between the trade-union and the Social-Democratic movements. Such people may argue that the later a country enters the arena of capitalism and, consequently, of the working-class movement, the more the socialists in that country may take part in, and support, the trade-union movement, and the less the reason for the existence of non-Social-Democratic trade unions. So far the argument is fully correct; unfortunately, however, some go beyond that and dream of a complete fusion of Social-Democracy with trade-unionism. We shall soon see, from the example of the Rules of the St. Petersburg League of Struggle, what a harmful effect such dreams have upon our plans of organisation.

The workers' organisations for the economic struggle should be trade-union organisations. Every Social-Democratic worker should as far as possible assist and actively work in these organisations. But, while this is true, it is certainly not in our interest to demand that only Social-Democrats should be eligible for membership in the "trade" unions, since that would only narrow the scope of our influence upon the masses. Let every worker who understands the need to unite for the struggle against the employers and the government join the trade unions. The very aim of the trade unions would be impossible of achievement, if they did not unite all who have attained at least this elementary degree of understanding, if they were not very *broad* organisations. The broader these organisations, the broader will be our influence over them —an influence due, not only to the "spontaneous" development of the economic struggle, but to the direct and conscious effort of the socialist trade-union members to influence their comrades. But a broad organisation cannot apply methods of strict secrecy (since this demands far greater training than is required for the economic struggle). How is the contradiction between the need for a large membership and the need for strictly secret methods to be reconciled? How are we to make the trade unions as public as possible? Generally speaking, there can be only two ways to this end: either the trade unions become legalised (in some countries this preceded the legalisation of the socialist and political unions), or the organisation is kept secret, but so "free" and amorphous, *lose**
as the Germans say, that the need for secret methods becomes almost negligible as far as the bulk of the members is concerned.

---

* *Lose* (German)—loose.—*Ed.*

The legalisation of non-socialist and non-political labour unions in Russia has begun, and there is no doubt that every advance made by our rapidly growing Social-Democratic working-class movement will multiply and encourage attempts at legalisation—attempts proceeding for the most part from supporters of the existing order, but partly also from the workers themselves and from liberal intellectuals. The banner of legality has already been hoisted by the Vasilyevs and the Zubatovs. Support has been promised and rendered by the Ozerovs and the Wormses, and followers of the new tendency are now to be found among the workers. Henceforth, we cannot but reckon with this tendency. How we are to reckon with it, on this there can be no two opinions among Social-Democrats. We must steadfastly expose any part played in this movement by the Zubatovs and the Vasilyevs, the gendarmes and the priests, and explain their real intentions to the workers. We must also expose all the conciliatory, "harmonious" notes that will be heard in the speeches of liberal politicians at legal meetings of the workers, irrespective of whether the speeches are motivated by an earnest conviction of the desirability of peaceful class collaboration, by a desire to curry favour with the powers that be, or whether they are simply the result of clumsiness. Lastly, we must warn the workers against the traps often set by the police, who at such open meetings and permitted societies spy out the "fiery ones" and try to make use of legal organisations to plant their *agents provocateurs* in the illegal organisations.

Doing all this does not at all mean forgetting that *in the long run* the legalisation of the working-class movement will be to our advantage, and not to that of the Zubatovs. On the contrary, it is precisely our campaign of exposure that will help us to separate the tares from the wheat. What the tares are, we have already indicated. By the wheat we mean attracting the attention of ever larger numbers, including the most backward sections, of the workers to social and political questions, and freeing ourselves, the revolutionaries, from functions that are essentially legal (the distribution of legal books, mutual aid, etc.), the development of which will inevitably provide us with an increasing quantity of material for agitation. In this sense, we may, and should, say to the Zubatovs and the Ozerovs: Keep at it, gentlemen, do your best! Whenever you place a trap in the path of the workers (either by way of direct provocation, or by the "honest" demoralisation of the workers with the aid of "Struveism"), we will see to it that you are exposed. But whenever you take a real step forward, though it be the most "timid zigzag", we will say: Please continue! And the only step that can be a real step forward is a real, if small, extension of the workers' field of action. Every such extension will be to our advantage and will help to hasten the advent of legal societies of the kind in, which it will not be *agents provocateurs* who are detecting socialists, but socialists who are gaining adherents. In a word, our task is to fight the tares. It is not our business to grow wheat in flower-pots. By pulling up the tares, we clear the soil for the wheat. And while the Afanasy Ivanoviches and Pulkheria Ivanovnas[56] are tending their flower-pot crops, we must prepare the reapers, not only to cut down the tares of today, but to reap the wheat of tomorrow.*

Thus, *we* cannot by means of legalisation *solve* the problem of creating a trade-union organisation that will be as little secret and as extensive as possible (but we should be extremely glad if the Zubatovs and the Ozerovs disclosed to us even a partial opportunity for such a solution—to this end, however, we must strenuously combat them). There remain secret trade-union organisations, and *we must* give all possible assistance to the workers who (as we definitely know) are adopting this course. Trade-union organisations, not only can be of tremendous value in developing and consolidating the economic struggle, but

---

* *Iskra*'s campaign against the tares evoked the following angry outburst from *Rabocheye Dyelo:* "For *Iskra*, the signs of the times lie not so much in the great events [of the spring], as in the miserable attempts of the agents of Zubatov to 'legalise' the working-class movement. It fails to see that these facts tell against it; for they testify that the working-class movement has assumed menacing proportions in the eyes of the government" (*Two Conferences*, p. 27). For all this we have to blame the "dogmatism" of the orthodox who "turn a deaf ear to the imperative demands of life". They obstinately refuse to see the yard-high wheat and are combating inch-high tares! Does this not reveal a "distorted sense of perspective in regard to the Russian working-class movement" (ibid., p. 27)?

can also become a very important auxiliary to political agitation and revolutionary organisation. In order to achieve this purpose, and in order to guide the nascent trade-union movement in the channels desired by Social-Democracy, we must first understand clearly the absurdity of the plan of organisation the St. Petersburg Economists have been nursing for nearly five years. That plan is set forth in the "Rules for a Workers' Mutual Benefit Fund" of July 1897 (*"Listok" Rabotnika,* No. 9-10, p. 46, taken from *Rabochaya Mysl,* No. 1), as well as in the "Rules for a Trade-Union Workers' Organisation", of October 1900 (special leaflet printed in St. Petersburg and referred to in *Iskra,* No. 1). Both these sets of rules have one main shortcoming: they set up the broad workers' organisation in a rigidly specified structure and confound it with the organisation of revolutionaries. Let us take the last-mentioned set of rules, since it is drawn up in greater detail. The body consists of *fifty-two* paragraphs. Twenty-three deal with the structure, the method of functioning, and the competence of the "workers' circles", which are to be organised in every factory ("a maximum of ten persons") and which elect "central (factory) groups". "The central group," says paragraph 2, "observes all that goes on in its factory or workshop and keeps a record of events." "The central group presents to subscribers a monthly financial account" (par. 17), etc. Ten paragraphs are devoted to the "district organisation", and nineteen to the highly complex interconnection between the Committee of the Workers' Organisation and the Committee of the St. Petersburg League of Struggle (elected representatives of each district and of the "executive groups"—"groups of propagandists, groups for maintaining contact with the provinces and with the organisation abroad, groups for managing stores, publications, and funds").

Social-Democracy="executive groups" in relation to the economic struggle of the workers! It would be difficult to show more glaringly how the Economists' ideas deviate from Social-Democracy to trade-unionism, and how alien to them is any idea that a Social-Democrat must concern himself first and foremost with an organisation of revolutionaries capable of guiding the *entire* proletarian struggle for emancipation. To talk of "the political emancipation of the working class" and of the struggle against "tsarist despotism", and at the same time to draft rules like these, means to have no idea whatsoever of the real political tasks of Social-Democracy. Not one of the fifty or so paragraphs reveals even a glimmer of understanding that it is necessary to conduct the widest possible political agitation among the masses, an agitation highlighting every aspect of Russian absolutism and the specific features of the various social classes in Russia. Rules like these are of no use even for the achievement of trade-union, let alone political, aims, since trade unions are organised by *trades*, of which no mention is made.

But most characteristic, perhaps, is the amazing top-heaviness of the whole "system", which attempts to bind each single factory and its "committee" by a permanent string of uniform and ludicrously petty rules and a three-stage system of election. Hemmed in by the narrow outlook of Economism, the mind is lost in details that positively reek of red tape and bureaucracy. In practice, of course, three-fourths of the clauses are never applied; on the other hand, a "secret" organisation of this kind, with its central group in each factory, makes it very easy for the gendarmes to carry out raids on a vast scale. The Polish comrades have passed through a similar phase in their movement, with everybody enthusiastic about the extensive organisation of workers' benefit funds; but they very quickly abandoned this idea when they saw that such organisations only provided rich harvests for the gendarmes. If we have in mind broad workers' organisations, and not widespread arrests, if we do not want to provide satisfaction to the gendarmes, we must see to it that these organisations remain without any rigid formal structure. But will they be able to function in that case?

Let us see what the functions are: "...To observe all that goes on in the factory and keep a record of events" (par. 2 of the Rules). Do we really require a formally established group for this purpose? Could not the purpose be better served by correspondence conducted in the illegal papers without the setting up of special groups? "...To lead the struggles of the workers for the improvement of their workshop conditions" (par. 3). This, too, requires no set organisational form. Any sensible agitator can in the course of ordinary conversation gather what the demands of the workers are and transmit them to a narrow —not a broad—organisation of revolutionaries for expression in a leaflet. "...To organise a fund ... to which subscriptions of two kopeks per ruble* should be made" (par. 9)—and then to present to subscribers a monthly financial account (par. 17), to expel members who fail to pay their contributions (par. 10), and so forth. Why, this is a very paradise for the police; for nothing would be easier for them than to penetrate into such a secrecy of a "central factory fund", confiscate the money, and arrest the best people. Would it not be simpler to issue one-kopek or two-kopek coupons bearing the official stamp of a well-known (very narrow and very secret) organisation, or to make collections without coupons of any kind and to print reports in a certain agreed code in an illegal paper? The object would thereby be attained, but it would be a hundred times more difficult for the gendarmes to pick up clues.

I could go on analysing the Rules, but I think that what has been said will suffice. A small, compact core of the most reliable, experienced, and hardened workers, with responsible representatives in the principal districts and connected by all the rules of strict secrecy with the organisation of revolutionaries, can, with the widest support of the masses and without any formal organisation, perform *all* the functions of a trade-union organisation, in a manner, moreover, desirable to Social-Democracy. Only in this way can we secure the *consolidation* and development of a *Social-Democratic* trade-union movement, despite all the gendarmes.

It may be objected that an organisation which is so *lose* that it is not even definitely formed, and which has not even an enrolled and registered membership, cannot be called an organisation at all. Perhaps so. Not the name is important. What is important is that this "organisation without members" shall do everything that is required, and from the very outset ensure a solid connection between our future trade unions and socialism. Only an incorrigible utopian would have a *broad* organisation of

---

*Of wages earned.—*Tr.*

workers, with elections, reports, universal suffrage, etc., under the autocracy.

The moral to be drawn from this is simple. If we begin with the solid foundation of a strong organisation of revolutionaries, we can ensure the stability of the movement as a whole and carry out the aims both of Social-Democracy and of trade unions proper. If, however, we begin with a broad workers' organisation, which is supposedly most "accessible" to the masses (but which is actually most accessible to the gendarmes and makes revolutionaries most accessible to the police), we shall achieve neither the one aim nor the other; we shall not eliminate our rule-of-thumb methods, and, because we remain scattered and our forces are constantly broken up by the police, we shall only make trade unions of the Zubatov and Ozerov type the more accessible to the masses.

What, properly speaking, should be the functions of the organisation of revolutionaries? We shall deal with this question in detail. First, however, let us examine a very typical argument advanced by our terrorist, who (sad fate!) in this matter also is a next-door neighbour to the Economist. *Svoboda*, a journal published for workers, contains in its first issue an article entitled "Organisation", the author of which tries to defend his friends, the Economist workers of Ivanovo-Voznesensk. He writes:

"It is bad when the masses are mute and unenlightened, when the movement does not come from the rank and file. For instance, the students of a university town leave for their homes during the summer and other holidays, and immediately the workers' movement comes to a standstill. Can a workers' movement which has to be pushed on from outside be a real force? No, indeed.... It has not yet learned to walk, it is still in leading-strings. So it is in all matters. The students go off, and everything comes to a standstill. The most capable are seized; the cream is skimmed—and the milk turns sour. If the 'committee' is arrested, everything comes to a standstill until a new one can be formed. And one never knows what sort of committee will be set up next—it may be nothing like the former. The first said one thing, the second may say the very opposite. Continuity between yesterday and tomorrow is broken, the experience of the past does not serve as a guide for the future. And all because no roots have been struck first in depth, in the masses; the work is carried on not by a hundred fools, but by a dozen wise men. A dozen wise men can be wiped out at a snap, but when the organisation embraces masses, everything proceeds from them, and nobody, however he tries, can wreck the cause" (p. 63).

The facts are described correctly. The picture of our amateurism is well drawn. But the conclusions are worthy of *Rabochaya Mysl*, both as regards their stupidity and their lack of political tact. They represent the height of stupidity, because the author confuses the philosophical and social-historical question of the "depth" of the "roots" of the movement with the technical and organisational question of the best method in combating the gendarmes. They represent the height of political tactlessness, because, instead of appealing from bad leaders to good leaders, the author appeals from the leaders in general to the "masses". This is as much an attempt to drag us back organisationally as the idea of substituting excitative terrorism for political agitation drags us back politically. Indeed, I am experiencing a veritable *embarras de richesses*, and hardly know where to begin to disentangle the jumble offered up by *Svoboda*. For clarity, let me begin by citing an example. Take the Germans. It will not be denied, I hope, that theirs is a mass organisation, that in Germany everything proceeds from the masses, that the working-class movement there has learned to walk. Yet observe how these millions value their "dozen" tried political leaders, how firmly they cling to them. Members of the hostile parties in parliament have often taunted the socialists by exclaiming: "Fine democrats you are indeed! Yours is a working-class movement only in name; in actual fact the same clique of leaders is always in evidence, the same Bebel and the same Liebknecht, year in and year out, and that goes on for decades. Your supposedly elected workers' deputies are more permanent than the officials appointed by the Emperor!" But the Germans only smile with contempt at these demagogic attempts to set the "masses" against the "leaders", to arouse bad and ambitious instincts in the former, and to rob the movement of its solidity and stability by undermining the confidence of the masses in their "dozen wise men". Political thinking is sufficiently developed among the Germans, and they have accumulated sufficient political experience to understand that without the "dozen" tried and talented leaders (and talented men are not born by the hundreds), professionally trained, schooled by long experience, and working in perfect harmony, no class in modern society can wage a determined struggle. The Germans too have had demagogues in their ranks who have flattered the "hundred fools", exalted them above the "dozen wise ‚men", extolled the "horny hand" of the masses, and (like Most and Hasselmann) have spurred them on to reckless "revolutionary" action and sown distrust towards the firm and steadfast leaders. It was only by stubbornly and relentlessly combating all demagogic elements within the socialist movement that German socialism has managed to grow and become as strong as it is. Our wiseacres, however, at a time when Russian Social-Democracy is passing through a crisis entirely due to the lack of sufficiently trained, developed, and experienced leaders to guide the spontaneously awakening masses, cry out with the profundity of fools: "It is a bad business when the movement does not proceed from the rank and file".

"A committee of students is of no use; it is not stable." Quite true. But the conclusion to be drawn from this is that we must have a committee of professional *revolutionaries*, and it is immaterial whether a student or a worker is capable of becoming a professional revolutionary. The conclusion you draw, however, is that the working-class movement must not be pushed on from outside! In your political innocence you fail to notice that you are playing into the hands of our Economists and fostering our amateurism. Wherein, may I ask, did our students "push on" our workers? *In the sense* that the student brought to the worker the fragments of political knowledge he himself possesses, the crumbs of socialist ideas he has managed to acquire (for the principal intellectual diet of the present-day student, legal Marxism, could furnish only the rudiments, only scraps of knowledge). There has never been too much of *such* "pushing on from outside"; on the contrary, there has so far been all too little of it in our movement, for we have been stewing too assiduously in our own juice; we have bowed far too slavishly to the elementary "economic struggle of the workers against the employers and the government". We professional revolutionaries must and will make it our business to engage in *this kind* of "pushing on" a hundred times more forcibly than we have done hitherto. But the very fact that you select so hideous a phrase as "pushing on from outside"

—a phrase which cannot but rouse in the workers (at least in the workers who are as unenlightened as you yourselves) a sense of distrust towards *all* who bring them political knowledge and revolutionary experience from outside, which cannot but rouse in them an instinctive desire to resist *all* such people—proves you to be *demagogues,* and demagogues are the worst enemies of the working class.

And, please—don't hasten howling about my "uncomradely methods" of debating. I have not the least desire to doubt the purity of your intentions. As I have said, one may become a demagogue out of sheer political innocence. But I have shown that you have descended to demagogy, and I will never tire of repeating that demagogues are the worst enemies of the working class. The worst enemies, because they arouse base instincts in the masses, because the unenlightened worker is unable to recognise his enemies in men who represent themselves, and sometimes sincerely so, as his friends. The worst enemies, because in the period of disunity and vacillation, when our movement is just beginning to take shape, nothing is easier than to employ demagogic methods to mislead the masses, who can realise their error only later by bitter experience. That is why the slogan of the day for the Russian Social-Democrat must be—resolute struggle against *Svoboda* and *Rabocheye Dyelo*, both of which have sunk to the level of demagogy. We shall deal with this further in greater detail.*

"A dozen wise men can be more easily wiped out than a hundred fools." This wonderful truth (for which the hundred fools will always applaud you) appears obvious only because in the very midst of the argument you have skipped from one question to another. You began by talking and continued to talk of the unearthing of a "committee", of the unearthing of an "organisation", and now you skip to the question of unearthing the movement's "roots" in their "depths". The fact is, of course,

---

* For the moment let us observe merely that our remarks on "pushing on from outside" and *Svoboda*'s other disquisitions on organisation apply *in their entirety* to *all* the Economists, including the adherents of *Rabocheye Dyelo*; for some of them have actively preached and defended such views on organisation, while others among them have drifted into them.

that our movement cannot be unearthed, for the very reason that it has countless thousands of roots deep down among the masses; but that is not the point at issue. As far as "deep roots" are concerned, we cannot be "unearthed" even now, despite all our amateurism, and yet we all complain, and cannot but complain, that the "*organisations*" are being unearthed and as a result it is impossible to maintain continuity in the movement. But since you raise the question of *organisations* being unearthed and persist in your opinion, I assert that it is far more difficult to unearth a dozen wise men than a hundred fools. This position I will defend, no matter how much you instigate the masses against me for my "anti-democratic" views, etc. As I have stated repeatedly, by "wise men", in connection with organisation, I mean *professional revolutionaries*, irrespective of whether they have developed from among students or working men. I assert: (1) that no revolutionary movement can endure without a stable organisation of leaders maintaining continuity; (2) that the broader the popular mass drawn spontaneously into the struggle, which forms the basis of the movement and participates in it, the more urgent the need for such an organisation, and the more solid this organisation must be (for it is much easier for all sorts of demagogues to side-track the more backward sections of the masses); (3) that such an organisation must consist chiefly of people professionally engaged in revolutionary activity; (4) that in an autocratic state, the more we *confine* the membership of such an organisation to people who are professionally engaged in revolutionary activity and who have been professionally trained in the art of combating the political police, the more difficult will it be to unearth the organisation; and (5) the *greater* will be the number of people from the working class and from the other social classes who will be able to join the movement and perform active work in it.

I invite our Economists, terrorists, and "Economists-terrorists"* to confute these propositions. At the moment,

---

* This term is perhaps more applicable to *Svoboda* than the former, for in an article entitled "The Regeneration of Revolutionism" the publication defends terrorism, while in the article at present under review it defends Economism. One might say of *Svoboda* that

I shall deal only with the last two points. The question as to whether it is easier to wipe out "a dozen wise men" or "a hundred fools" reduces itself to the question, above considered, whether it is possible to have a mass *organisation* when the maintenance of strict secrecy is essential. We can never give a mass organisation that degree of secrecy without which there can be no question of persistent and continuous struggle against the government. To concentrate all secret functions in the hands of as small a number of professional revolutionaries as possible does not mean that the latter will "do the thinking for all" and that the rank and file will not take an active part in the *movement*. On the contrary, the membership will promote increasing numbers of the professional revolutionaries from its ranks; for it will know that it is not enough for a few students and for a few working men waging the economic struggle to gather in order to form a "committee", but that it takes years to train oneself to be a professional revolutionary; and the rank and file will "think", not only of amateurish methods, but of such training. Centralisation of the secret functions of the *organisation* by no means implies centralisation of all the functions of the *movement*. Active participation of the widest masses in the illegal press will not diminish because a "dozen" professional revolutionaries centralise the secret functions connected with this work; on the contrary, it will *increase* tenfold. In this way, and in this way alone, shall we ensure that reading the illegal press, writing for it, and to some extent even distributing it, will *almost cease to be secret work*, for the police will soon come to realise the folly and impossibility of judicial and administrative red-tape procedure over every copy of a publication that is being distributed in the thousands. This holds not only

---

"it would if it could, but it can't". Its wishes and intentions are of the very best—but the result is utter confusion; this is chiefly due to the fact that, while *Svoboda* advocates continuity of organisation, it refuses to recognise continuity of revolutionary thought and Social-Democratic theory. It wants to revive the professional revolutionary ("The Regeneration of Revolutionism"), and to that end proposes, first, excitative terrorism, and, secondly, "an organisation of average workers" (*Svoboda*, No. 1, p. 66, et seq.), as less likely to be "pushed on from outside". In other words, it proposes to pull the house down to use the timber for heating it.

for the press, but for every function of the movement, even for demonstrations. The active and widespread participation of the masses will not suffer; on the contrary, it will benefit by the fact that a "dozen" experienced revolutionaries, trained professionally no less than the police, will centralise all the secret aspects of the work—the drawing up of leaflets, the working out of approximate plans; and the appointing of bodies of leaders for each urban district, for each factory district, and for each educational institution, etc. (I know that exception will be taken to my "undemocratic" views, but I shall reply below fully to this anything but intelligent objection.) Centralisation of the most secret functions in an organisation of revolutionaries will not diminish, but rather increase the extent and enhance the quality of the activity of a large number of other organisations, that are intended for a broad public and are therefore as loose and as non-secret as possible, such as workers' trade unions; workers' self-education circles and circles for reading illegal literature; and socialist, as well as democratic, circles among *all* other sections of the population; etc., etc. We must have such circles, trade unions, and organisations everywhere in *as large a number as possible* and with the widest variety of functions; but it would be absurd and harmful *to confound* them with the organisation of *revolutionaries*, to efface the border-line between them, to make still more hazy the all too faint recognition of the fact that in order to "serve" the mass movement we must have people who will devote themselves exclusively to Social-Democratic activities, and that such people must *train* themselves patiently and steadfastly to be professional revolutionaries.

Yes, this recognition is incredibly dim. Our worst sin with regard to organisation consists in the fact that *by our primitiveness we have lowered the prestige of revolutionaries in Russia*. A person who is flabby and shaky on questions of theory, who has a narrow outlook, who pleads the spontaneity of the masses as an excuse for his own sluggishness, who resembles a trade-union secretary more than a spokesman of the people, who is unable to conceive of a broad and bold plan that would command the respect even of opponents, and who is inexperienced and clumsy in his own professional art—the art of combating the political police—such a man is not a revolutionary, but a wretched amateur!

Let no active worker take offence at these frank remarks, for as far as insufficient training is concerned, I apply them first and foremost to myself. I used to work in a study circle[57] that set itself very broad, all-embracing tasks; and all of us, members of that circle, suffered painfully and acutely from the realisation that we were acting as amateurs at a moment in history when we might have been able to say, varying a well-known statement: "Give us an organisation of revolutionaries, and we will overturn Russia!" The more I recall the burning sense of shame I then experienced, the bitterer become my feelings towards those pseudo-Social-Democrats whose preachings "bring disgrace on the calling of a revolutionary", who fail to understand that our task is not to champion the degrading of the revolutionary to the level of an amateur, but *to raise* the amateurs to the level of revolutionaries.

D. The Scope of Organisational Work

We have heard B—v tell us about "the lack of revolutionary forces fit for action which is felt not only in St. Petersburg, but throughout Russia". Hardly anyone will dispute this fact. But the question is, how is it to be explained? B—v writes:

"We shall not go into an explanation of the historical causes of this phenomenon; we shall merely state that a society, demoralised by prolonged political reaction and split by past and present economic changes, promotes from its own ranks *an extremely small number of persons fit for revolutionary work*; that the working class does produce revolutionary workers who to some extent reinforce the ranks of the illegal organisations, but that the number of such revolutionaries is inadequate to meet the requirements of the times. This is all the more so because the worker who spends eleven and a half hours a day in the factory is in such a position that he can, in the main, perform only the functions of an agitator; but propaganda and organisation, the delivery and reproduction of illegal literature, the issuance of leaflets, etc., are duties which must necessarily fall mainly upon the shoulders of an extremely small force of intellectuals" (*Rabocheye Dyelo*, No. 6, pp. 38-39).

On many points we disagree with B—v, particularly with those we have emphasised, which most saliently reveal that, although weary of our amateurism (as is every thinking practical worker), B—v cannot find the way out of this intolerable situation, because he is weighted down by Economism. The fact is that society produces very *many* persons fit for "the cause", but we are unable to make use of them all. The critical, transitional state of our movement in this respect may be formulated as follows: *There are no people—yet there is a mass of people.* There is a mass of people, because the working class and increasingly varied social strata, year after year, produce from their ranks an increasing number of discontented people who desire to protest, who are ready to render all the assistance they can in the struggle against absolutism, the intolerableness of which, though not yet recognised by all, is more and more acutely sensed by increasing masses of the people. At the same time, we have no people, because we have no leaders, no political leaders, no talented organisers capable of arranging extensive and at the same time uniform and harmonious work that would employ all forces, even the most inconsiderable. "The growth and development of the revolutionary organisations" lag, not only behind the growth of the working-class movement, which even B—v admits, but behind that of the general democratic movement among all strata of the people. (In passing, probably B—v would now regard this as supplementing his conclusion.) The scope of revolutionary work is too narrow, as compared with the breadth of the spontaneous basis of the movement. It is too hemmed in by the wretched theory of "economic struggle against the employers and the government". Yet, at the present time, not only Social-Democratic political agitators, but Social-Democratic organisers must "go among all classes of the population".* There is hardly a single practical worker who will doubt that the Social-Democrats could distribute the thousand and one minute

---

* Thus, an undoubted revival of the democratic spirit has recently been observed among persons in military service, partly as a consequence of the more frequent street battles with "enemies" like workers and students. As soon as our available forces permit, we must without fail devote the most serious attention to propaganda and agitation among soldiers and officers, and to the creation of "military organisations" affiliated to our Party.

functions of their organisational work among individual representatives of the most varied classes. Lack of specialisation is one of the most serious defects of our technique, about which B—v justly and bitterly complains. The smaller each separate "operation" in our common cause the more people we can find capable of carrying out such operations (people who, in the majority of cases, are completely incapable of becoming professional revolutionaries); the more difficult will it be for the police to "net" all these "detail workers", and the more difficult will it be for them to frame up, out of an arrest for some petty affair, a "case" that would justify the government's expenditure on "security". As for the number of people ready to help us, we referred in the preceding chapter to the gigantic change that has taken place in this respect in the last five years or so. On the other hand, in order to unite all these tiny fractions into one whole, in order not to break up the movement while breaking up its functions, and in order to imbue the people who carry out the minute functions with the conviction that their work is necessary and important, without which conviction they will never do the work,* it is necessary to have a strong or-

---

* I recall that once a comrade told me of a factory inspector who wanted to help the Social-Democrats, and actually did, but complained bitterly that he did not know whether his "information" reached the proper revolutionary centre, how much his help was really required, and what possibilities there were for utilising his small and petty services. Every practical worker can, of course, cite many similar instances in which our primitiveness deprived us of allies. These services, each "small" in itself, but invaluable when taken in the mass, could and would be rendered to us by office employees and officials, not only in factories, but in the postal service, on the railways, in the Customs, among the nobility, among the clergy, and in *every* other walk of life, including even the police and the Court! Had we a real party, a real militant organisation of revolutionaries, we would not make undue demands on every one of these "aides", we would not hasten always and invariably to bring them right into the very heart of our "illegality", but, on the contrary, we would husband them most carefully and would even train people especially for such functions, bearing in mind that many students could be of much greater service to the Party as "aides" holding some official post than as "short-term" revolutionaries. But, I repeat, only an organisation that is firmly established and has no lack of active forces would have the right to apply such tactics.

ganisation of tried revolutionaries. The more secret such an organisation is, the stronger and more widespread will be the confidence in the Party. As we know, in time of war, it is not only of the utmost importance to imbue one's own army with confidence in its strength, but it is important also to convince the enemy and all *neutral* elements of the strength; friendly neutrality may sometimes decide the issue. If such an organisation existed, one built up on a firm theoretical foundation and possessing a Social-Democratic organ, we should have no reason to fear that the movement might be diverted from its path by the numerous "outside" elements that are attracted to it. (On the contrary, it is precisely at the present time, with amateurism prevalent, that we see many Social-Democrats leaning towards the *Credo* and only imagining that they are Social-Democrats.) In a word, specialisation necessarily presupposes centralisation, and in turn imperatively calls for it.

But B—v himself, who has so excellently described the necessity for specialisation, underestimates its importance, in our opinion, in the second part of the argument we have quoted. The number of working-class revolutionaries is inadequate, he says. This is perfectly true, and once again we stress that the "valuable communication of a close observer" fully confirms our view of the causes of the present crisis in Social-Democracy, and, consequently, of the means required to overcome it. Not only are revolutionaries in general lagging behind the spontaneous awakening of the masses, but even worker-revolutionaries are lagging behind the spontaneous awakening of the working-class masses. This *fact* confirms with clear evidence, from the "practical" point of view, too, not only the absurdity but even the *politically reactionary nature* of the "pedagogics" to which we are so often treated in the discussion of our duties to the workers. This fact proves that our very first and most pressing duty is to help to train working-class revolutionaries who will be on the same level *in regard to Party activity* as the revolutionaries from amongst the intellectuals (we emphasise the words "in regard to Party activity", for, although necessary, it is neither so easy nor so pressingly necessary to bring the workers up to the level of intellectuals in other respects). Attention, therefore, must be devoted *principally* to *raising* the workers to the level of revolutionaries; it is not at all our task *to descend* to the level of the "working masses" as the Economists wish to do, or to the level of the "average worker", as *Svoboda* desires to do (and by this ascends to the second grade of Economist "pedagogics"). I am far from denying the necessity for popular literature for the workers, and especially popular (of course, not vulgar) literature for the especially backward workers. But what annoys me is this constant confusion of pedagogics with questions of politics and organisation. You, gentlemen, who are so much concerned about the "average worker", as a matter of fact, rather insult the workers by your desire *to talk down* to them when discussing working-class politics and working-class organisation. Talk about serious things in a serious manner; leave pedagogics to the pedagogues, and not to politicians and organisers! Are there not advanced people, "average people", and "masses" among the intelligentsia too? Does not everyone recognise that popular literature is also required for the intelligentsia, and is not such literature written? Imagine someone, in an article on organising college or high-school students, repeating over and over again, as if he had made a new discovery, that first of all we must have an organisation of "average students". The author of such an article would be ridiculed, and rightly so. Give us your ideas on organisation, if you have any, he would be told, and we ourselves will decide who is "average", who above average, and who below. But if you have no organisational ideas *of your own*, then all your exertions in behalf of the "masses" and "average people" will be simply boring. You must realise that these questions of "politics" and "organisation" are so serious in themselves that they cannot be dealt with in any other but a serious way. We can and must *educate* workers (and university and Gymnasium students) so that we *may be able to discuss* these questions with them. But once you do bring up these questions, you must give real replies to them; do not fall back on the "average", or on the "masses"; do not try to dispose of the matter with facetious remarks and mere phrases.*

To be fully prepared for his task, the worker-revolutionary must likewise become a professional revolutionary. Hence B—v is wrong in saying that since the worker spends eleven and a half hours in the factory, the brunt of all other revolutionary functions (apart from agitation) *"must necessarily* fall mainly upon the shoulders of an extremely small force of intellectuals". But this condition does not obtain out of sheer "necessity". It obtains because we are backward, because we do not recognise our duty to assist every capable worker to become a *professional* agitator, organiser, propagandist, literature distributor, etc., etc. In this respect, we waste our strength in a positively shameful manner; we lack the ability to husband that which should be tended and reared with special care. Look at the Germans: their forces are a hundredfold greater than ours. But they understand perfectly well that really capable agitators, etc., are not often promoted from the ranks of the "average". For this reason they immediately try to place every capable working man in conditions that will enable him to develop and apply his abilities to the fullest: he is made a professional agitator; he is encouraged to widen the field of his activity, to spread it from one factory to the whole of the industry, from a single locality to the whole country. He acquires experience and dexterity in his profession; he broadens his outlook and increases his knowledge; he observes at close quarters the prominent political leaders from other localities and of other parties; he strives to rise to their level and combine in himself the knowledge of the working-class environment and the freshness of socialist convictions with professional skill, without which the prole-

---

* *Svoboda*, No. 1, p. 66, in the article "Organisation": "The heavy tread of the army of workers will reinforce all the demands that will be advanced in behalf of Russian Labour"—Labour with a capital L, of course. And the author exclaims: "I am not in the least hostile towards the intelligentsia, but [*but*—the word that Shchedrin translated as meaning: The ears never grow higher than the forehead!]—but I always get frightfully annoyed when a man comes to me uttering beautiful and charming words and demands that they be accepted for their [his?] beauty and other virtues" (p. 62). Yes, I "always get frightfully annoyed", too.

tariat *cannot* wage a stubborn struggle against its excellently trained enemies. In this way alone do the working masses produce men of the stamp of Bebel and Auer. But what is to a great extent automatic in a politically free country must in Russia be done deliberately and systematically by our organisations. A worker-agitator who is at all gifted and "promising" *must not be left* to work eleven hours a day in a factory. We must arrange that he be maintained by the Party; that he may go underground in good time; that he change the place of his activity, if he is to enlarge his experience, widen his outlook, and be able to hold out for at least a few years in the struggle against the gendarmes. As the spontaneous rise of their movement becomes broader and deeper, the working-class masses promote from their ranks not only an increasing number of talented agitators, but also talented organisers, propagandists, and "practical workers" in the best sense of the term (of whom there are so few among our intellectuals who, for the most part, in the Russian manner, are somewhat careless and sluggish in their habits). When we have forces of specially trained worker-revolutionaries who have gone through extensive preparation (and, of course, revolutionaries "of all arms of the service"), no political police in the world will then be able to contend with them, for these forces, boundlessly devoted to the revolution, will enjoy the boundless confidence of the widest masses of the workers. We are directly *to blame* for doing too little to "stimulate" the workers to take this path, common to them and to the "intellectuals", of professional revolutionary training, and for all too often dragging them back by our silly speeches about what is "accessible" to the masses of the workers, to the "average workers", etc.

In this, as in other respects, the narrow scope of our organisational work is without a doubt due directly to the fact (although the overwhelming majority of the "Economists" and the novices in practical work do not perceive it) that we restrict our theories and our political tasks to a narrow field. Subservience to spontaneity seems to inspire a fear of taking even one step away from what is "accessible" to the masses, a fear of rising too high above mere attendance on the immediate and direct requirements of the masses. Have no fear, gentlemen! Remember that we stand so low on the plane of organisation that the very idea that we *could* rise *too* high is absurd!

E. "Conspiratorial" Organisation and "Democratism"

Yet there are many people among us who are so sensitive to the "voice of life" that they fear it more than anything in the world and charge the adherents of the views here expounded with following a Narodnaya Volya line, with failing to understand "democratism", etc. These accusations, which, of course, have been echoed by *Rabocheye Dyelo,* need to be dealt with.

The writer of these lines knows very well that the St. Petersburg Economists levelled the charge of Narodnaya Volya tendencies also against *Rabochaya Gazeta* (which is quite understandable when one compares it with *Rabochaya Mysl*). We were not in the least surprised, therefore, when, soon after the appearance of *Iskra*, a comrade informed us that the Social-Democrats in the town of X describe *Iskra* as a Narodnaya Volya organ. We, of course, were flattered by this accusation; for what decent Social-Democrat has not been accused by the Economists of being a Narodnaya Volya sympathiser?

These accusations are the result of a twofold misunderstanding. First, the history of the revolutionary movement is so little known among us that the name "Narodnaya Volya" is used to denote any idea of a militant centralised organisation which declares determined war upon tsarism. But the magnificent organisation that the revolutionaries had in the seventies, and that should serve us as a model, was not established by the Narodnaya Volya, but by the *Zemlya i Volya*, which split up into the Chorny Peredel and the Narodnaya Volya. Consequently, to regard a militant revolutionary organisation as something specifically Narodnaya Volya in character is absurd both historically and logically; for *no* revolutionary trend, if it seriously thinks of struggle, can dispense with such an organisation. The mistake the Narodnaya Volya committed was not in striving to enlist *all* the discontented in the organisation and to direct this organisation to resolute struggle against the autocracy; on the contrary, that was its great historical merit. The mistake was in relying on a theory which in substance was not a revolutionary theory at all, and the Narodnaya Volya members either did not know how, or were unable, to link their movement inseparably with the class struggle in the developing capitalist society. Only a gross failure to understand Marxism (or an "understanding" of it in the spirit of "Struveism") could prompt the opinion that the rise of a mass, spontaneous working-class movement *relieves* us of the duty of creating as good an organisation of revolutionaries as the Zemlya i Volya had, or, indeed, an incomparably better one. On the contrary, this movement *imposes* the duty upon us; for the spontaneous struggle of the proletariat will not become its genuine "class struggle" until this struggle is led by a strong organisation of revolutionaries.

Secondly, many people, including apparently B. Krichevsky (*Rabocheye Dyelo*, No. 10, p. 18), misunderstand the polemics that Social-Democrats have always waged against the "conspiratorial" view of the political struggle. We have always protested, and will, of course, continue to protest against *confining* the political struggle to conspiracy.* But this does not, of course, mean that we deny the need for a strong revolutionary organisation. Thus, in the pamphlet mentioned in the preceding footnote, after the polemics against reducing the political struggle to a conspiracy, a description is given (as a Social-Democratic ideal) of an organisation so strong as to be able to "resort to ... rebellion" and to every "other form of attack", in order to "deliver a smashing blow against absolutism".**

---

* Cf. *The Tasks of the Russian Social-Democrats*, p. 21, polemics against P. L. Lavrov. (See *Collected Works*, Vol. 2, pp. 340-41.—*Ed.*)
** *The Tasks of the Russian Social-Democrats*, p. 23. (See *Collected Works*, Vol. 2, p. 342.—*Ed.*) Apropos, we shall give another illustration of the fact that *Rabocheye Dyelo* either does not understand what it is talking about or changes its views "with the wind". In No. 1 of *Rabocheye Dyelo*, we find the following passage in italics: "*The substance set forth in the pamphlet accords entirely with the editorial programme of Rabocheye Dyelo*" (p. 142). Really? Does the view that the overthrow of the autocracy must not be set as the first task of the mass movement accord with the views expressed in *The Tasks of the Russian Social-Democrats*? Do the

In *form* such a strong revolutionary organisation in an autocratic country may also be described as a "conspiratorial" organisation, because the French word "conspiration" is the equivalent of the Russian word *"zagovor"* ("conspiracy"), and such an organisation must have the utmost secrecy. Secrecy is such a necessary condition for this kind of organisation that all the other conditions (number and selection of members, functions, etc.) must be made to conform to it. It would be extremely naïve indeed, therefore, to fear the charge that we Social-Democrats desire to create a conspiratorial organisation. Such a charge should be as flattering to every opponent of Economism as the charge of following a Narodnaya Volya line.

The objection may be raised that such a powerful and strictly secret organisation, which concentrates in its hands all the threads of secret activities, an organisation which of necessity is centralised, may too easily rush into a premature attack, may thoughtlessly intensify the movement before the growth of political discontent, the intensity of the ferment and anger of the working class, etc., have made such an attack possible and necessary. Our reply to this is: Speaking abstractly, it cannot be denied, of course, that a militant organisation *may* thoughtlessly engage in battle, which *may* end in a defeat entirely avoidable under other conditions. But we cannot confine ourselves to abstract reasoning on such a question, because every battle bears within itself the abstract possibility of defeat, and there is no way of *reducing* this possibility except by organised preparation for battle. If, however, we proceed from the concrete conditions at present obtaining in Russia, we must come to the positive conclusion that a strong revolutionary organisation is absolutely necessary precisely for the purpose of giving stability to the movement and of *safeguarding* it against the possibility of making thoughtless attacks. Precisely at the present time, when no such organisation yet exists, and

theory of "the economic struggle against the employers and the government" and the stages theory accord with the views expressed in that pamphlet? We leave it to the reader to judge whether a periodical that understands the meaning of "accordance in opinion" in this peculiar manner can have firm principles.

when the revolutionary movement is rapidly and spontaneously growing, we *already observe* two opposite extremes (which, as is to be expected, "meet"). These are: the utterly unsound Economism and the preaching of moderation, and the equally unsound "excitative terror", which strives "artificially to call forth symptoms of the end of the movement, which is developing and strengthening itself, when this movement is as yet nearer to the start than to the end" (V. Zasulich, in *Zarya*, No. 2-3, p. 353). And the instance of *Rabocheye Dyelo* shows that *there exist* Social-Democrats who give way to both these extremes. This is not surprising, for, apart from other reasons, the "economic struggle against the employers and the government" can *never* satisfy revolutionaries, and opposite extremes will therefore always appear here and there. Only a centralised, militant organisation that consistently carries out a Social-Democratic policy, that satisfies, so to speak, all revolutionary instincts and strivings, can safeguard the movement against making thoughtless attacks and prepare attacks that hold out the promise of success.

A further objection may be raised, that the views on organisation here expounded contradict the "democratic principle". Now, while the earlier accusation was specifically Russian in origin, this one is *specifically foreign* in character. And only an organisation abroad (the Union of Russian Social-Democrats Abroad) was capable of giving its Editorial Board instructions like the following:

"*Organisational Principle.* In order to secure the successful development and unification of Social-Democracy, the broad democratic principle of Party organisation must be emphasised, developed, and fought for; this is particularly necessary in view of the anti-democratic tendencies that have revealed themselves in the ranks of our Party" (*Two Conferences*, p. 18).

We shall see in the next chapter how *Rabocheye Dyelo* combats *Iskra*'s "anti-democratic tendencies". For the present, we shall examine more closely the "principle" that the Economists advance. Everyone will probably agree that "the broad democratic principle" presupposes the two following conditions: first, full publicity, and secondly, election to all offices. It would be absurd to speak of democracy without publicity, moreover, without a publicity that is not limited to the membership of the organisation. We call the German Socialist Party a democratic organisation because all its activities are carried out publicly; even its party congresses are held in public. But no one would call an organisation democratic that is hidden from every one but its members by a veil of secrecy. What is the use, then, of advancing "the *broad* democratic principle" when the fundamental condition for this principle *cannot be fulfilled* by a secret organisation? "The broad principle" proves itself simply to be a resounding but hollow phrase. Moreover, it reveals a total lack of understanding of the urgent tasks of the moment in regard to organisation. Everyone knows how great the lack of secrecy is among the "broad" masses of our revolutionaries. We have heard the bitter complaints of B—v on this score and his absolutely just demand for a "strict selection of members" (*Rabocheye Dyelo*, No. 6, p. 42). Yet, persons who boast a keen "sense of realities" *urge*, in a situation like this, not the strictest secrecy and the strictest (consequently, more restricted) selection of members, but "the *broad* democratic principle"! This is what you call being wide off the mark.

Nor is the situation any better with regard to the second attribute of democracy, the principle of election. In politically free countries, this condition is taken for granted. "They are members of the Party who accept the principles of the Party programme and render the Party all possible support," reads Clause 1 of the Rules of the German Social-Democratic Party. Since the entire political arena is as open to the public view as is a theatre stage to the audience, this acceptance or non-acceptance, support or opposition, is known to all from the press and from public meetings. Everyone knows that a certain political figure began in such and such a way, passed through such and such an evolution, behaved in a trying moment in such and such a manner, and possesses such and such qualities; consequently, *all* party members, knowing all the facts, can elect or refuse to elect this person to a particular party office. The general control (in the literal sense of the term) exercised over every act of a party man in the political field brings into existence an automatically operating mechanism which produces what in biology is called the "survival of the fittest". "Natural selection" by full publicity, election, and general control provides the assurance that, in the last analysis, every political figure will be "in his proper place", do the work for which he is best fitted by his powers and abilities, feel the effects of his mistakes on himself, and prove before all the world his ability to recognise mistakes and to avoid them.

Try to fit this picture into the frame of our autocracy! Is it conceivable in Russia for all "who accept the principles of the Party programme and render the Party all possible support" to control every action of the revolutionary working in secret? Is it possible for all to elect one of these revolutionaries to any particular office, when, in the very interests of the work, the revolutionary *must* conceal his identity from nine out of ten of these "all"? Reflect somewhat over the real meaning of the high-sounding phrases to which *Rabocheye Dyelo* gives utterance, and you will realise that "broad democracy" in Party organisation, amidst the gloom of the autocracy and the domination of gendarmerie, is nothing more than a *useless and harmful toy*. It is a useless toy because, in point of fact, no revolutionary organisation has ever practised, or could practise, *broad* democracy, however much it may have desired to do so. It is a harmful toy because any attempt to practice "the broad democratic principle" will simply facilitate the work of the police in carrying out large-scale raids, will perpetuate the prevailing primitiveness, and will divert the thoughts of the practical workers from the serious and pressing task of training themselves to become professional revolutionaries to that of drawing up detailed "paper" rules for election systems. Only abroad, where very often people with no opportunity for conducting really active work gather, could this "playing at democracy" develop here and there, especially in small groups.

To show the unseemliness of *Rabocheye Dyelo*'s favourite trick of advancing the plausible "principle" of democracy in revolutionary affairs, we shall again summon a witness. This witness, Y. Serebryakov, editor of the London magazine, *Nakanune*, has a soft spot for *Rabocheye Dyelo* and is filled with a great hatred for Plekhanov and the "Plekhanovites". In its articles on the split in the Union of Russian Social-Democrats Abroad, *Nakanune* definitely sided with *Rabocheye Dyelo* and poured a stream of petty abuse upon Plekhanov. All the more valuable, therefore, is this witness in the question at issue. In *Nakanune* for July (No. 7) 1899, in an article entitled "Concerning the Manifesto of the Self-Emancipation of the Workers Group", Serebryakov argued that it was "indecent" to talk about such things as "self-deception, leadership, and the so-called Areopagus in a serious revolutionary movement" and, *inter alia*, wrote:

"Myshkin, Rogachov, Zhelyabov, Mikhailov, Perovskaya, Figner, and others never regarded themselves as leaders, and no one ever elected or appointed them as such, although in actuality, they were leaders, because, in the propaganda period, as well as in the period of the struggle against the government, they took the brunt of the work upon themselves, they went into the most dangerous places, and their activities were the most fruitful. They became leaders, not because they wished it, but because the comrades surrounding them had confidence in their wisdom, in their energy, in their loyalty. To be afraid of some kind of Areopagus (if it is not feared, why write about it?) that would arbitrarily govern the movement is far too naïve. Who would pay heed to it?"

We ask the reader, in what way does the "Areopagus" differ from "anti-democratic tendencies"? And is it not evident that *Rabocheye Dyelo*'s "plausible" organisational principle is equally naïve and indecent; naïve, because no one would pay heed to the "Areopagus", or people with "anti-democratic tendencies", if "the comrades surrounding them had" no "confidence in their wisdom, energy, and loyalty"; indecent, because it is a demagogic sally calculated to play on the conceit of some, on the ignorance of others regarding the actual state of our movement, and on the lack of training and the ignorance of the history of the revolutionary movement on the part of still others. The only serious organisational principle for the active workers of our movement should be the strictest secrecy, the strictest selection of members, and the training of professional revolutionaries. Given these qualities, something even more than "democratism" would be guaranteed to us, namely, complete, comradely, mutual confidence among revolutionaries. This is absolutely essential for us, because there can be no question of replacing it by general democratic control in Russia. It would be a great mistake to believe that the impossibility of establishing real "democratic" control renders the members of the revolutionary organisation beyond control altogether. They have not the time to think about toy forms of democratism (democratism within a close and compact body of comrades in which complete, mutual confidence prevails), but they have a lively sense of their *responsibility*, knowing as they do from experience that an organisation of real revolutionaries will stop at nothing to rid itself of an unworthy member. Moreover, there is a fairly well-developed public opinion in Russian (and international) revolutionary circles which has a long history behind it, and which sternly and ruthlessly punishes every departure from the duties of comradeship (and "democratism", real and not toy democratism, certainly forms a component part of the conception of comradeship). Take all this into consideration and you will realise that this talk and these resolutions about "anti-democratic tendencies" have the musty odour of the playing at generals which is indulged in abroad.

It must be observed also that the other source of this talk, viz., naïveté, is likewise fostered by the confusion of ideas concerning the meaning of democracy. In Mr. and Mrs. Webb's book on the English trade unions there is an interesting chapter entitled "Primitive Democracy". In it the authors relate how the English workers, in the first period of existence of their unions, considered it an indispensable sign of democracy for all the members to do all the work of managing the unions; not only were all questions decided by the vote of all the members, but all official duties were fulfilled by all the members in turn. A long period of historical experience was required for workers to realise the absurdity of such a conception of democracy and to make them understand the necessity for representative institutions, on the one hand, and for full-time officials, on the other. Only after a number of cases of financial bankruptcy of trade-union treasuries occurred did the workers realise that the rates of contributions and benefits cannot be decided merely by a democratic vote, but that this requires also the advice of insurance experts. Let us take also Kautsky's book on parliamentarism and legislation by the people. There we find that the conclusions drawn by the Marxist theoretician coincide with the lessons learned from many years of practical experience by the workers who organised "spontaneously". Kautsky strongly protests against Rittinghausen's primitive conception of democracy; he ridicules those who in the name of democracy demand that "popular newspapers shall be edited directly by the people"; he shows the need for *professional* journalists, parliamentarians, etc., for the Social-Democratic leadership of the proletarian class struggle; he attacks the "socialism of anarchists and *littérateurs*", who in their "striving for effect" extol direct legislation by the whole people, completely failing to understand that this idea can be applied only relatively in modern society.

Those who have performed practical work in our movement know how widespread the "primitive" conception of democracy is among the masses of the students and workers. It is not surprising that this conception penetrates also into rules of organisations and into literature. The Economists of the Bernsteinian persuasion included in their rules the following: "§ 10. All affairs affecting the interests of the whole of the union organisation shall be decided by a majority vote of all its members". The Economists of the terrorist persuasion repeat after them: "The decisions of the committee shall become effective only after they have been referred to all the circles" (*Svoboda*, No. 1, p. 67). Observe that this proposal for a widely applied referendum is advanced *in addition* to the demand that *the whole of* the organisation be built on an elective basis! We would not, of course, on this account condemn practical workers who have had too few opportunities for studying the theory and practice of real democratic organisations. But when *Rabocheye Dyelo,* which lays claim to leadership, confines itself, under such conditions, to a resolution on broad democratic principles, can this be described as anything but a mere "striving for effect"?

F. Local and All-Russian Work

The objections raised against the plan of organisation here outlined on the grounds that it is undemocratic and conspiratorial are totally unsound. Nevertheless, there remains a question which is frequently put and which deserves detailed examination. This is the question of the relations between local work and All-Russian work. Fears are expressed that the formation of a centralised organisation may shift the centre of gravity from the former to the latter, damage the movement through weakening our contacts with the working masses and the continuity of local agitation generally. To these fears we reply that our movement in the past few years has suffered precisely from the fact that local workers have been too absorbed in local work; that therefore it is absolutely necessary to shift the centre of gravity somewhat to national work; and that, far from weakening, this would strengthen our ties and the continuity of our local agitation. Let us take the question of central and local newspapers. I would ask the reader not to forget that we cite the publication of newspapers only as *an example* illustrating an immeasurably broader and more varied revolutionary activity in general.

In the first period of the mass movement (1896-98), an attempt was made by local revolutionary workers to publish an All-Russian paper—*Rabochaya Gazeta*. In the next period (1898-1900), the movement made an enormous stride forward, but the attention of the leaders was wholly absorbed by local publications. If we compute the total number of the local papers that were published, we shall find that on the average one issue per month was published.* Does this not clearly illustrate our amateurism? Does this not clearly show that our revolutionary organisation lags behind the spontaneous growth of the movement? If *the same number* of issues had been published, not by scattered local groups, but by a single organisation, we would not only have saved an enormous amount of effort, but we would have secured immeasurably greater stability and continuity in our work. This simple point is frequently lost sight of by those practical workers who work *actively* and almost exclusively on local publications (unfortunately this is true even now in the overwhelming majority of cases), as well as by the publicists who display an astonishing quixotism on this question. The practical workers usually rest content with the argument that "it is difficult"**

---

* See *Report to the Paris Congress*,[58] p. 14. "From that time (1897) to the spring of 1900, thirty issues of various papers were published in various places.... On an average, over one issue per month was published."

** This difficulty is more apparent than real. In fact, *there is not* for local workers to engage in the organisation of an All-Russian newspaper, and that local newspapers are better than no newspapers at all. This argument is, of course, perfectly just, and we, no less than any practical worker, appreciate the enormous importance and usefulness of local newspapers *in general*. But not this is the point. The point is, can we not overcome the fragmentation and primitiveness that are so glaringly expressed in the thirty issues of local newspapers that have been published throughout Russia in the course of two and a half years? Do not restrict yourselves to the indisputable, but too general, statement about the usefulness of local newspapers generally; have the courage frankly to admit their negative aspects revealed by the experience of two and a half years. This experience has shown that under the conditions in which we work, these local newspapers prove, in the majority of cases, to be unstable in their principles, devoid of political significance, extremely costly in regard to expenditure of revolutionary forces, and totally unsatisfactory from a technical point of view (I have in mind, of course, not the technique of printing, but the frequency and regularity of publication). These defects are not accidental; they are the inevitable outcome of the fragmentation which, on the one hand, explains the predominance of local newspapers in the period under review, and, on the other, is *fostered by* this predominance. It is positively *beyond the strength* of a separate local organisation to raise its newspaper to the level of a political organ maintaining stability of principles; it is *beyond its strength* to collect and utilise sufficient material to shed light on the whole of our political life. The argument usually advanced to support the need for numerous local newspapers in free countries that the cost of printing by local workers is low and that the people can be kept more fully and quickly informed—this *argument*, as experience has shown, speaks *against* local newspapers in Russia. They turn out to be excessively costly in regard to the expenditure of revolutionary forces, and appear *very* rarely, for the simple reason that the publication of an *illegal* newspaper, how-

---

a single local study circle that lacks the opportunity of taking up some function or other in connection with All-Russian work. "Don't say, I can't; say, I won't."

ever small its size, requires an extensive secret apparatus, such as is possible with large-scale factory production; for this apparatus cannot be created in a small, handicraft workshop. Very frequently, the primitiveness of the secret apparatus (every practical worker can cite numerous cases) enables the police to take advantage of the publication and distribution of one or two issues to make *mass* arrests, which result in such a clean sweep that it becomes necessary to start all over again. A well-organised secret apparatus requires professionally well-trained revolutionaries and a division of labour applied with the greatest consistency, but both these requirements are beyond the strength of a separate local organisation, however strong it may be at any given moment. Not only the general interests of our movement as a whole (training of the workers in consistent socialist and political principles) but also specifically local interests are *better served by non-local newspapers*. This may seem paradoxical at first sight, but it has been proved to the hilt by the two and a half years of experience referred to. Everyone will agree that had all the local forces that were engaged in the publication of the thirty issues of newspapers worked on a single newspaper, sixty, if not a hundred, issues could easily have been published, with a fuller expression, in consequence, of all the specifically local features of the movement. True, it is no easy matter to attain such a degree of organisation, but we must realise the need for it. Every local study circle must think about it and *work actively* to achieve it, without waiting for an impetus from outside, without being tempted by the popularity and closer proximity of a local newspaper which, as our revolutionary experience has shown, proves to a large extent to be illusory.

And it is a bad service indeed those publicists render to the practical work who, thinking themselves particularly close to the practical workers, fail to see this illusoriness, and make shift with the astoundingly hollow and cheap argument that we must have local newspapers, we must have district newspapers, and we must have All-Russian newspapers. Generally speaking, of course, all these are necessary, but once the solution of a concrete organisational problem is undertaken, surely time and circumstances must be taken into consideration. Is it not quixotic for

Svoboda (No. 1, p. 68) to write in a special article "dealing with *the question of a newspaper*": "It seems to us that every locality, with any appreciable number of workers, should have its own workers' newspaper; not a newspaper imported from somewhere, but its very own." If the publicist who wrote these words refuses to think of their meaning, then at least the reader may do it for him. How many scores, if not hundreds, of "localities with any appreciable number of workers" there are in Russia, and what a perpetuation of our amateurish methods this would mean if indeed every local organisation set about publishing its own newspaper! How this diffusion would facilitate the gendarmerie's task of netting—and without "any appreciable" effort—the local revolutionary workers at the very outset of their activity and of preventing them from developing into real revolutionaries. A reader of an All-Russian newspaper, continues the author, would find little interest in the descriptions of the malpractices of the factory owners and the "details of factory life in various towns not his own". But "an inhabitant of Orel would not find Orel affairs dull reading. In every issue he would learn who had been 'picked for a lambasting' and who had been 'flayed', and he would be in high spirits" (p. 69). Certainly, the Orel reader is in high spirits, but our publicist's flights of imagination are also high—too high. He should have asked himself whether such concern with trivialities is tactically in order. We are second to none in appreciating the importance and necessity of factory exposures, but it must be borne in mind that we have reached a stage when St. Petersburg folk find it dull reading the St. Petersburg correspondence of the St. Petersburg *Rabochaya Mysl*. Leaflets are the medium through which local factory exposures have always been *and must continue* to be made, but we must raise the level of the *newspaper*, not lower it to the level of a factory leaflet. What we ask of a newspaper is not so much "petty" exposures, as exposures of the major, typical evils of factory life, exposures based on especially striking facts and capable, therefore, of arousing the interest of *all* workers and all leaders of the movement, of really enriching their knowledge, broadening their outlook, and serving as a starting-point for awakening new districts and workers from ever-newer trade areas.

"Moreover, in a local newspaper, all the malpractices of the factory administration and other authorities may be denounced then and there. In the case of a general, distant newspaper, however, by the time the news reaches it the facts will have been forgotten in the source localities. The reader, on getting the paper, will exclaim: 'When was that—who remembers it?' " (ibid.). Precisely—who remembers it! From the same source we learn that the 30 issues of newspapers which appeared in the course of two and a half years were published in six cities. This averages *one issue per city per half-year*! And even if our frivolous publicist *trebled* his estimate of the productivity of local work (which would be wrong in the case of an average town, since it is impossible to increase productivity to any considerable extent by our rule-of-thumb methods), we would still get only one issue every two months, i.e., nothing at all like "denouncing then and there". It would suffice, however, for ten local organisations to combine and send their delegates to take an active part in organising a general newspaper, to enable us every fortnight to "denounce", *over the whole of Russia,* not petty, but really outstanding and typical evils. No one who knows the state of affairs in our organisations can have the slightest doubt on that score. As for catching the enemy red-handed—if we mean it seriously and not merely as a pretty phrase— that is quite beyond the ability of an illegal paper generally. It can be done only by a leaflet, because the time limit for exposures of that nature can be a day or two at the most (e.g., the usual brief strikes, violent factory clashes, demonstrations, etc.).

"The workers live not only at the factory, but also in the city," continues our author, rising from the particular to the general, with a strict consistency that would have done honour to Boris Krichevsky himself; and he refers to matters like municipal councils, municipal hospitals, municipal schools, and demands that workers' newspapers should not ignore municipal affairs in general.

This demand—excellent in itself—serves as a particularly vivid illustration of the empty abstraction to which discussions of local newspapers are all too frequently limited. In the first place, if indeed newspapers appeared "in every locality with any appreciable number of workers" with such detailed information on municipal affairs as *Svoboda* desires, this would, under our Russian conditions, inevitably degenerate into actual concern with trivialities, lead to a weakening of the consciousness of the importance of an All-Russian revolutionary assault upon the tsarist autocracy, and strengthen the extremely virile shoots—not uprooted but rather hidden or temporarily suppressed—of the tendency that has become noted as a result of the famous remark about revolutionaries who talk a great deal about non-existent parliaments and too little about existent municipal councils. We say "inevitably", in order to emphasise that *Svoboda* obviously does not desire this, but the contrary, to come about. But good intentions are not enough. For municipal affairs to be dealt with in their proper perspective, in relation to our entire work, this perspective must *first* be clearly conceived, firmly established, not only by argument, but by numerous examples, so that it may acquire the stability of a *tradition*. This is still far from being the case with us. Yet this must be done *first*, before we can allow ourselves to think and talk about an extensive local press.

Secondly, to write really well and interestingly about municipal affairs, one must have first-hand knowledge, not book knowledge, of the issues. But there are hardly any Social-Democrats *anywhere in Russia* who possess such knowledge. To be able to write in newspapers (not in popular pamphlets) about municipal and state affairs, one must have fresh and varied material gathered and written up by able people. And in order to be able to gather and write up such material, we must have something more than the "primitive democracy" of a primitive circle, in which everybody does everything and all entertain themselves by playing at referendums. It is necessary to have a staff of expert writers and correspondents, an army of Social-Democratic reporters who establish contacts far and wide, who are able to fathom all sorts of "state secrets" (the knowledge of which makes the Russian government official so puffed up, but the blabbing of which is such an easy matter to him), who are able to penetrate "behind the scenes"—an army of people who must, as their "official duty" be ubiquitous and omniscient. And we, the Party that fights against *all* economic, political, social, and

national oppression, can and must find, gather, train, mo-
bilise, and set into motion such an army of omniscient
people—all of which requires still to be done. Not only has
not a single step in this direction been taken in the overwhelming majority of localities, but even the *recognition*
of its necessity is very often lacking. One will search in
vain in our Social-Democratic press for lively and interesting articles, correspondence, and exposures dealing with
our big and little affairs—diplomatic, military, ecclesiasti-
cal, municipal, financial, etc., etc. There is *almost nothing*,
or very little, about these matters.* That is why "it always
annoys me frightfully when a man comes to me, utters
beautiful and charming words" about the need for newspapers in "every locality with any appreciable number of
workers" that will expose factory, municipal, and government evils.

The predominance of the local papers over a central
press may be a sign of either poverty or luxury. Of poverty,
when the movement has not yet developed the forces for
large-scale production, continues to flounder in amateurism,
and is all but swamped with "the petty details of factory
life". Of luxury, when the movement *has fully mastered*
the task of comprehensive exposure and comprehensive
agitation, and it becomes necessary to publish numerous
local newspapers in addition to the central organ. Let each
decide for himself what the predominance of local newspapers implies in present-day Russia. I shall limit myself
to a precise formulation of my own conclusion, to leave
no grounds for misunderstanding. Hitherto, the majority
of our local organisations have thought almost exclusively

---

* That is why even examples of exceptionally good local newspapers fully confirm our point of view. For example, *Yuzhny Rabochy* is an excellent newspaper, entirely free of instability of principle. But it has been unable to provide what it desired for the local
movement, owing to the infrequency of its publication and to extensive police raids. Principled presentation of the fundamental questions of the movement and wide political agitation, which our Party
most urgently requires at the present time, has proved too big a
job for the local newspaper. The material of particular value it has
published, like the articles on the mine owners' convention and on
unemployment, was not strictly local material, *it was required for
the whole of Russia*, not for the South alone. No such articles have
appeared in any of our Social-Democratic newspapers.

in terms of local newspapers, and have devoted almost all their activities to this work. This is abnormal; the very opposite should have been the case. The majority of the local organisations should think principally of the publication of an All-Russian newspaper and devote their activities chiefly to it. Until this is done, we shall *not* be able to establish a *single* newspaper capable, to any degree, of serving the movement with *comprehensive* press agitation. When this is done, however, normal relations between the necessary central newspaper and the necessary local newspapers will be established automatically.

* * *

It would seem at first glance that the conclusion on the necessity for shifting the centre of gravity from local to All-Russian work does not apply to the sphere of the specifically economic struggle. In this struggle, the immediate enemies of the workers are the individual employers or groups of employers, who are not bound by any organisation having even the remotest resemblance to the purely military, strictly centralised organisation of the Russian Government—our immediate enemy in the political struggle—which is led in all its minutest details by a single will.

But that is not the case. As we have repeatedly pointed out, the economic struggle is a trade struggle, and for that reason it requires that the workers be organised according to trades, not only according to place of employment. Organisation by trades becomes all the more urgently necessary, the more rapidly our employers organise in all sorts of companies and syndicates. Our fragmentation and our amateurism are an outright hindrance to this work of organisation which requires the existence of a single, All-Russian body of revolutionaries capable of giving leadership to the All-Russian trade unions. We have described above the type of organisation that is needed for this purpose; we shall now add but a few words on the question of our press in this connection.

Hardly anyone will doubt the necessity for every Social-Democratic newspaper to have a *special department* devoted to the trade-union (economic) struggle. But the growth of the trade-union movement compels us to think about the creation of a trade-union press. It seems to us, however, that with rare exceptions, there can be no question of trade-union newspapers in Russia at the present time; they would be a luxury, and many a time we lack even our daily bread. The form of trade-union press that would suit the conditions of our illegal work and is already required at the present time is *trade-union pamphlets*. In these pamphlets, *legal** and illegal material should be gathered and grouped systematically, on the working conditions in a given trade, on the differences in this respect in the various parts of Russia; on the main demands advanced by the workers in the given trade; on the inadequacies of legislation affecting that trade; on outstanding instances of economic struggle by the workers in the trade; on the beginnings, the present state, and the requirements of their trade-union organisation, etc. Such pamphlets would, in the first place, relieve our Social-Democratic press of a mass of trade details that are of interest only to workers in the given trade. Secondly, they would record the results

---

* Legal material is particularly important in this connection, and we are particularly behind in our ability to gather and utilise it systematically. It would not be an exaggeration to say that one could somehow compile a trade-union pamphlet on the basis solely of legal material, but it could not be done on the basis of illegal material alone. In gathering illegal material from workers on questions like those dealt with in the publications of *Rabochaya Mysl*, we waste a great deal of the efforts of revolutionaries (whose place in this work could very easily be taken by legal workers), and yet we never obtain good material. The reason is that a worker who very often knows only a single department of a large factory and almost always the economic results, but not the general conditions and standards of his work, cannot acquire the knowledge which is possessed by the office staff of a factory, by inspectors, doctors, etc., and which is scattered in petty newspaper reports and in special industrial, medical, Zemstvo, and other publications.

I vividly recall my "first experiment", which I would never like to repeat. I spent many weeks "examining" a worker, who would often visit me, regarding every aspect of the conditions prevailing in the enormous factory at which he was employed. True, after great effort, I managed to obtain material for a description (of the one single factory!), but at the end of the interview the worker would wipe the sweat from his brow, and say to me smilingly: "I find it easier to work overtime than to answer your questions."

The more energeticaly we carry on our revolutionary struggle, the more the government will be compelled to legalise part of the "trade-union" work, thereby relieving us of part of our burden.

of our experience in the trade-union struggle, they would preserve the gathered material, which now literally gets lost in a mass of leaflets and fragmentary correspondence; and they would summarise this material. Thirdly, they could serve as guides for agitators, because working conditions change relatively slowly and the main demands of the workers in a given trade are extremely stable (cf. for example, the demands advanced by the weavers in the Moscow district in 1885 and in the St. Petersburg district in 1896). A compilation of such demands and needs might serve for years as an excellent handbook for agitators on economic questions in backward localities or among the backward strata of the workers. Examples of successful strikes in a given region, information on higher living standards, on improved working conditions, in one locality, would encourage the workers in other localities to take up the fight again and again. Fourthly, having made a start in generalising the trade-union struggle and in this way strengthening the link between the Russian trade-union movement and socialism, the Social-Democrats would at the same time see to it that our trade-union work occupied neither too small nor too large a place in our Social-Democratic work as a whole. A local organisation that is cut off from organisations in other towns finds it very difficult, sometimes almost impossible, to maintain a correct sense of proportion (the example of *Rabochaya Mysl* shows what a monstrous exaggeration can be made in the direction of trade-unionism). But an All-Russian organisation of revolutionaries that stands undeviatingly on the basis of Marxism, that leads the entire political struggle and possesses a staff of professional agitators, will never find it difficult to determine the proper proportion.

V

The "Plan" for an All-Russian Political Newspaper

"The most serious blunder *Iskra* committed in this connection," writes B. Krichevsky (*Rabocheye Dyelo*, No. 10, p. 30), charging us with a tendency to "convert theory into a lifeless doctrine by isolating it from practice", "was its 'plan' for a general party organisation" (viz., the article entitled "Where To Begin"*). Martynov echoes this idea in declaring that "*Iskra's* tendency to belittle the significance of the forward march of the drab everyday struggle in comparison with the propaganda of brilliant and completed ideas ... was crowned with the plan for the organisation of a party which it sets forth in the article entitled 'Where To Begin' in issue No. 4" (ibid., p. 61). Finally, L. Nadezhdin has of late joined in the chorus of indignation against this "plan" (the quotation marks were meant to express sarcasm). In his pamphlet, which we have just received, entitled *The Eve of the Revolution* (published by the "Revolutionary-Socialist Group" *Svoboda,* whose acquaintance we have made), he declares (p. 126): "To speak now of an organisation held together by an All-Russian newspaper means propagating armchair ideas and armchair work" and represents a manifestation of "bookishness", etc.

That our terrorist turns out to be in argeement with the champions of the "forward march of the drab everyday struggle" is not surprising, since we have traced the roots of this intimacy between them in the chapters on politics and organisation. But we must draw attention here to the fact that Nadezhdin is the only one who has conscientiously tried to grasp the train of thought in an article he disliked and has made an attempt to reply to the point, whereas *Rabocheye Dyelo* has said nothing that is material to the subject, but has tried merely to confuse the question by a series of unseemly, demagogic sallies. Unpleasant though the task may be, we must first spend some time in cleansing this Augean stable.

A. Who Was Offended by the Article "Where to Begin"

Let us present a small selection of the expletives and exclamations that *Rabocheye Dyelo* hurled at us. "It is not a newspaper that can create a party organisation, but vice versa...." "A newspaper, standing *above* the party, *outside of its control,* and independent of it, thanks to its having

---

* See *Collected Works,* Vol. 5, pp. 13-24.—*Ed.*

its own staff of agents...." "By what miracle has *Iskra* forgotten about the actually existing Social-Democratic organisations of the party to which it belongs?..." "Those who possess firm principles and a corresponding plan are the supreme regulators of the real struggle of the party and dictate to it their plan...." "The plan drives our active and virile organisations into the kingdom of shadows and desires to call into being a fantastic network of agents...." "Were *Iskra's* plan carried into effect, every trace of the Russian Social-Democratic Labour Party, which is taking shape, would be obliterated...." "A propagandist organ becomes an uncontrolled autocratic law-maker for the entire practical revolutionary struggle...." "How should our Party react to the suggestion that it be *completely* subordinated to an autonomous editorial board?", etc., etc.

As the reader can see from the contents and the tone of these above quotations, *Rabocheye Dyelo has taken offence.* Offence, not for its own sake, but for the sake of the organisations and committees of our Party which it alleges *Iskra* desires to drive into the kingdom of shadows and whose very traces it would obliterate. How terrible! But a curious thing should be noted. The article "Where To Begin" appeared in May 1901. The articles in *Rabocheye Dyelo* appeared in September 1901. Now we are in mid-January 1902. During these five months (prior to and after September), *not a single* committee and *not a single* organisation of the Party protested formally against this monster that seeks to drive them into the kingdom of shadows; and yet scores and hundreds of communications from all parts of Russia have appeared during this period in *Iskra*, as well as in numerous local and non-local publications. How could it happen that those who would be driven into the realm of shadows are not aware of it and have not taken offence, though a third party has?

The explanation is that the committees and other organisations are engaged in real work and are not playing at "democracy". The committees read the article "Where To Begin", saw that it represented an attempt "to elaborate a definite plan for an organisation, *so that its formation may be undertaken from all aspects*"; and since they knew and saw very well that *not one* of these "sides" would dream of "setting about to build it" until it was convinced of its necessity, and of the correctness of the architectural plan, it has naturally never occurred to them to take offence at the boldness of the people who said in *Iskra*: "In view of the pressing importance of the question, we, on our part, take the liberty of submitting to the comrades a skeleton plan to be developed in greater detail in a pamphlet now in preparation for the print." With a conscientious approach to the work, was it possible to view things otherwise than that if the comrades *accepted* the plan submitted to them, they would carry it out, not because they are "subordinate", but because they would be convinced of its necessity for our common cause, and that if they *did not accept it*, then the "skeleton" (a pretentious word, is it not?) would remain merely a skeleton? Is it not demagogy to fight against the skeleton of a plan, not only by "picking it to pieces" and advising comrades to reject it, but by *inciting* people inexperienced in revolutionary matters against its authors *merely on the grounds* that they *dare* to "legislate" and come out as the "supreme regulators", i.e., because they dare *to propose* an outline of a plan? Can our Party develop and make progress if an attempt *to raise* local functionaries to broader views, tasks, plans, etc., is objected to, not only with the claim that these views are erroneous, but on the grounds that the very "desire" *to "raise"* us gives "offence"? Nadezhdin, too, "picked" our plan "to pieces", but he did not sink to such demagogy as cannot be explained solely by naïvete or by primitiveness of political views. From the outset, he emphatically rejected the charge that we intended to establish an "inspectorship over the Party". That is why Nadezhdin's criticism of the plan can and should be answered on its merits, while *Rabocheye Dyelo* deserves only to be treated with contempt.

But contempt for a writer who sinks so low as to shout about "autocracy" and "subordination" does not relieve us of the duty of disentangling the confusion that such people create in the minds of their readers. Here we can clearly demonstrate to the world the nature of catchwords like "broad democracy". We are accused of forgetting the committees, of desiring or attempting to drive them into the kingdom of shadows, etc. How can we reply to these charges when, out of considerations of secrecy, we *can give* the reader *almost no facts* regarding our real relationships with the committees? Persons hurling vehement accusations calculated to provoke the crowd prove to be ahead of us because of their brazenness and their disregard of the duty of a revolutionary to conceal carefully from the eyes of the world the relationships and contacts which he maintains, which he is establishing or trying to establish. Naturally, we refuse once and for all to compete with such people in the field of "democratism". As to the reader who is not initiated in all Party affairs, the only way in which we can discharge our duty to him is to acquaint him, not with what is and what is *im Werden* but with *a particle* of what has taken place and what may be told as a thing of the past.

The Bund hints that we are "impostors"*; the Union Abroad accuses us of attempting to obliterate all traces of the Party. Gentlemen, you will get complete satisfaction when we relate to the public *four facts* concerning the past.

First fact.** The members of one of the Leagues of Struggle, who took a direct part in founding our Party and in sending a delegate to the Inaugural Party Congress, reached agreement with a member of the *Iskra* group regarding the publication of a series of books for workers that were to serve the entire movement. The attempt to publish the series failed, and the pamphlets written for it, *The Tasks of the Russian Social-Democrats* and *The New Factory Law*,*** by a circuitous course and through the medium of third parties, found their way abroad, where they were published.[60]

Second fact. Members of the Central Committee of the Bund approached a member of the *Iskra* group with the proposal to organise what the Bund then described as a "literary laboratory". In making the proposal, they stated that unless this was done, the movement would greatly retrogress. The result of these negotiations was the appear-

---

* *Iskra*, No. 8. The reply of the Central Committee of the General Jewish Union of Russia and Poland to our article on the national question.
** We deliberately refrain from relating these facts in the sequence of their occurrence.[59]
*** See *Collected Works*, Vol. 2, pp. 323-51 and 267-315.—*Ed.*

ance of the pamphlet *The Working-Class Cause in Russia.*[*]

Third fact. The Central Committee of the Bund, via a provincial town, approached a member of the *Iskra* group with the proposal that he undertake the editing of the revived *Rabochaya Gazeta* and, of course, obtained his consent. The offer was later modified: the comrade in question was invited to act as a contributor, in view of a new plan for the composition of the Editorial Board. Also this proposal, of course, obtained his consent.[62] Articles were sent (which we managed to preserve): "Our Programme", which was a direct protest against Bernsteinism, against the change in the line of the legal literature and of *Rabochaya Mysl*; "Our Immediate Task" ("to publish a Party organ that shall appear regularly and have close contacts with all the local groups"; the drawbacks of the prevailing "amateurism"); "An Urgent Question" (an examination of the objection that it is necessary *first* to develop the activities of local groups before undertaking the publication of a common organ; an insistence on the paramount importance of a "revolutionary organisation" and on the necessity of "developing organisation, discipline, and the technique of secrecy to the highest degree of perfection").[**] The proposal to resume publication of *Rabochaya Gazeta* was not carried out, and the articles were not published.

Fourth fact. A member of the committee that was organising the second regular congress of our Party communicated to a member of the *Iskra* group the programme of the congress and proposed that group as editorial board of the revived *Rabochaya Gazeta*. This preliminary step, as it were, was later sanctioned by the committee to which this member belonged, and by the Central Committee of the Bund.[63] The *Iskra* group was notified of the place and time of the congress and (uncertain of being able, for certain reasons, to send a delegate) drew up a written report for

---

[*] The author requests me to state that, like his previous pamphlets, this one was sent to the Union Abroad on the assumption that its publications were edited by the Emancipation of Labour group (owing to certain circumstances, he could not then—February 1899—know of the change in editorship). The pamphlet will be republished by the League[61] at an early date.

[**] See *Collected Works*, Vol. 4, pp. 210-14, 215-20, 221-26.—*Ed.*

the congress. In the report, the idea was suggested that the mere election of a Central Committee would not only fail to solve the question of unification at a time of such complete disorder as the present, but would even compromise the grand idea of establishing a party, in the event of an early, swift, and thorough police round-up, which was more than likely in view of the prevailing lack of secrecy; that therefore, a beginning should be made by inviting all committees and all other organisations to support the revived common organ, which would establish *real* contacts between all the committees and *really* train a group of leaders for the entire movement; and that the committees and the Party would very easily be able to transform such a group into a Central Committee as soon as the group had grown and become strong. In consequence of a number of police raids and arrests, however, the congress could not take place. For security reasons the report was destroyed, having been read only by a few comrades, including the representatives of one committee.

Let the reader now judge for himself the character of the methods employed by the Bund in hinting that we were impostors, or by *Rabocheye Dyelo,* which accuses us of trying to relegate the committees to the kingdom of shadows and to "substitute" for the organisation of a party an organisation disseminating the ideas advocated by a single newspaper. It was to the committees, *on the repeated invitation*, that we reported on the necessity for adopting a definite plan of concerted activities. It was precisely for the Party organisation that we elaborated this plan, in articles sent to *Rabochaya Gazeta*, and in the report to the Party congress, again on the invitation of those who held such an influential position in the Party that they took the initiative in its (actual) restoration. Only after the *twice* repeated attempts of the Party organisation, *in conjunction with ourselves, officially* to revive the central organ of the Party had failed, did we consider it our bounden duty to publish an *unofficial* organ, in order that with the *third* attempt the comrades might have before them the results of *experience* and not merely conjectural proposals. Now certain results of this experience are present for all to see, and all comrades may now judge whether we properly understood our duties and what should be thought of people that strive to mislead those unacquainted with the immediate past, simply because they are piqued at our having pointed out to some their inconsistency on the "national" question, and to others the inadmissibility of their vacillation in matters of principle.

B. Can a Newspaper Be a Collective Organiser?

The quintessence of the article "Where To Begin" consists in the fact that it discusses *precisely* this question and gives an affirmative reply to it. As far as we know, the only attempt to examine this question on its merits and to prove that it must be answered in the negative was made by L. Nadezhdin, whose argument we reproduce in full:

"... It pleased us greatly to see *Iskra* (No. 4) present the question of the need for an All-Russian newspaper; but we cannot agree that this presentation bears relevance to the title 'Where To Begin'. Undoubtedly this is an extremely important matter, but neither a newspaper, nor a series of popular leaflets, nor a mountain of manifestos, can serve as the basis for a militant organisation in revolutionary times. We must set to work to build strong political organisations in the localities. We lack such organisations; we have been carrying on our work mainly among enlightened workers, while the masses have been engaged almost exclusively in the economic struggle. *If strong political organisations are not trained locally, what significance will even an excellently organised All-Russian newspaper have?* It will be a burning bush, burning without being consumed, but firing no one! *Iskra* thinks that round it and in the activities in its behalf people will gather and organise. *But they will find it far easier to gather and organise round activities that are more concrete.* This something more concrete must and should be the extensive organisation of local newspapers, the immediate preparation of the workers' forces for demonstrations, the constant activity of local organisations among the unemployed (indefatigable distribution of pamphlets and leaflets, convening of meetings, appeals to actions of protest against the government, etc.). We must begin live political work in the localities, and when the time comes to unite on this real basis, it will not be an artificial, paper unity; not by means of newspapers can such a unification of local work into an All-Russian cause be achieved!" (*The Eve of the Revolution*, p. 54.)

We have emphasised the passages in this eloquent tirade that most clearly show the author's incorrect judgement of our plan, as well as the incorrectness of his point of view in general, which is here contraposed to that of *Iskra*.

Unless we train strong political organisations in the localities, even an excellently organised All-Russian newspaper will be of no avail. This is incontrovertible. But the whole point is that *there is no other way of training* strong political organisations except through the medium of an All-Russian newspaper. The author missed the most important statement *Iskra* made *before it proceeded* to set forth its "plan": that it was necessary "to call for the formation of a revolutionary organisation, capable of uniting all forces and guiding the movement in actual practice and *not in name alone, that is, an organisation ready at any time to support every protest and every outbreak* and use it to build up and consolidate the fighting forces suitable for the decisive struggle". But now after the February and March events, everyone will agree with this in principle, continues *Iskra*. Yet what we need is not a solution of the question in principle, but its *practical solution*; we must immediately advance a definite constructive plan through which all may immediately set to work to build *from every side*. Now we are again being dragged away from the practical solution towards something which in principle is correct, indisputable, and great, but which is entirely inadequate and incomprehensible to the broad masses of workers, namely, "to rear strong political organisations"! This is not the point at issue, most worthy author. The point is *how* to go about the rearing and how to accomplish it.

It is not true to say that "we have been carrying on our work mainly among enlightened workers, while the masses have been engaged almost exclusively in the economic struggle". Presented in such a form, the thesis reduces itself to *Svoboda*'s usual but fundamentally false contraposition of the enlightened workers to the "masses". In recent years, even the enlightened workers have been "engaged almost exclusively in the economic struggle". That is the first point. On the other hand, the masses will never learn to conduct the political struggle until we help *to train* leaders for this struggle, both from among the enlightened workers and from among the intellectuals. Such leaders can acquire training *solely* by systematically evaluating *all* the everyday aspects of our political life, *all attempts* at protest and struggle on the part of the various classes and on various grounds. Therefore, to talk of "rearing political organisations" and at the same time *to contrast* the "paper work" of a political newspaper to "live political work in the localities" is plainly ridiculous. *Iskra* has adapted its "plan" for a newspaper to the "plan" for creating a "militant preparedness" to support the unemployed movement, peasant revolts, discontent among the Zemstvo people, "popular indignation against some tsarist bashi-bazouk on the rampage", etc. Any one who is at all acquainted with the movement knows fully well that the vast majority of local organisations have *never even dreamed* of these things; that many of the prospects of "live political work" here indicated *have neve*r been realised by a single organisation; that the attempt, for example, to call attention to the growth of discontent and protest among the Zemstvo intelligentsia rouses feelings of consternation and perplexity in Nadezhdin ("Good Lord, is this newspaper intended for Zemstvo people?"—*The Eve*, p. 129), among the Economists (Letter to *Iskra*, No. 12), and among many practical workers. Under these circumstances, it is possible to "begin" *only* by inducing people *to think* about all these things, to summarise and generalise all the divers signs of ferment and active struggle. In our time, when Social-Democratic tasks are being degraded, *the only way* "live political work" can be *begun* is with live political agitation, which is impossible unless we have an All-Russian newspaper, frequently issued and regularly distributed.

Those who regard the *Iskra* "plan" as a manifestation of "bookishness" have totally failed to understand its substance and take for the goal that which is suggested as the most suitable means for the present time. These people have not taken the trouble to study the two comparisons that were drawn to present a clear illustration of the plan. *Iskra* wrote: The publication of an All-Russian political newspaper must be *the main line* by which we may unswervingly develop, deepen, and expand the organisation (viz., the revolutionary organisation that is ever ready to support every protest and every outbreak). Pray tell me, when bricklayers lay bricks in various parts of an enormous, unprecedentedly large structure, is it "paper" work to use a line to help them find the correct place for the bricklaying; to indicate to them the ultimate goal of the common work; to enable them to use, not only every brick, but even every piece of brick which, cemented to the bricks laid before and after it, forms a finished, continuous line? And are we not now passing through precisely such a period in our Party life when we have bricks and bricklayers, but lack the guide line for all to see and follow? Let them shout that in stretching out the line, we want to command. Had we desired to command, gentlemen, we would have written on the title page, not "*Iskra*, No. 1", but "*Rabo-chaya Gazeta*, No. 3", as we were invited to do by certain comrades, and *as we would have had a perfect right to do* after the events described above. But we did not do that. We wished to have our hands free to wage an irreconcilable struggle against all pseudo-Social-Democrats; we wanted our line, if properly laid, to be respected because it was correct, and not because it had been laid by an official organ.

"The question of uniting local activity in central bodies runs in a vicious circle," Nadezhdin lectures us; "unification requires homogeneity of the elements, and the homogeneity can be created only by something that unites; but the unifying element may be the product of strong local organisations which at the present time are by no means distinguished for their homogeneity." This truth is as revered and as irrefutable as that we must train strong political organisations. And it is equally barren. *Every* question "runs in a vicious circle" because political life as a whole is an endless chain consisting of an infinite number of links. The whole art of politics lies in finding and taking as firm a grip as we can of the link that is least likely to be struck from our hands, the one that is most important at the given moment, the one that most of all guarantees its possessor the possession of the whole chain.* If we had a crew of experienced bricklayers who had learned to work so well together that they could lay their bricks exactly as required without a guide line (which, speaking abstractly,

_____

* Comrade Krichevsky and Comrade Martynov! I call your attention to this outrageous manifestation of "autocracy", "uncontrolled authority", "supreme regulating", etc. Just think of it: a desire *to possess* the whole chain!! Send in a complaint at once. Here you have a ready-made topic for two leading articles for No. 12 of *Rabocheye Dyelo*!

is by no means impossible), then perhaps we might take hold of some other link. But it is unfortunate that as yet we have no experienced bricklayers trained for teamwork, that bricks are often laid where they are not needed at all, that they are not laid according to the general line, but are so scattered that the enemy can shatter the structure as if it were made of sand and not of bricks.

Another comparison: "A newspaper is not only a collective propagandist and a collective agitator, it is also a collective organiser. In this respect *it may be compared to the scaffolding* erected round a building under construction; it marks the contours of the structure and facilitates communication between the builders, permitting them to distribute the work and to view the common results achieved by their organised labour."* Does this sound anything like the attempt of an armchair author to exaggerate his role? The scaffolding is not required at all for the dwelling; it is made of cheaper material, is put up only temporarily, and is scrapped for firewood as soon as the shell of the structure is completed. As for the building of revolutionary organisations, experience shows that sometimes they may be built without scaffolding, as the seventies showed. But at the present time we cannot even imagine the possibility of erecting the building we require without scaffolding.

Nadezhdin desagrees with this, saying: "*Iskra* thinks that around it and in the activities in its behalf people will gather and organise. *But they will find it far easier* to gather and organise around *activities that are more concrete!*" Indeed, "far easier around activities that are more concrete". A Russian proverb holds: "Don't spit into a well, you may want to drink from it." But there are people who do not object to drinking from a well that has been spat into. What despicable things our magnificent, legal "Critics of Marxism" and illegal admirers of *Rabochaya Mysl* have said in the name of this something more concrete! How restricted our movement is by our own narrowness, lack of initiative, and hesitation, which are justified with the traditional argument about finding it "far easier to gather

---

* Martynov, in quoting the first sentence of this passage in *Rabocheye Dyelo* (No. 10, p. 62), omitted the second, as if desiring to emphasise either his unwillingness to discuss the essentials of the question or his inability to understand them.

around something more concrete"! And Nadezhdin—who regards himself as possessing a particularly keen sense of the "realities of life", who so severely condemns "armchair" authors and (with pretensions to wit) accuses *Iskra* of a weakness for seeing Economism everywhere, and who sees himself standing far above the division between the orthodox and the Critics—fails to see that with his arguments he contributes to the narrowness that arouses his indignation and that he is drinking from the most spat-in well! The sincerest indignation against narrowness, the most passionate desire to raise its worshippers from their knees, will not suffice if the indignant one is swept along without sail or rudder and, as "spontaneously" as the revolutionaries of the seventies, clutches at such things as "excitative terror", "agrarian terror", "sounding the tocsin", etc. Let us take a glance at these "more concrete" activities around which he thinks it will be "far easier" to gather and organise: (1) local newspapers; (2) preparations for demonstrations; (3) work among the unemployed. It is immediately apparent that all these things have been seized upon at random as a pretext for saying something; for, however we may regard them, it would be absurd to see in them anything especially suitable for "gathering and organising". The selfsame Nadezhdin says a few pages further: "It is time we simply stated the fact that activity of a very pitiable kind is being carried on in the localities, the committees are not doing a tenth of what they could do ... the co-ordinating centres we have at present are the purest fiction, representing a sort of revolutionary bureaucracy, whose members mutually grant generalships to one another; and so it will continue until strong local organisations grow up." These remarks, though exaggerating the position somewhat, no doubt contain many a bitter truth; but can it be said that Nadezhdin does not perceive the connection between the pitiable activity in the localities and the narrow mental outlook of the functionaries, the narrow scope of their activities, inevitable in the circumstances of the lack of training of Party workers confined to local organisations? Has he, like the author of the article on organisation, published in *Svoboda*, forgotten how the transition to a broad local press (from 1898) was accompanied by a strong intensification of Economism and "primitiveness"? Even if a "broad local press" could be established at all satisfactorily (and we have shown this to be impossible, save in very exceptional cases)—even then the local organs could not "gather and organise" *all* the revolutionary forces for a *general* attack upon the autocracy and for leadership of the *united* struggle. Let us not forget that we are here discussing *only* the "rallying", organising significance of the newspaper, and we could put to Nadezhdin, who defends fragmentation, the question he himself has ironically put: "Have we been left a legacy of 200,000 revolutionary organisers?" Furthermore, "preparations for demonstrations" cannot be *contraposed* to *Iskra*'s plan, for the very reason that this plan includes the organisation of the broadest possible demonstrations *as one of its aims*; the point under discussion is the selection of the practical *means*. On this point also Nadezhdin is confused, for he has lost sight of the fact that only forces that are "gathered and organised" can "prepare for" demonstrations (which hitherto, in the overwhelming majority of cases, have taken place spontaneously) and that we *lack* precisely *the ability* to rally and organise. "Work among the unemployed." Again the same confusion; for this too represents one of the field operations of the mobilised forces and not a plan for mobilising the forces. The extent to which Nadezhdin here too underestimates the harm caused by our fragmentation, by our lack of "200,000 organisers", can be seen from the fact that: many people (including Nadezhdin) have reproached *Iskra* for the paucity of the news it gives on unemployment and for the casual nature of the correspondence it publishes about the most common affairs of rural life. The reproach is justified; but *Iskra* is "guilty without sin". We strive "to stretch a line" through the countryside too, where there are hardly any bricklayers anywhere, and we are *obliged* to encourage *everyone* who informs us even as regards the most common facts, in the hope that this will increase the number of our contributors in the given field and will ultimately *train us all* to select facts that are really the most outstanding. But the material on which we can train is so scanty that, unless we generalise it for the whole of Russia, we shall have very little to train on at all. No doubt, one with at least as much ability as an agitator and as much knowledge of the life of the vagrant as Nadezhdin manifests could render price-less service to the movement by carrying on agitation among the unemployed; but such a person would be simply hiding his light under a bushel if he failed to inform *all* comrades in Russia as regards every step he took in his work, so that others, who, in the mass, still lack the ability to undertake new kinds of work, might learn from his example.

All without exception now talk of the importance of unity, of the necessity for "gathering and organising"; but in the majority of cases what is lacking is a definite idea of where to begin and how to bring about this unity. Probably all will agree that if we "unite", say, the district circles in a given town, it will be necessary to have for this purpose *common institutions*, i.e., not merely the common title of "League", but genuinely *common* work, exchange of material, experience, and forces, distribution of functions, not only by districts, but through specialisation on a town-wide scale. All will agree that a big secret apparatus will not pay its way (to use a commercial expression) "with the resources" (in both money and manpower, of course) of a single district, and that this narrow field will not provide sufficient scope for a specialist to develop his talents. But the same thing applies to the co-ordination of activities of a number of towns, since even a specific locality *will be* and, in the history of our Social-Democratic movement, has proved to be, far too narrow a field; we have demonstrated this above in detail with regard to political agitation and organisational work. What we require foremost and imperatively is to broaden the field, establish *real* contacts between the towns on the basis of *regular, common* work; for fragmentation weighs down on the people and they are "stuck in a hole" (to use the expression employed by a correspondent to *Iskra*), not knowing what is happening in the world, from whom to learn, or how to acquire experience and satisfy their desire to engage in broad activities. I continue to insist that we can *start* establishing *real* contacts only with the aid of a common newspaper, as the only regular, All-Russian enterprise, one which will summarise the results of the most divers forms of activity and thereby *stimulate* people to march forward untiringly along *all* the innumerable paths leading to revolution, in

the same way as all roads lead to Rome. If we do not want
unity in name only, we must arrange for all local study
circles *immediately to assign*, say, a fourth of their forces
to *active* work for the *common* cause, and the newspaper
will immediately convey to them* the general design, scope,
and character of the cause; it will give them a precise indi-
cation of the most keenly felt shortcomings in the All-Russian activity, where agitation is lacking and contacts are
weak, and it will point out which little wheels in the vast
general mechanism a given study circle might repair or
replace with better ones. A study circle that has not yet
begun to work, but which is only just seeking activity,
could then start, not like a craftsman in an isolated little
workshop unaware of the earlier development in "industry" or of the general level of production methods prevailing in industry, but as a participant in an extensive enterprise that *reflects* the whole general revolutionary attack
on the autocracy. The more perfect the finish of each little
wheel and the larger the number of detail workers engaged
in the common cause, the closer will our network become
and the less will be the disorder in the ranks consequent
on inevitable police raids.

The mere function of distributing a newspaper would
help to establish *actual* contacts (if it is a newspaper worthy
of the name, i.e., if it is issued regularly, not once a month
like a magazine, but at least four times a month). At the
present time, communication between towns on revolutionary business is an extreme rarity, and, at all events,
is the exception rather than the rule. If we had a newspaper, however, such communication would become the rule
and would secure, not only the distribution of the newspaper, of course, but (what is more important) an exchange
of experience, of material, of forces, and of resources. Organisational work would immediately acquire much greater

---

* *A reservation*: that is, if a given study circle sympathises with
the policy of the newspaper and considers it useful to become a
collaborator, meaning by that, not only for literary collaboration,
but for revolutionary collaboration generally. *Note for Rabocheye
Dyelo*: Among revolutionaries who attach value to the cause and
not to playing at democracy, who do not separate "sympathy" from
the most active and lively participation, this reservation is taken for
granted.

scope, and the success of one locality would serve as a standing encouragement to further perfection; it would arouse the desire to utilise the experience gained by comrades working in other parts of the country. Local work would become far richer and more varied than it is at present. Political and economic exposures gathered from all over Russia would provide mental food for workers of all trades and *all stages of development*; they would provide material and occasion for talks and readings on the most divers subjects, which would, in addition, be suggested by hints in the legal press, by talk among the people, and by "shamefaced" government statements. Every outbreak, every demonstration, would be weighed and discussed in its every aspect in all parts of Russia and would thus stimulate a desire to keep up with, and even surpass, the others (we socialists do not by any means flatly reject all emulation or all "competition"!) and consciously prepare that which at first, as it were, sprang up spontaneously, a desire to take advantage of the favourable conditions in a given district or at a given moment for modifying the plan of attack, etc. At the same time, this revival of local work would obviate that desperate, "convulsive" exertion of *all* efforts and risking of *all* forces which every single demonstration or the publication of every single issue of a local newspaper now frequently entails. On the one hand, the police would find it much more difficult to get at the "roots", if they did not know in what district to dig down for them. On the other hand, regular common work would train our people to adjust the force of a *given* attack to the strength of the given contingent of the common army (at the present time hardly anyone ever thinks of doing that, because in nine cases out of ten these attacks occur spontaneously); such regular common work would facilitate the "transportation" from one place to another, not only of literature, but also of revolutionary forces.

In a great many cases these forces are now being bled white on restricted local work, but under the circumstances we are discussing it would be possible to transfer a capable agitator or organiser from one end of the country to the other, and the occasion for doing this would constantly arise. Beginning with short journeys on Party business at the Party's expense, the comrades would become accustomed to being maintained by the Party, to becoming professional revolutionaries, and to training themselves as real political leaders.

And if indeed we succeeded in reaching the point when all, or at least a considerable majority, of the local committees, local groups, and study circles took up active work for the common cause, we could, in the not distant future, establish a weekly newspaper for regular distribution in tens of thousands of copies throughout Russia. This newspaper would become part of an enormous pair of smith's bellows that would fan every spark of the class struggle and of popular indignation into a general conflagration. Around what is in itself still a very innocuous and very small, but regular and *common*, effort, in the full sense of the word, a regular army of tried fighters would systematically gather and receive their training. On the ladders and scaffolding of this general organisational structure there would soon develop and come to the fore Social-Democratic Zhelyabovs from among our revolutionaries and Russian Bebels from among our workers, who would take their place at the head of the mobilised army and rouse the whole people to settle accounts with the shame and the curse of Russia.

That is what we should dream of!

* * *

"We should dream!" I wrote these words and became alarmed. I imagined myself sitting at a "unity conference" and opposite me were the *Rabocheye Dyelo* editors and contributors. Comrade Martynov rises and, turning to me, says sternly: "Permit me to ask you, has an autonomous editorial board the right to dream without first soliciting the opinion of the Party committees?" He is followed by Comrade Krichevsky, who (philosophically deepening Comrade Martynov, who long ago rendered Comrade Plekhanov more profound) continues even more sternly: "I go further. I ask, has a Marxist any right at all to dream, knowing that according to Marx mankind always sets itself the tasks it can solve and that tactics is a process of the growth of Party tasks which grow together with the Party?"

The very thought of these stern questions sends a cold shiver down my spine and makes me wish for nothing but a place to hide in. I shall try to hide behind the back of Pisarev.

"There are rifts and rifts," wrote Pisarev of the rift between dreams and reality. "My dream may run ahead of the natural march of events or may fly off at a tangent in a direction in which no natural march of events will ever proceed. In the first case my dream will not cause any harm; it may even support and augment the energy of the working men.... There is nothing in such dreams that would distort or paralyse labour-power. On the contrary, if man were completely deprived of the ability to dream in this way, if he could not from time to time run ahead and mentally conceive, in an entire and completed picture, the product to which his hands are only just beginning to lend shape, then I cannot at all imagine what stimulus there would be to induce man to undertake and complete extensive and strenuous work in the sphere of art, science, and practical endeavour.... The rift between dreams and reality causes no harm if only the person dreaming believes seriously in his dream, if he attentively observes life, compares his observations with his castles in the air, and if, generally speaking, he works conscientiously for the achievement of his fantasies. If there is some connection between dreams and life then all is well."[64]

Of this kind of dreaming there is unfortunately too little in our movement. And the people most responsible for this are those who boast of their sober views, their "closeness" to the "concrete", the representatives of legal criticism and of illegal "tail-ism".

C. What Type of Organisation Do We Require?

From what has been said the reader will see that our "tactics-as-plan" consists in rejecting an immediate *call* for assault; in demanding "to lay effective siege to the enemy fortress"; or, in other words, in demanding that all efforts be directed towards gathering, organising, and *mobilising* a permanent army. When we ridiculed *Rabocheye Dyelo* for its leap from Economism to shouting for an assault (for which it clamoured in *April* 1901, in *"Listok"* Rabo-

chevo Dyela, No. 6), it of course came down on us with accusations of being "doctrinaire", of failing to understand our revolutionary duty, of calling for caution, etc. Of course, we were not in the least surprised to hear these accusations from those who totally lack principles and who evade all arguments by references to a profound "tactics-as-process", any more than we were surprised by the fact that these charges were repeated by Nadezhdin, who in general has a supreme contempt for durable programmes and the fundamentals of tactics.

It is said that history does not repeat itself. But Nadezhdin exerts every effort to cause it to repeat itself and he zealously imitates Tkachov in strongly condemning "revolutionary culturism", in shouting about "sounding the tocsin" and about a special "eve-of-the-revolution point of view", etc. Apparently, he has forgotten the well-known maxim that while an original historical event represents a tragedy, its replica is merely a farce.[65] The attempt to seize power, which was prepared by the preaching of Tkachov and carried out by means of the "terrifying" terror that did really terrify, had grandeur, but the "excitative" terror of a Tkachov the Little is simply ludicrous, particularly so when it is supplemented with the idea of an organisation of average people.

"If *Iskra* would only emerge from its sphere of bookishness," wrote Nadezhdin, "it would realise that these [instances like the worker's letter to *Iskra*, No. 7, etc.] are symptoms of the fact that soon, very soon, the 'assault' will begin, and to speak now [*sic!*] of an organisation linked with an All-Russian newspaper means to propagate arm chair ideas and armchair activity." What an unimaginable muddle—on the one hand, excitative terror and an "organisation of average people", along with the opinion that it is far "easier" to gather around something "more concrete", like a local newspaper, and, on the other, the view that to talk "now" about an All-Russian organisation means to propagate armchair thoughts, or, bluntly put, "now" it is already too late! But what of the "extensive organisation of local newspapers"—is it not too late for that, my dear L. Nadezhdin? And compare with this *Iskra*'s point of view and tactical line: excitative terror is nonsense; to talk of an organisation of average people and of the *extensive* publication of local newspapers means to fling the door wide open to Economism. We must speak of a single All-Russian organisation of revolutionaries, and it will never be too late to talk of that until the real, not a paper, assault begins.

"Yes, as far as organisation is concerned the situation is anything but brilliant," continues Nadezhdin. "Yes, *Iskra* is entirely right in saying that the mass of our fighting forces consists of volunteers and insurgents.... You do well to give such a sober picture of the state of our forces. But why, at the same time, do you forget that *the masses are not ours at all*, and consequently, *will not ask us* when to begin military operations; they will simply go and 'rebel'.... When the crowd itself breaks out with its elemental destructive force it *may* overwhelm and sweep aside the 'regular troops' among whom we prepared all the time to introduce extremely systematic organisation, but never *managed* to do so." (Our italics.)

Astounding logic! *For the very reason* that the "masses are not ours" it is stupid and unseemly to shout about an immediate "assault", for assault means attack by regular troops and not a spontaneous mass upsurge. For the very reason that the masses *may* overwhelm and sweep aside the regular troops we must without fail "manage to keep up" with the spontaneous upsurge by our work of "introducing extremely systematic organisation" in the regular troops, for the more we "manage" to introduce such organisation the more probably will the regular troops not be overwhelmed by the masses, but will take their place at their head. Nadezhdin is confused because he imagines that troops in the course of systematic organisation are engaged in something that isolates them from the masses, when in actuality they are engaged exclusively in all-sided and all-embracing political agitation, i.e., precisely in work that *brings closer and merges into a single whole* the elemental destructive force of the masses and the conscious destructive force of the organisation of revolutionaries. You, gentlemen, wish to lay the blame where it does not belong. For it is precisely the *Svoboda* group that, by including terror *in its programme*, calls for an organisation of terrorists, and such an organisation would indeed prevent our troops from establishing closer contacts with the masses, which, unfortunately, are still not ours, and which, unfortunately, do not yet ask us, or rarely ask us, when and how to launch their military operations.

"We shall miss the revolution itself," continues Nadezhdin in his attempt to scare *Iskra*, "in the same way as we missed the recent events, which came upon us like a bolt from the blue." This sentence, taken in connection with what has been quoted above, clearly demonstrates the absurdity of the "eve-of-the-revolution point of view" invented by *Svoboda*.* Plainly put, this special "point of view" boils down to this that it is too late "now" to discuss and prepare. If that is the case, most worthy opponent of "bookishness", what was the use of writing a pamphlet of 132 pages on "questions of theory** and tactics"? Don't you think it would have been more becoming for the "eve-of-the-revolution point of view" to have issued 132,000 leaflets containing the summary call, "Bang them—knock 'em down!"?

Those who make nation-wide political agitation the cornerstone of their programme, *their tactics, and their organisational work*, as *Iskra* does, stand the least risk of missing the revolution. The people who are now engaged throughout Russia in weaving the network of connections that spread from the All-Russian newspaper not only did not miss the spring events, but, on the contrary, gave us an opportunity to foretell them. Nor did they miss the demonstrations that were described in *Iskra*, Nos. 13 and

---

* *The Eve of the Revolution*, p. 62.
** In his *Review of Questions of Theory*, Nadezhdin, by the way, made almost no contribution whatever to the discussion of questions of theory, apart, perhaps, from the following passage, a most peculiar one from the "eve-of-the-revolution point of view": "Bernsteinism, on the whole, is losing its acuteness for us at the present moment, as is the question whether Mr. Adamovich will prove that Mr. Struve has already earned a lacing, or, on the contrary, whether Mr. Struve will refute Mr. Adamovich and will refuse to resign—it really makes no difference, because the hour of revolution has struck" (p. 110). One can hardly imagine a more glaring illustration of Nadezhdin's infinite disregard for theory. We have proclaimed "the eve of the revolution", *therefore* "it really makes no difference" whether or not the orthodox will succeed in finally driving the Critics from their positions! Our wiseacre fails to see that it is precisely during the revolution that we shall stand in need of the results of our theoretical battles with the Critics in order to be able resolutely to combat their *practical* positions!

14; on the contrary, they took part in them, clearly realising that it was their duty to come to the aid of the spontaneously rising masses and, at the same time, through the medium of the newspaper, help all the comrades in Russia to inform themselves of the demonstrations and to make use of their gathered experience. And if they live they will not miss the revolution, which, first and foremost, will demand of us experience in agitation, ability to support (in a Social-Democratic manner) every protest, as well as direct the spontaneous movement, while safeguarding it from the mistakes of friends and the traps of enemies.

We have thus come to the last reason that compels us so strongly to insist on the plan of an organisation centred round an All-Russian newspaper, through the common work for the common newspaper. Only such organisation will ensure the *flexibility* required of a militant Social-Democratic organisation, viz., the ability to adapt itself immediately to the most divers and rapidly changing conditions of struggle, the ability, "on the one hand, to avoid an open battle against an overwhelming enemy, when the enemy has concentrated all his forces at one spot and yet, on the other, to take advantage of his unwieldiness and to attack him when and where he least expects it".* It would be a grievous error indeed to build the Party organisation in anticipation only of outbreaks and street fighting, or only upon the "forward march of the drab everyday struggle". We must *always* conduct our everyday work and always be prepared for every situation, because very fre-

---

* *Iskra*, No. 4, "Where To Begin". "Revolutionary culturists, who do not accept the eve-of-the-revolution point of view, are not in the least perturbed by the prospect of working for a long period of time," writes Nadezhdin (p. 62). This brings us to observe: Unless we are able to devise political tactics and an organisational plan for *work over a very long period*, while ensuring, in *the very process of this work*, our Party's readiness to be at its post and fulfil its duty in every contingency whenever the march of events is accelerated—unless we succeed in doing this, we shall prove to be but miserable political adventurers. Only Nadezhdin, who began but yesterday to describe himself as a Social-Democrat, can forget that the aim of Social-Democracy is to transform radically the conditions of life of the whole of mankind and that for this reason it is not permissible for a Social-Democrat to be "perturbed" by the question of the duration of the work.

quently it is almost impossible to foresee when a period of outbreak will give way to a period of calm. In the instances, however, when it is possible to do so, we could not turn this foresight to account for the purpose of reconstructing our organisation; for in an autocratic country these changes take place with astonishing rapidity, being sometimes connected with a single night raid by the tsarist janizaries.[66] And the revolution itself must not by any means be regarded as a single act (as the Nadezhdins apparently imagine), but as a series of more or less powerful outbreaks rapidly alternating with periods of more or less complete calm. For that reason, the principal content of the activity of our Party organisation, the focus of this activity, should be work that is both possible and essential in the period of a most powerful outbreak as well as in the period of complete calm, namely, work of political agitation, connected throughout Russia, illuminating all aspects of life, and conducted among the broadest possible strata of the masses. But this work is *unthinkable* in present-day Russia without an All-Russian newspaper, issued very frequently. The organisation, which will form round this newspaper, the organisation of its *collaborators* (in the broad sense of the word, i.e., all those working for it), will be ready *for everything*, from upholding the honour, the prestige, and the continuity of the Party in periods of acute revolutionary "depression" to preparing for, appointing the time for, and carrying out the *nationwide armed uprising*.

Indeed, picture to yourselves a very ordinary occurrence in Russia—the total round-up of our comrades in one or several localities. In the absence of a *single*, common, regular activity that combines *all* the local organisations, such round-ups frequently result in the interruption of the work for many months. If, however, all the local organisations had one common activity, then, even in the event of a very serious round-up, two or three energetic persons could in the course of a few weeks establish contact between the common centre and new youth circles, which, as we know, spring up very quickly even now. And when the common activity, hampered by the arrests, is apparent to all, new circles will be able to come into being and make connections with the centre even more rapidly.

On the other hand, picture to yourselves a popular uprising. Probably everyone will now agree that we must think of this and prepare for it. But *how*? Surely the Central Committee cannot appoint agents to all localities for the purpose of preparing the uprising. Even if we had a Central Committee, it could achieve absolutely nothing by such appointments under present-day Russian conditions. But a network of agents* that would form in the course of establishing and distributing the common newspaper would not have to "sit about and wait" for the call for an uprising, but could carry on the regular activity that would guarantee the highest probability of success in the event of an uprising. Such activity would strengthen our contacts with the broadest strata of the working masses and with all social strata that are discontented with the autocracy, which is of such importance for an uprising. Precisely such activity would serve to cultivate the ability to estimate correctly the general political situation and, consequently, the ability to select the proper moment for an uprising. Precisely such activity would train *all* local organisations to respond simultaneously to the same political questions, incidents, and events that agitate the whole of Russia and to react to such "incidents" in the most vigorous, uniform, and expedient manner possible; for an uprising is in essence the most vigorous, most uniform, and most expedient "answer" of the entire people to the government. Lastly, it is precisely such activity that would train all revolutionary organisations throughout Russia to maintain the most continuous, and at the same time the

---

* Alas, alas! Again I have let slip that awful word "agents", which jars so much on the democratic ears of the Martynovs! I wonder why this word did not offend the heroes of the seventies and yet offends the amateurs of the nineties? I like the word, because it clearly and trenchantly indicates *the common cause* to which all the agents bend their thoughts and actions, and if I had to replace this word by another, the only word I might select would be the word "collaborator", if it did not suggest a certain bookishness and vagueness. The thing we need is a military organisation of agents. However, the numerous Martynovs (particularly abroad), whose favourite pastime is "mutual grants of generalships to one another", may instead of saying "passport agent" prefer to say, "Chief of the Special Department for Supplying Revolutionaries with Passports", etc.

most secret, contacts with one another, thus creating *real* Party unity; for without such contacts it will be impossible collectively to discuss the plan for the uprising and to take the necessary preparatory measures on the eve, measures that must be kept in the strictest secrecy.

In a word, the "plan for an All-Russian political newspaper", far from representing the fruits of the labour of armchair workers, infected with dogmatism and bookishness (as it seemed to those who gave but little thought to it), is the most practical plan for immediate and all-round preparation of the uprising, with, at the same time, no loss of sight for a moment of the pressing day-to-day work.

Conclusion

The history of Russian Social-Democracy can be distinctly divided into three periods:

The first period embraces about ten years, approximately from 1884 to 1894. This was the period of the rise and consolidation of the theory and programme of Social-Democracy. The adherents of the new trend in Russia were very few in number. Social-Democracy existed without a working-class movement, and as a political party it was at the embryonic stage of development.

The second period embraces three or four years—1894-98. In this period Social-Democracy appeared on the scene as a social movement, as the upsurge of the masses of the people, as a political party. This is the period of its childhood and adolescence. The intelligentsia was fired with a vast and general zeal for struggle against Narodism and for going among the workers; the workers displayed a general enthusiasm for strike action. The movement made enormous strides. The majority of the leaders were young people who had not reached "the age of thirty-five", which to Mr. N. Mikhailovsky appeared to be a sort of natural border-line. Owing to their youth, they proved to be untrained for practical work and they left the scene with astonishing rapidity. But in the majority of cases the scope of their activity was very wide. Many of them had begun their revolutionary thinking as adherents of Narodnaya Volya. Nearly all had in their early youth enthusiastically worshipped the terrorist heroes. It required a struggle to abandon the captivating impressions of those heroic traditions, and the struggle was accompanied by the breaking off of personal relations with people who were determined to remain loyal to the Narodnaya Volya and for whom the young Social-Democrats had profound respect. The struggle compelled the youthful leaders to educate themselves, to read illegal literature of every trend, and to study closely the questions of legal Narodism. Trained in this struggle, Social-Democrats went into the working-class movement without "for a moment" forgetting either the theory of Marxism, which brightly illumined their path, or the task of overthrowing the autocracy. The formation of the Party in the spring of 1898 was the most striking and at the same time the *last* act of the Social-Democrats of this period.

The third period, as we have seen, was prepared in 1897 and it definitely cut off the second period in 1898 (1898-?). This was a period of disunity, dissolution, and vacillation. During adolescence a youth's voice breaks. And so, in this period, the voice of Russian Social-Democracy began to break, to strike a false note—on the one hand, in the writings of Messrs. Struve and Prokopovich, of Bulgakov and Berdayev, and on the other, in those of V. I—n and R. M., of B. Krichevsky and Martynov. But it was only the leaders who wandered about separately and drew back; the movement itself continued to grow, and it advanced with enormous strides. The proletarian struggle spread to new strata of the workers and extended to the whole of Russia, at the same time indirectly stimulating the revival of the democratic spirit among the students and among other sections of the population. The political consciousness of the leaders, however, capitulated before the breadth and power of the spontaneous upsurge; among the Social-Democrats, another type had become dominant—the type of functionaries, trained almost exclusively on "legal Marxist" literature, which proved to be all the more inadequate the more the spontaneity of the masses demanded political consciousness on the part of the leaders. The leaders not only lagged behind in regard to theory ("freedom of criticism") and practice ("primitiveness"), but they sought to justify their backwardness by all manner of high-flown arguments. Social-Democracy was degraded to the level of trade-unionism by the Brentano adherents in legal literature, and by the tail-enders in illegal literature. The *Credo* programme began to be put into operation, especially when the "primitive methods" of the Social-Democrats caused a revival of revolutionary non-Social-Democratic tendencies.

If the reader should feel critical that I have dealt at too great length with a certain *Rabocheye Dyelo*, I can say only that *Rabocheye Dyelo* acquired "historical" significance because it most notably reflected the "spirit" of this third period.* It was not the consistent R. M., but the weathercock Krichevskys and Martynovs who were able properly to express the disunity and vacillation, the readiness to make concessions to "criticism", to "Economism", and to terrorism. Not the lofty contempt for practical work displayed by some worshipper of the "absolute" is characteristic of this period, but the combination of petti-fogging practice and utter disregard for theory. It was not so much in the direct rejection of "grandiose phrases" that the heroes of this period engaged as in their vulgarisation. Scientific socialism ceased to be an integral revolutionary theory and became a hodgepodge "freely" diluted with the content of every new German textbook that appeared; the slogan "class struggle" did not impel to broader and more energetic activity, but served as a balm, since "the economic struggle is inseparably linked with the political struggle"; the idea of a party did not serve as a call for the creation of a militant organisation of revolutionaries, but was used to justify some sort of "revolutionary bureaucracy" and infantile playing at "democratic" forms.

When the third period will come to an end and the fourth (now heralded by many portents) will begin we do not know. We are passing from the sphere of history to the sphere of the present and, partly, of the future. But we firmly believe that the fourth period will lead to the consolidation of militant Marxism, that Russian Social-Democracy will emerge from the crisis in the full flower of manhood, that the opportunist rearguard will be "replaced" by the genuine vanguard of the most revolutionary class.

In the sense of calling for such a "replacement" and by way of summing up what has been expounded above, we may meet the question, What is to be done? with the brief reply:

Put an End to the Third Period.

---

* I could also reply with the German proverb: *Den Sack schlägt man, den Esel meint man* (you beat the sack, but you mean the donkey). Not *Rabocheye Dyelo* alone, but also *the broad mass* of practical workers *and theoreticians* was carried away by the "criticism" *à la mode*, becoming confused in regard to the question of spontaneity and lapsing from the Social-Democratic to the trade-unionist conception of our political and organisational tasks.

The Attempt to Unite *Iskra* with
Rabocheye Dyelo

It remains for us to describe the tactics adopted and consistently pursued by *Iskra* in its organisational relations with *Rabocheye Dyelo*. These tactics were fully expressed in *Iskra*, No. 1, in the article entitled "The Split in the Union of Russian Social-Democrats Abroad".* From the outset we adopted the point of view that the *real* Union of Russian Social-Democrats Abroad, which at the First Congress of our Party was recognised as its representative abroad, *had split* into two organisations; that the question of the Party's representation remained an open one, having been settled only temporarily and conditionally by the election, at the International Congress in Paris, of two members to represent Russia on the International Socialist Bureau, one from each of the two sections of the divided Union Abroad. We declared that fundamentally *Rabocheye Dyelo was wrong*; in principle we emphatically took the side of the Emancipation of Labour group, at the same time refusing to enter into the details of the split and noting the services rendered by the Union Abroad in the sphere of purely practical work.**

Consequently, ours was, to a certain extent, a waiting policy. We made a concession to the opinions prevailing among the majority of the Russian Social-Democrats that the most determined opponents of Economism could work

---

* See *Collected Works*, Vol. 4, pp. 378-79.—*Ed.*
** Our judgement of the split was based, not only upon a study of the literature on the subject, but also on information gathered abroad by several members of our organisation.

hand in hand with the Union Abroad because it had repeatedly declared its agreement in principle with the Emancipation of Labour group, without, allegedly, taking an independent position on fundamental questions of theory and tactics. The correctness of our position was indirectly proved by the fact that almost simultaneously with the appearance of the first issue of *Iskra* (December 1900) three members separated from the Union, formed the so-called "Initiators' Group", and offered their services: (1) to the foreign section of the *Iskra* organisation, (2) to the revolutionary *Sotsial-Demokrat* organisation, and (3) to the Union Abroad, as mediators in negotiations for reconciliation. The first two organisations at once announced their agreement; *the third turned down* the offer. True, when a speaker related these facts at the "Unity" Conference last year, a member of the Administrative Committee of the Union Abroad declared the rejection of the offer to have been due *entirely* to the fact that the Union Abroad was dissatisfied with the composition of the Initiators' Group. While I consider it my duty to cite this explanation, I cannot, however, refrain from observing that it is an unsatisfactory one; for, knowing that two organisations had agreed to enter into negotiations, the Union Abroad could have approached them through another intermediary or directly.

In the spring of 1901 both *Zarya* (No. 1, April) and *Iskra* (No. 4, May)* entered into open polemics with *Rabocheye Dyelo*. *Iskra* particularly attacked the article "A Historic Turn" in *Rabocheye Dyelo*, which, in its *April* supplement, that is, after the spring events, revealed instability on the question of terror and the calls for "blood", with which many had been carried away at the time. Notwithstanding the polemics, the Union Abroad agreed to resume negotiations for reconciliation through the instrumentality of a new group of "conciliators". A preliminary conference of representatives of the three. cited organisations, held in June, framed a draft agreement on the basis of a very detailed "accord on principles", which the Union Abroad published in the pamphlet *Two Conferences*, and the

---

* See *Collected Works*, Vol. 5, pp. 13-24.—*Ed.*

League Abroad in the pamphlet *Documents of the "Unity" Conference*.

The contents of this accord on principles (more frequently named the Resolutions of the June Conference) make it perfectly clear that we put forward as an absolute condition for unity *the most emphatic* repudiation of any and every manifestation of opportunism generally, and of Russian opportunism in particular. Paragraph 1 reads: "We repudiate all attempts to introduce opportunism into the proletarian class struggle—attempts that have found expression in the so-called Economism, Bernsteinism, Millerandism, etc." "The sphere of Social-Democratic activities includes ... ideological struggle against all opponents of revolutionary Marxism" (4, c); "In every sphere of organisational and agitational activity Social-Democracy must never for a moment forget that the immediate task of the Russian proletariat is the overthrow of the autocracy" (5, a); "...agitation, not only on the basis of the everyday struggle between wagelabour and capital" (5, b); "...we do not recognise ... a stage of purely economic struggle and of struggle for partial political demands" (5, c); "...we consider it important for the movement to criticise tendencies that make a principle of the elementariness ... and narrowness of the lower forms of the movement" (5, d). Even a complete outsider, having read these resolutions at all attentively, will have realised from their very formulations that they are directed against people who were opportunists and "Economists", who, even for a moment, forgot the task of overthrowing the autocracy, who recognised the theory of stages, who elevated narrowness to a principle, etc. Anyone who has the least acquaintance with the polemics conducted by the Emancipation of Labour group, *Zarya*, and *Iskra* against *Rabocheye Dyelo* cannot doubt for a single moment that these resolutions repudiate, point by point, the very errors into which *Rabocheye Dyelo* strayed. Hence, when a member of the Union Abroad declared at the "Unity" Conference that the articles in No. 10 of *Rabocheye Dyelo* had been prompted, not by a new "historic turn" on the part of the Union Abroad, but by the excessive "abstractness" of the resolutions,* the assertion was justly ridiculed by one of

---

* This assertion is repeated in *Two Conferences*, p. 25.

the speakers. Far from being abstract, he said, the resolutions were incredibly concrete: one could see at a glance that they were "trying to catch somebody".

This remark occasioned a characteristic incident at the Conference. On the one hand, Krichevsky, seizing upon the word "catch" in the belief that this was a slip of the tongue which betrayed our evil intentions ("to set a trap"), pathetically exclaimed: "Whom are they out to catch?" "Whom indeed?" rejoined Plekhanov sarcastically. "Let me come to the aid of Comrade Plekhanov's lack of perspicacity", replied Krichevsky. "Let me explain to him that the trap was set *for the Editorial Board of Rabocheye Dyelo* [general laughter] but we have not allowed ourselves to be caught!" (A remark from the left: "All the worse for you!") On the other hand, a member of the Borba group (a group of conciliators), opposing the amendments of the Union Abroad to the resolutions and desiring to defend our speaker, declared that obviously tne word "catch" was dropped by chance in the heat of polemics.

For my part, I think the speaker responsible for uttering the word will hardly be pleased with this "defence". I think the words "trying to catch somebody" were "true words spoken in jest"; we have always accused *Rabocheye Dyelo* of instability and vacillation, and, naturally, we *had* to try *to catch* it in order to put a stop to the vacillation. There is not the slightest suggestion of evil intent in this, for we were discussing instability of principles. And we succeeded in "catching" the Union Abroad in such a comradely manner* that Krichevsky himself and one other member of the

---

* Precisely: In the introduction to the June resolutions we said that Russian Social-Democracy as a whole always stood by the principles of the Emancipation of Labour group and that the particular service of the Union Abroad was its publishing and organising activity. In other words, we expressed our complete readiness to forget the past and to recognise the usefulness (for the cause) of the work of our comrades of the Union Abroad *provided* it completely ceased the vacillation we tried to "catch". Any impartial person reading the June resolutions will only thus interpret them. If the Union Abroad, after having *caused* a split by its new turn towards Economism (in its articles in No. 10 and in the amendments), now solemnly charges us with *untruth* (*Two Conferences*, p. 30), because of what we said about its services, then of course, such an accusation can only evoke a smile.

Administrative Committee of the Union signed the June resolutions.

The articles in *Rabocheye Dyelo*, No. 10 (our comrades saw the issue for the first time when they arrived at the Conference, a few days before the meetings started) clearly showed that a new turn had taken place in the Union Abroad in the period between the summer and the autumn: the Economists had once more gained the upper hand, and the Editorial Board, which veered with every "wind", again set out to defend "the most pronounced Bernsteinians" and "freedom of criticism", to defend "spontaneity", and through the lips of Martynov to preach the "theory of restricting" the sphere of our political influence (for the alleged purpose of rendering this influence more complex). Once again Parvus' apt observation that it is difficult to catch an opportunist with a formula has been proved correct. An opportunist will readily put his name to *any* formula and as readily abandon it, because opportunism means precisely a lack of definite and firm principles. Today, the opportunists have repudiated *all* attempts to introduce opportunism, repudiated *all* narrowness, solemnly promised "never for a moment to forget about the task of overthrowing the autocracy" and to carry on "agitation not only on the basis of the everyday struggle between wage-labour and capital", etc., etc. But tomorrow they will change their form of expression and revert to their old tricks on the pretext of defending spontaneity and the forward march of the drab everyday struggle, of extolling demands promising palpable results, etc. By continuing to assert that in the articles in No. 10 "the Union Abroad did not and does not now see any heretical departure from the general principles of the draft adopted at the conference" (*Two Conferences*, p. 26), the Union Abroad merely reveals a complete lack of ability, or of desire, to understand the essential points of the disagreements.

After the tenth issue of *Rabocheye Dyelo*, we could make only one effort: open a general discussion in order to ascertain whether all the members of the Union Abroad agreed with the articles and with the Editorial Board. The Union Abroad is particularly displeased with us because of this and accuses us of trying to sow discord in its ranks, of interfering in other people's business, etc. These accusations are obviously unfounded, since with an elected editorial board that "veers" with every wind, however light, everything depends upon the direction of the wind, and we defined that direction at private meetings at which no one was present, except members of the organisations intending to unite. The amendments to the June resolutions submitted in the name of the Union Abroad have removed the last shadow of hope of arriving at agreement. The amendments are documentary evidence of the new turn towards Economism and of the fact that the majority of the Union members are in agreement with *Rabocheye Dyelo*, No. 10. It was moved to delete the words "so-called Economism" from the reference to manifestations of opportunism (on the plea that "the meaning" of these words "was vague"; but if that were so, all that was required was a more precise definition of the nature of the widespread error), and to delete "Millerandism" (although Krichevsky had defended it in *Rabocheye Dyelo*, No. 2-3, pp. 83-84, and still more openly in *Vorwärts**). Notwithstanding the fact that the June resolutions definitely indicated that the task of Social-Democracy is "to guide *every* manifestation of the proletarian struggle against *all* forms of political, *economic*, and social oppression", thereby calling for the introduction of system and unity in all these manifestations of the struggle, the Union Abroad added the wholly superfluous words that "the economic struggle is a powerful stimulus to the mass movement" (taken by itself, this assertion cannot be disputed, but with the existence of narrow Economism it could not but give occasion for false interpretations). Moreover, even the direct *constriction* of "politics" was suggested for the June resolutions, both by the deletion of the words "not for a moment" (to forget the aim of overthrowing the autocracy) and by the addition of the words "the economic struggle is the *most widely* applicable means of drawing the masses into active political struggle". Naturally, upon the submission of such amendments, the speakers on our side refused, one after another, to take the floor, considering it hopeless to continue ne-

---

* A polemic on the subject started in *Vorwärts* between its present editor, Kautsky, and the Editorial Board of *Zarya*. We shall not fail to acquaint the Russian reader with this controversy.[68]

gotiations with people who were again turning towards Economism and were striving to secure for themselves freedom to vacillate.

"It was precisely the preservation of the independent features and the autonomy of *Rabocheye Dyelo*, considered by the Union to be the *sine qua non* of the durability of our future agreement, that *Iskra* regarded as the stumbling-block to agreement" (*Two Conferences*, p. 25). This is most inexact. We never had any designs against *Rabocheye Dyelo*'s autonomy.* We did indeed *absolutely refuse to recognise* the independence of its features, if by "independent features" is meant independence on questions of principle in theory and tactics. The June resolutions contain an utter repudiation of *such* independence of features, because, in practice, such "independence of features" has always meant, as we have pointed out, all manner of vacillations fostering the disunity which prevails among us and which is intolerable from the Party point of view. *Rabocheye Dyelo*'s articles in its tenth issue, together with its "amendments", clearly revealed its desire to preserve this kind of independence of features, and such a desire naturally and inevitably led to a rupture and a declaration of war. But all of us were ready to recognise *Rabocheye Dyelo*'s "independence of features" in the sense that it should concentrate on definite literary functions. A proper distribution of these functions naturally called for: (1) a theoretical magazine, (2) a political newspaper, and (3) popular collections of articles and popular pamphlets. Only by agreeing to such a distribution of functions would *Rabocheye Dyelo* have proved that it *sincerely* desired to abandon once and for all its errors, against which the June resolutions were directed. Only such a distribution of functions would have removed all possibility of friction, effectively guaranteed a durable agreement, and, at the same time, served as a basis for a revival and for new successes of our movement.

At present not a single Russian Social-Democrat can have any doubts that the final rupture between the revolution-

---

* That is, if the editorial consultations in connection with the establishment of a joint supreme council of the combined organisations are not to be regarded as a restriction of autonomy. But in June *Rabocheye Dyelo* agreed to this.

ary and the opportunist tendencies was caused, not by any "organisational" circumstances, but by the desire of the opportunists to consolidate the independent features of opportunism and to continue to cause confusion of mind by the disquisitions of the Krichevskys and Martynovs.

Correction to *What Is To Be Done?*

The Initiators' Group of whom I speak in the pamphlet *What Is To Be Done?*, p. 141,* have asked me to make the following correction to my description of the part they played in the attempt to reconcile the Social-Democratic organisations abroad: "Of the three members of this group, only one left the Union Abroad at the end of 1900; the others left in 1901, only after becoming convinced that it was impossible to obtain the Union's consent to a conference with the *Iskra* organisation abroad and the revolutionary *Sotsial-Demokrat* organisation, which the Initiators' Group had proposed. The Administrative Committee of the Union Abroad at first rejected this proposal, contending that the persons comprising the Initiators' Group were 'not competent' to act as mediators, and it expressed the desire to enter into direct contact with the *Iskra* organisation abroad. Soon thereafter, however, the Administrative Committee of the Union Abroad informed the Initiators' Group that following the appearance of the first number of *Iskra* containing the report of the split in the Union, it had altered its decision and no longer desired to maintain relations with *Iskra*. After this, how can one explain the statement made by a member of the Administrative Committee of the Union Abroad that the latter's rejection of a conference was called forth *entirely* by its dissatisfaction with the composition of the Initiators' Group? It is true that it is equally difficult to explain why the Administrative Committee of the Union Abroad agreed to

_____
* See pp. 178-79 of this pamphlet.—*Ed.*

a conference in June of last year; for the article in the first issue of *Iskra* still remained in force and *Iskra*'s 'negative' attitude to the Union Abroad was still more strongly expressed in the first issue of *Zarya*, and in No. 4 of *Iskra*, both of which appeared prior to the June Conference."

N. Lenin

Iskra, No. 19, April 1, 1902

Notes

[1] *What Is To Be Done? Burning Questions of Our Movement*—a book written by Lenin in the latter part of 1901 and in the beginning of 1902. In "Where To Begin", published in *Iskra*, No. 4 (May 1901), Lenin wrote that the article represents "a skeleton plan to be developed in greater detail in a pamphlet now in preparation for print".

Lenin began the actual writing of the book in the autumn of 1901. In his "Preface to the Pamphlet *Documents of the 'Unity' Conference*", written in November 1901, Lenin stated that the book was in preparation "to be published in the near future". Lenin subsequently described his article, "A Talk With Defenders of Economism" (*Iskra*, No. 12, December 1901), as a synopsis of *What Is To Be Done?* In February 1902 Lenin wrote the preface to the book, which appeared in the early days of March in Stuttgart where it was published by Dietz. An announcement of its publication was printed in *Iskra*, No. 18, March 10, 1902.

In republishing *What Is To Be Done?* in 1907 in the collection *Twelve Years*, Lenin omitted section A of Chapter V "Who Was Offended by the Article 'Where To Begin'" and announced in the preface that the book was being published "with very slight abridgements, omitting only details concerning organisational relationships and minor polemical remarks". Lenin added five footnotes to the new edition.

The text of *What Is To Be Done?* given in Vol. 5 of V. I. Lenin's *Collected Works* (from which this translation has been made) follows the 1902 edition, checked with the text of the 1907 edition.

[2] *Iskra (The Spark)*—the first All-Russian illegal Marxist newspaper, founded by Lenin in 1900. It played a decisive role in the struggle for the creation of a Marxist party, in smashing the Economists, in uniting the isolated Social-Democratic circles and preparing the ground for the Second Congress of the R.S.D.L.P.

The publication of a revolutionary newspaper in Russia was impossible owing to police persecution. While still in exile in Siberia, Lenin worked out all the details of a plan to publish the paper abroad and proceeded to carry out this plan as soon as his term of exile ended in January 1900.

The first issue of Lenin's *Iskra* appeared on December 11 (24), 1900, in Leipzig, after which it was published in Munich, London (from July 1902), and, beginning with the spring of 1903, in Geneva.

The Editorial Board of *Iskra* was made up of V. I. Lenin, G. V. Plekhanov, L. Martov (Y. O. Tsederbaum), P. B. Axelrod, A. N. Potresov and V. I. Zasulich. N. K. Krupskaya became secretary of the Editorial Board in the spring of 1901. Lenin was the factual Editor-in-Chief and leader of all *Iskra*'s activities. His articles in *Iskra* dealt with the fundamental problems of building the Party and of the class struggle of the proletariat in Russia as well as with outstanding events on the international scene.

Groups and committees of the R.S.D.L.P. supporting the Lenin-*Iskra* line were organised in a number of cities of Russia, including St. Petersburg and Moscow.

Iskra organisations were founded by and worked under the direct guidance of professional revolutionaries trained by Lenin (N. E. Bauman, I. V. Babushkin, S. I. Gusev, M. I. Kalinin and others).

On Lenin's initiative, and with his immediate participation, the *Iskra* Editorial Board drew up a Draft Programme of the Party (published in issue No. 21), and prepared the Second Congress of the R.S.D.L.P., which was held in July-August 1903.

By that time most of the Social-Democratic organisations in Russia had associated themselves with *Iskra*, approved its tactics, programme and organisational plan, and recognised it as their leading organ. In a special resolution the Second Congress recorded the exceptional role of the paper in the struggle to create the Party and adopted *Iskra* as the Central Organ of the R.S.D.L.P.

The Second Congress appointed an Editorial Board consisting of Lenin, Plekhanov and Martov. Contrary to the Congress decision, Martov refused to serve on the board, and issues 46-51 of *Iskra* were edited by Lenin and Plekhanov. Subsequently, Plekhanov took his stand with the Mensheviks and demanded that all the former Menshevik editors, who had been rejected by the Congress, be included in the Editorial Board. Lenin could not agree to this, and on October 19 (November 1), 1903, resigned from the Editorial Board in order to entrench himself in the Central Committee of the Party and to strike at the Menshevik opportunists from this position. Issue 52 of *Iskra* was edited by Plekhanov alone. On November 13 (26), 1903, acting on his own accord, and in defiance of the will of the Congress, Plekhanov co-opted the former Menshevik editors to the Editorial Board. Beginning with the 52nd issue of *Iskra*, the Mensheviks converted it into their organ. A new, opportunist Menshevik *Iskra* now appeared to take the place of the old, Leninist Bolshevik *Iskra*.   p. 5

3 *Rabocheye Dyelo* (*Workers' Cause*)—a magazine published by the Economists at irregular intervals from April 1899 to February 1902 in Geneva. Organ of the Union of Russian Social-Democrats Abroad edited by B. N. Krichevsky, A. S. Martynov and V. P. Ivan-

shin. Altogether 12 issues (of which three were double issues) appeared.   p. 5

⁴ *Rabochaya Gazeta (Workers' Gazette)*—illegal organ of the Kiev Social-Democratic group. Two issues appeared: No. 1 in August, and No. 2 in December (dated November) 1897. The First Congress of the R.S.D.L.P. adopted *Rabochaya Gazeta* as the official organ of the Party, but it discontinued publication after the Congress as a result of a police raid on the printing press and the arrest of the Central Committee.   p. 6

⁵ *Lassalleans* and *Eisenachers*—two parties in the German working class movement in the sixties and early seventies of the last century.

Lassalleans—adherents and followers of Ferdinand Lassalle. The General Association of German Workers, founded by Lassalle in 1863, made up the core of the movement. Proceeding from the possibility of a peaceful transformation of capitalism into socialism with the aid of workers' associations supported by the capitalist state, the Lassalleans advocated the struggle for universal franchise and peaceful parliamentary activities as a substitute for the revolutionary struggle of the working class.

Marx trenchantly criticised the Lassalleans, pointing out that "over a course of several years they were a hindrance to the organisation of the proletariat and ended up by becoming no more than a tool in the hands of the police". Marx gives an appraisal of the theoretical views of the Lassalleans and of their tactics in *Critique of the Gotha Programme, Alleged Splits in the International* and in correspondence with Engels.

Eisenachers—supporters of Marxism, were under the ideological influence of Marx and Engels. Led by Wilhelm Liebknecht and August Bebel, they founded the Social-Democratic Workers' Party of Germany at the Eisenach Congress in 1869.

The two parties fought each other bitterly.

The rise of the workers' movement and intensified reprisals by the government impelled both parties to merge. The merger was effected at the Gotha Congress in 1875, when a single Socialist Workers' Party of Germany was formed, in which the Lassalleans represented the opportunist wing.

Lenin characterises the Lassalleans and Eisenachers in his article "August Bebel", written in August 1913 (*Collected Works*, Vol. 19).   p. 8

⁶ *Guesdists* and *Possibilists*—two trends in the French socialist movement; they originated in 1882 following the split in the French Workers' Party.

Guesdists—supporters of Jules Guesde. They represented the Left, Marxist trend and maintained that the proletariat must pursue an independent revolutionary policy. In 1901 the Guesdists founded the Socialist Party of France.

Possibilists—a petty-bourgeois, reformist trend which sought to deflect the proletariat from revolutionary methods of struggle. They proposed to confine the activities of the working class to what was "possible" under capitalism. In 1902, in conjunction with other reformist groups, they founded the French Socialist Party. The Socialist Party of France and the French Socialist Party merged in 1905. During the imperialist war of 1914-18 Jules Guesde, in common with the leadership of the French Socialist Party, took his stand as a social-chauvinist.   p. 8

7 *Fabians*—members of the reformist and opportunist Fabian Society, founded in England in 1884 by a group of bourgeois intellectuals. The Fabians took their name from the Roman General Quintus Fabius Maximus called Cunctator ("the Delayer"), famous for his procrastinating tactics and avoidance of decisive battles. The Fabians sought to deflect the proletariat from the class struggle and advocated the possibility of a peaceful transition from capitalism to socialism by means of petty reforms.

Engels characterises the Fabians in a letter to Sorge, January 18, 1893 (Marx and Engels, *Selected Correspondence*, p. 452). Lenin characterises the Fabians in several of his works—see his "Preface to the Russian Translation of 'Letters by Johannes Becker, Joseph Dietzgen, Frederick Engels, Karl Marx, and Others to Friedrich Sorge and Others'", "The Agrarian Programme of Social-Democracy in the Russian Revolution", "British Pacifism and British Dislike of Theory", etc.   p. 8

8 *Narodnaya Volya*—a secret Narodnik society founded in 1879 for revolutionary struggle against the tsarist autocracy.

The Narodnaya Volya was smashed by the tsarist government soon after its members had assassinated Alexander II on March 1 (13), 1881. Following this the majority of the Narodniks abandoned the revolutionary struggle against tsarism, began to advocate reconciliation, agreement with the tsarist autocracy. These Epigoni of Narodism, the liberal Narodniks of the eighties and nineties actually voiced the interests of the kulaks.   p. 8

9 See Marx and Engels, *Selected Works*, Vol. I, Moscow 1962, p. 245.
                                                                              p. 10

10 *Union of Russian Social-Democrats Abroad*—founded in Geneva in 1894 on the initiative of the Emancipation of Labour Group which at first supervised its activities and edited its publications. Opportunist elements (the "young" Social-Democrats, the Economists) subsequently gained the upper hand in the Union. In November 1898, at the Union's first congress, the Emancipation of Labour Group declined to bear further responsibility for the editorship of its publications. The final break with the Union and the secession of the Emancipation of Labour Group occurred in April 1900, at the Union's second congress, when the Emancipation of Labour Group and its followers left the congress and founded their own organisation, the *Sotsial-Demokrat* group.   p. 12

11 *Zarya* (*Dawn*)—a Marxist journal of politics published in Stuttgart by the Editors of *Iskra* in 1901-02.

The following articles by V. I. Lenin appeared in *Zarya*: "Casual Notes", "The Persecutors of the Zemstvo and the Hannibals of Liberalism", the first four chapters of "The Agrarian Question and the 'Critics of Marx'" (the *Zarya* title was "The 'Critics' on the Agrarian Question"), "Review of Home Affairs", "The Agrarian Programme of Russian Social-Democracy". Four issues of the magazine appeared: No. 1 in April 1901 (acually on March 23, new style), Nos. 2-3 in December 1901, and No. 4 in August 1902. p. 12

[12] *Cadets* (the Constitutional-Democratic Party)—the principal bourgeois party in Russia, the party of the liberal-monarchist bourgeoisie. Was formed in October 1905. Under the cloak of pseudo-democratism and calling themselves the party of "people's freedom", the Cadets tried to win the peasantry to their side. They strove to preserve tsarism in the form of a constitutional monarchy. After the victory of the October Socialist Revolution the Cadets organised counter-revolutionary conspiracies and revolts against the Soviet Republic. p. 12

[13] *Bezzaglavtsi*—the group that founded and edited the magazine *Bez Zaglaviya* (*Without a Title*), published in St. Petersburg in 1906. The group, which included S. N. Prokopovich, Y. D. Kuskova, V. Y. Bogucharsky and others, openly advocated revisionism, supported the Mensheviks and liberals and was opposed to the proletariat pursuing an independent policy. Lenin called the Bezzaglavtsi pro-Menshevik Cadets or pro-Cadet Mensheviks. p. 12

[14] *Ilovaisky, D. I.* (1832-1920)—historian, author of numerous official text-books on history, widely used in elementary and secondary schools in Russia prior to the revolution. Ilovaisky interpreted history as consisting mainly of the acts of tsars and generals, and explained the historical process by secondary and incidental factors. p. 13

[15] *Exceptional Law Against the Socialists* was introduced in Germany in 1878. It provided for the prohibition of all Social-Democratic organisations, mass labour organisations, the labour press, the confiscation of socialist literature and the persecution of Social-Democrats. The law was repealed in 1890 under the pressure of the mass working-class movement. p. 13

[16] *Vorwärts* (*Forward*)—central organ of the German Social-Democratic Party. It began publication in 1876, with Wilhelm Liebknecht as editor. In its columns Frederick Engels combated all manifestations of opportunism. In the latter half of the nineties, after Engels's death, *Vorwärts* began to print systematically articles by opportunists, who dominated the German Social-Democratic Party and the Second International. p. 14

[17] *The Katheder-Socialists* (*Socialists of the Chair*)—a trend in bourgeois political economy, originated in Germany in the seventies and eighties of the nineteenth century. The Katheder-Socialists used their position as university lecturers to preach bourgeois liberal reformism under the guise of socialism. Their contention was that the bourgeois state stood above classes, was capable of reconciling hostile classes, gradually introducing "socialism" without encroaching on the interests of the capitalists and, as far as possible, of taking into account the demands of the workers. The views of the Katheder-Socialists were advocated in Russia by the "legal Marxists". p. 14

[18] *Nozdryov*—the allusion to the landowner Nozdryov, a trouble-maker and rascal, a character in Gogol's *Dead Souls*. Gogol called Nozdryov a "historical" personage because wherever he appeared he left behind a "history" of troublemaking.   p. 14

[19] *The Hanover resolution* regarding "attacks on the fundamental views and tactics of the party", adopted by the Congress of the German Social-Democratic Party in Hanover, September 27 to October 2 (October 9-14), 1899. The discussion of this question at the congress and the adoption of a special resolution were necessitated by the fact that the opportunists, led by Bernstein, advocated the revision of Marxist theory and demanded a reconsideration of Social-Democratic revolutionary policy and tactics. The Hanover resolution rejected the demand of the revisionists but failed to criticise or expose Bernsteinism. Bernstein's supporters voted for the resolution.   p. 14

[20] *The Lübeck resolution*—adopted at the congress of the German Social-Democratic Party in Lübeck, September 9-15 (22-28), 1901. The central issue at the congress was the struggle against revisionism, which by that time had taken shape as the Right wing of the Party with its own programme and press organ, the *Sozialistische Monatshefte* (*Socialist Monthly*). The leader of the revisionists, Bernstein, who had been advocating a revision of scientific socialism long before the congress, demanded in his congress speech "freedom to crit-icise" Marxism. The congress rejected the resolution moved by Bernstein's supporters and adopted a resolution which, though directly warning Bernstein, did not lay down the principle that Bern-steinian views were incompatible with membership in the working-class party.   p. 14

[21] *The Stuttgart Congress* of the German Social-Democratic Party, held on September 21-26 (October 3-8), 1898, was the first congress to discuss the question of revisionism in the German Social-Democratic movement. It heard a statement from Bernstein, who was not present at the congress, in which he set forth and defended his opportunist views, expounded earlier in a number of articles. Bern-stein's opponents at the congress failed to take a united stand. One section (Bebel, Kautsky and others) advocated ideological struggle against Bernstein and criticism of his mistakes, but did not agree to take organisational measures against him. Another section, the minority headed by Rosa Luxemburg, was more resolute in its op-position to Bernsteinism.   p. 15

[22] *Starover*—pseudonym of A. N. Potresov, member of the Editorial Board of *Iskra*, subsequently a Menshevik.   p. 16

[23] *The Author Who Got a Swelled Head*—the title of one of Maxim Gorky's early stories.   p. 17

[24] Lenin refers to the collection *Material for a Characterisation of Our Economic Development*, printed legally in 2,000 copies in April 1895. The symposium contained Lenin's article (signed *K. Tulin*) "The Economic Content of Narodism and the Criticism of It in Mr.

Struve's Book (*The Reflection of Marxism in Bourgeois Literature*)", directed against the "legal Marxists". (See V. I. Lenin, *Collected Works*, Vol. 1.) p. 18

25 *Zubatov*—chief of the Moscow secret police, the moving spirit of "police socialism" in Russia. Zubatov set up bogus labour organisations under the aegis of the gendarmes and police, in an effort to deflect the workers from the revolutionary movement. p. 19

26 *A Protest by Russian Social-Democrats* was written by Lenin in 1899, during his exile. It was directed against the *Credo* of a group of Economists (S. N. Prokopovich, Y. D. Kuskova and others who subsequently became Cadets). On receiving a copy of the *Credo* through his sister, A. I. Yelizarova, Lenin wrote a sharp protest in which he exposed the nature of this declaration.

The Protest was discussed and unanimously endorsed by a meeting of 17 exiled Marxists, convened by Lenin in the village of Yermakovskoye, Minusinsk District (Siberia). The exiles in the Turukhansk District (Siberia) and in Orlovo (Vyatka Gubernia) subsequently associated themselves with it.

Lenin forwarded a copy of the Protest to the Emancipation of Labour Group abroad, where it was published in the beginning of 1900 by G. V. Plekhanov in his *Vademecum (Guide) for the Editors of Rabocheye Dyelo*. p. 20

27 *Rabochaya Mysl* (*Workers' Thought*)—newspaper of the Economists, published from October 1897 to December 1902. Sixteen issues appeared: Nos. 3 to 11, and 16 in Berlin, and the others in St. Petersburg. Edited by K. M. Takhtaryov and others.

Lenin criticises the views expounded by *Rabochaya Mysl*, as the Russian variety of international opportunism, in a number of his writings, particularly in his *Iskra* articles and in this work. p. 20

28 *Vademecum for the Editors of Rabocheye Dyelo*—the title of a collection of materials and documents compiled and prefaced by G. V. Plekhanov and published by the Emancipation of Labour Group in Geneva in 1900. It exposed the opportunist views of the Union of Russian Social-Democrats Abroad and of the Editors of its organ, *Rabocheye Dyelo*. p. 20

29 *Profession de foi*—a leaflet setting forth the opportunist views of the Kiev Committee, issued at the close of 1899. On many points it was identical with the notorious Economist *Credo*. It is criticised by Lenin in his article "Apropos of the *Profession de foi*" (V. I. Lenin, *Collected Works*, Vol. 4). p. 20

30 "*Separate Supplement*" to *Rabochaya Mysl*—a pamphlet published by the editors of the Economist *Rabochaya Mysl* in September 1899. The pamphlet, and in particular the article "Our Reality" which appeared over the signature of R. M., frankly set forth the opportunist views of the Economists. Lenin criticises this pamphlet in his article "A Retrograde Trend in Russian Social-Democracy" and in this work. p. 23

31 *Emancipation of Labour Group*—the first Russian Marxist group,

organised by G. V. Plekhanov in Geneva in 1883. The group did a great deal to disseminate Marxism in Russia. p. 24

[32] See Marx and Engels, *Selected Works*, Vol. II, Moscow 1962, p. 16. p. 25

[33] See Marx and Engels, *Selected Works*, Vol. I, Moscow 1962, pp. 652-54. p. 29

[34] *The St. Petersburg League of Struggle for the Emancipation of the Working Class* was formed by V. I. Lenin in the autumn of 1895 and united all the Marxist workers' circles in St. Petersburg. It was headed by a Central Group that was directed by Lenin. The League of Struggle was the first organisation in Russia to combine socialism with the working-class movement and to pass over from the propaganda of Marxism among a small circle of advanced workers to political agitation among the broad masses of the working class.

According to Lenin, the St. Petersburg League of Struggle for the Emancipation of the Working Class was the first real *rudiment of a revolutionary party which was backed by the working-class movement*. p. 32

[35] *Russkaya Starina* (*The Russian Antiquary*)—a monthly journal of history published in St. Petersburg from 1870 to 1918. p. 33

[36] *S. Peterburgsky Rabochy Listok* (*St. Petersburg Workers' Paper*) —an illegal newspaper, organ of the St. Petersburg League of Struggle for the Emancipation of the Working Class. Two issues appeared: No. 1 in February (marked January) 1897 (mimeographed in Russia in 300-400 copies); and No. 2 in September 1897 in Geneva. p. 33

[37] *A private meeting* referred to by Lenin was held in St. Petersburg between February 14 and 17 (February 26-March 1, new style), 1897. It was attended by V. I. Lenin, A. A. Vaneyev, G. M. Krzhizhanovsky and other members of the St. Petersburg League of Struggle for the Emancipation of the Working Class, that is, by the "veterans" who had been released from prison for three days, before being sent to exile in Siberia, and the "young" leaders of the League of Struggle who took over after Lenin's arrest. p. 35

[38] *"Listok" Rabotnika* (*The Workingman's Paper*)—published in Geneva by the Union of Russian Social-Democrats Abroad from 1896 to 1899; ten issues appeared. Issues 1 to 8 were edited by the Emancipation of Labour Group, which, with the majority of the Union swinging to Economism, refused to continue editing its publications. Nos. 9-10 were brought out by a new editorial board formed by the Union. p. 35

[39] *An article by V. I.*—reference is to an article by V. P. Ivanshin. p. 36

[40] The tsarist gendarmes wore blue uniforms. p. 36

[41] *V. V.*—pseudonym of V. P. Vorontsov, one of the ideologists of liberal Narodism in the eighties and nineties of last century. Lenin's

words "the V. V.'s of Russian Social-Democracy" are an allusion to the Economists, who represented the opportunist trend in the Russian Social-Democratic movement. p. 37

[42] *The Hirsch-Duncker unions*—founded by the bourgeois liberals Hirsch and Duncker in 1868 in Germany. Hirsch and Duncker advocated "harmony of class interests", drew the workers away from the revolutionary class struggle against the bourgeoisie, reduced the tasks and role of trade union organisations to those of benefit societies and educational clubs. p. 42

[43] *Self-Emancipation of the Workers· Group*—a small group of Economists formed in St. Petersburg in the autumn of 1898. The group, which existed only a few months, published a manifesto setting forth its aims (printed in *Nakanune*—a journal appearing in London), a set of rules and several leaflets for distribution among the workers. p. 44

[44] *Nakanune (On the Eve)*—a journal of the Narodnik trend published in London from January 1899 to February 1902. Thirty-seven issues appeared. *Nakanune* served as a rallying point for representatives of diverse petty-bourgeois parties. p. 44

[45] Under the pseudonym of N. Beltov, G. V. Plekhanov published his well-known book *The Development of the Monist View of History*, which appeared legally in St. Petersburg in 1895. p. 51

[46] Reference is to the satirical poem "Anthem of the Super-Modern Russian Socialist" by Y. O. Martov, published in *Zarya* No. 1, April 1901, over the signature "Nartsis Tuporylov". It ridiculed the Economists and their adaptation to the spontaneous movement. p. 51

[47] Reference is to the Union of Russian Social-Democrats Abroad. p. 58

[48] *Rural superintendents*—officials in tsarist Russia appointed from the landed nobility and exercising administrative and juridical rights. p. 58

[49] *Bund*—the General Jewish Workers' Union of Lithuania, Poland and Russia. Founded in 1897, it embraced mainly the Jewish artisans in the western regions of Russia. The Bund joined the R.S.D.L.P. at the latter's First Congress in March 1898. At the Second R.S.D.L.P. Congress the Bund delegates insisted on their organisation being recognised as the sole representative of the Jewish proletariat in Russia. The Congress rejected this organisational nationalism, whereupon the Bund withdrew from the Party.

In 1906, following the Fourth ("Unity") Congress, the Bund reaffiliated to the R.S.D.L.P. The Bundists constantly supported the Mensheviks and waged an incessant struggle against the Bolsheviks. Despite its formal affiliation to the R.S.D.L.P., the Bund was an organisation of a bourgeois-nationalist character. As opposed to the Bolshevik programme demand for the right of nations to self-determination, the Bund put forward the demand for cultural-national autonomy. During the First World War of 1914-18 the

Bundists took the stand of social-chauvinism. In 1917, the Bund supported the counter-revolutionary Provisional Government and fought on the side of the enemies of the October Socialist Revolution. During the Civil War prominent Bundists joined forces with the counter-revolution. At the same time a turn began among the rank-and-file members of the Bund in favour of collaboration with the Soviet government. When the victory of the proletarian dictatorship over the internal counter-revolution and foreign interventionists became evident the Bund declared its abandonment of the struggle against Soviet system. In March 1921, the Bund went into voluntary liquidation and part of its membership joined the R.S.P.(B.) in the ordinary way.   p. 60

[50] *Redemption payments*—by its Decree of February 19, 1861 on the abolition of serfdom in Russia, the tsarist government forced the peasants to pay redemption fees for "their own peasant lands watered with their sweat and blood" (Lenin). The prices set were two to three times higher than the actual value of the plots allotted to the peasants. By the time redemption payments were stopped in 1907, the peasants had payed the landlords a total of 2,000 million rubles.   p. 63

[51] *Iskra*, No. 7 (August 1901), carried in its section "Workers' Movement and Letters from the Factories" a letter from a weaver which testified to the vast influence Lenin's *Iskra* exercised on the advanced workers. The letter reads in part:

"...I showed *Iskra* to many fellow-workers and the copy was read to tatters; but we treasure it ... *Iskra* writes about our cause, about the All-Russian cause which cannot be evaluated in kopeks or measured in hours of work; when you read the paper you understand why the gendarmes and police are afraid of us workers and of the intellectuals whom we follow. It is a fact that they do not simply make the bosses tremble for their pocket-books, but inspire fear in the tsar, the employers and the rest.... It will not take much now to set the working folk aflame. All that is wanted is a spark to kindle the fire that is already smouldering among the people. How true are the words 'the spark will kindle a flame!'... In the past every strike was an event, but today everyone sees that strikes alone are not enough, that we must now strive for liberty, win it by might and main. Today everyone, old and young, is eager to read, but the sad thing is that there are no books. Last Sunday I gathered eleven people and read them 'Where To Begin', and we discussed it till late in the evening. How true it expresses everything, how it gets to the very heart of things.... And we would like to write a letter to your *Iskra*, to ask you to teach us not only how to begin, but how to live and how to die."   p. 88

[52] *Rossiya* (*Russia*)—a moderate liberal newspaper published in St. Petersburg from 1899 to 1902.   p. 93

[53] *L. Brentano*—a German bourgeois economist, advocate of so-called "state socialism", who tried to prove the possibility of attaining social equality within the framework of capitalism by introducing

reforms and conciliating the interests of the capitalists and workers. Using Marxist phraseology as a cover, Brentano and his followers endeavoured to subordinate the working-class movement to the interests of the bourgeoisie.   p. 95

[54] Reference is to the Workers' Group for the Struggle Against Capital, a small group with views similar to those of the Economists. Formed in St. Petersburg in the spring of 1899, it issued a mimeographed leaflet entitled "Our Programme", which, however, was not circulated owing to the arrest of the group.   p. 101

[55] *N. N.*—S. N. Prokopovich, an active Economist and later a Cadet.
                                                                          p. 107

[56] *Afanasy Ivanovich and Pulkheria Ivanovna*—small provincial landowners described by Gogol in *Old Time Landowners.*   p. 113

[57] Lenin is referring to his revolutionary activity in St. Petersburg in 1893-95.   p. 124

[58] Reference is to the pamphlet *Report on the Russian Social-Democratic Movement to the International Socialist Congress in Paris, 1900.* The report was submitted to the Congress by the Editorial Board of *Rabocheye Dyelo* on behalf of the Union of Russian Social-Democrats Abroad and was issued in a separate pamphlet in Geneva in 1901. The pamphlet also contained the report of the Bund ("The History of the Jewish Working-Class Movement in Russia and Poland").   p. 140

[59] This footnote was inserted by Lenin for the sake of secrecy. The facts are enumerated here in the order in which they actually took place.   p. 153

[60] Reference is to the negotiations of the St. Petersburg League of Struggle for the Emancipation of the Working Class with Lenin, who in the second half of 1897 wrote the two pamphlets mentioned in the text.   p. 153

[61] *League*—reference is to the League of Russian Revolutionary Social-Democrats Abroad, founded in October 1901 on Lenin's initiative. Affiliated to the League were the foreign section of the *Iskra* and the *Zarya* organisation and the *Sotsial-Demokrat* organisation (which included the Emancipation of Labour Group). The League was the representative of *Iskra* abroad. It published several issues of its *Bulletin* and a number of pamphlets, including one by V. I. Lenin, *To the Rural Poor.* The Second Congress of the R.S.D.L.P. endorsed the League as the sole party organisation abroad with the status of a Party committee. Following the Second Congress, the Mensheviks entrenched themselves in the League and from this position waged a struggle against Lenin and the Bolsheviks.   p. 154

[62] Reference is to the negotiations between the Central Committee of the Bund and V. I. Lenin.   p. 154

[63] In relating the *"fourth fact"*, Lenin has in view the attempt of the Union of Russian Social-Democrats Abroad and the Bund to convene

ihe Second Congress of the Party in the spring of 1900. The *"Member of the Committee"* mentioned by Lenin is I. Kh. Lalayants (member of the Ekaterinoslav Social-Democratic Committee), who came to Moscow in February 1900 for talks with V. I. Lenin.   p. 154

[64] Lenin is quoting from D. I. Pisarev's article "Blunders of Immature Thought".   p. 167

[65] Lenin refers here to the following passage in Marx's *The Eighteenth Brumaire of Louis Bonaparte*:

"Hegel remarks somewhere that all facts and personages of great importance in world history occur, as it were, twice. He forgot to add: the first time as tragedy, the second as farce." (Marx and Engels, *Selected Works*, Vol. I, Moscow 1962, p. 247.)   p. 168

[66] *Janizaries*—elite rifle troops of the Ottoman Empire, abolished in 1826. The janizaries were known for their plunder of the population and wanton brutality. Lenin uses the term to describe the tsarist police.   p. 172

[67] This appendix was omitted by Lenin when *What Is To Be Done?* was republished in 1907 in the collection *Twelve Years*.   p. 178

[68] *Iskra*, No. 18 (March 10, 1902), published in its section "From the Party" an item entitled *"Zarya's Polemics With Vorwärts"* which summed up the controversy.   p. 183

ADDENDUM

Among the books mentioned in the editor's notes, the following are currently available in editions by International Publishers:

Frederick Engels, THE PEASANT WAR IN GERMANY
Karl Marx, CRITIQUE OF THE GOTHA PROGRAM
Karl Marx, THE 18TH BRUMAIRE OF LOUIS BONAPARTE
K. Marx and F. Engels, SELECTED CORRESPONDENCE, 1846–1895
George V. Plekhanov, IN DEFENSE OF MATERIALISM (Development of the Monist View of History)

In addition, a number of articles referred to in Lenin, Collected Works *and in Marx and Engels,* Selected Works (2 vol. edition) *are also available in:*

V. I. Lenin, SELECTED WORKS, in three volumes
K. Marx and F. Engels, SELECTED WORKS (one-volume edition)